DEAR SCIENCE AND OTHER STORIES

D1570589

ERRANTRIES

A series edited by Simone Browne,
Deborah Cowen, and Katherine McKittrick

SERIES EDITORIAL ADVISORY BOARD
Jacqueline Nassy Brown, Paul Gilroy,
Gayatri Gopinath, Avery Gordon, Richa Nagar,
AbdouMaliq Simone, Françoise Vergès,
Ruth Wilson Gilmore, and Bobby Wilson

DEAR SCIENCE *and Other Stories*

Katherine McKittrick

DUKE UNIVERSITY PRESS DURHAM AND LONDON 2021

© 2021 Duke University Press
All rights reserved

Printed in the United States of America on acid-free paper ∞
Designed by Amy Ruth Buchanan
Typeset in Arno Pro and Trade Gothic by Copperline Book Services

Library of Congress Cataloging-in-Publication Data
Names: McKittrick, Katherine, author.
Title: Dear science and other stories / Katherine McKittrick.
Other titles: Errantries.
Description: Durham : Duke University Press, 2021. | Series: Errantries |
Includes bibliographical references and index.
Identifiers: LCCN 2020016402 (print)
LCCN 2020016403 (ebook)
ISBN 9781478010005 (hardcover)
ISBN 9781478011040 (paperback)
ISBN 9781478012573 (ebook)
Subjects: LCSH: African Americans—Study and teaching. |
African Americans—Social conditions. | Race—Philosophy. | African
American feminists. | Cross-cultural studies.
Classification: LCC E185.86 .M355 2021 (print) |
LCC E185.86 (ebook) |
DDC 305.896/073—dc23
LC record available at https://lccn.loc.gov/2020016402
LC ebook record available at https://lccn.loc.gov/2020016403

Cover art: Farley Hill National Park, Barbados.
Photo by Katherine McKittrick.

For Sylvia.

For Ellison,

again.

CONTENTS

There is no life that is not geographic.

—RUTH WILSON GILMORE

HE LIKED TO SAY THAT THIS LOVE WAS
THE RESULT OF A CLINICAL ERROR

Ray Zilli
Ellison Zilli
Simone Browne
Alexander Weheliye
Dina Georgis
Ruth Wilson Gilmore
Craig Gilmore
Demetrius Eudell
M. NourbeSe Philip
Cindi Katz
Eric Lott
Sammi King
Carmen Kynard
Barby Asante
Ken Wissoker
Nik Theodore
Barrington Walker
Kiese Laymon
Kara Keeling
Trish Salah
Richard Iton
Fred Moten
Laura Harris
Lidia Curti
Iain Chambers
Marcus Gilroy-Ware
Charmaine Lurch

Ricky Varghese
Deb Cowen
Sarah Haley
Treva Ellison
Nikolas Sparks
Mark V. Campbell
Nick Mitchell
Barnor Hesse
OmiSoore Dryden
Razia Dawood
Asha Tall
Tia-Simone Gardner
Dylan Robinson
Cora Gilroy-Ware
Steven Osuna
Temi Odumosu
Linda Peake
Esther Harvey
Karen de Souza
Bedour Alagraa
Kara Melton
Kendall Witaszek
Maya Stitski
David Scott
Avery Gordon
Jenny Burman
Minelle Mahtani

Ashon Crawley
Ben Carrington
Elleza Kelley
SA Smythe
Tanya Titchkosky
Scott Morgensen
Andy Kent
Nik Heynen
Sharad Chari
LaMonda Stallings
Mecca Sullivan
Grace Adeniyi-
    Ogunyankin
Tau Lewis
Vinay Gidwani
Terrie Easter Sheen
Shana Redmond
Saidiya Hartman
Erika Ibrahim
Yasmine Djerbal
Esther Kim
Danyel Haughton
Yaniya Lee
Carl James
Elliott Jun
Krista Franklin
Daniella Rose King

Stephanie Simpson
Liz Millward
Olivia Gross
Hunter Knight
Lynn Ly
Kim Khanh Tran
Chanda Prescod-
 Weinstein
Sharon Y. Rodgers
Tariq Jazeel
Sandra Brewster
Jenny Pickerill
Hazel Carby
AbdouMaliq Simone
Dionne Brand
Bianca Beauchemin

Sunny Kerr
Adam Elliott-Cooper
Clyde Woods
Kristin Moriah
Ken Hewitt
Fe Hewitt
Romi Morrison
Sivamohan Valluvan
Shana M. Griffin
Kate Mariner
Prince
Scott Rutherford
Renée Green
Leslie Sanders
Joshua Tranen
Errol Nazareth

Richa Nagar
Carolyn Prouse
Jessica Ryan
Carole Boyce
 Davies
Jacqueline Nassy
 Brown
Brittany Meché
Darcel Bullen
Jade Brooks
Robin D. G. Kelley
Beverley Mullings
Lisa Lowe
Vron Ware
Paul Gilroy
Sylvia Wynter

I have been experimenting with these and other stories for a long time. Thank you to the many students, faculty, staff, who invited me to share these ideas, as well as colleagues and friends who participated in panels, symposia, workshops, conversations. The feedback has been, and is, invaluable, admired, and appreciated. Many thanks to all those who administered and arranged travel, accommodations, and day-to-day activities during visits elsewhere. The referee comments are cherished. The readers encouraged me to think with and through this project and imagine sites-citations unseen. My parents, Valerie Brodrick and Robert McKittrick, have provided decades of support and love for which I am grateful. In addition to camaraderie and an indescribable critical eye, Simone Browne read a few iterations of *Dear Science*—thank you for taking the time to support these stories in a world that effaces black time. Ruthie Gilmore offered generosity, notes, time, stories, space, futures, friendship. Sylvia Wynter's conversation, kindness, and commitment to black intellectual life is admired, always. Zilli, endlessly curious and studied, provided scaffolding, contexts, walls, shelves, books, writings, ideas, love, photographs, songs, codes, mechanics, guitar tabs, notations, grooves that are immeasurable. Shortcomings weigh; the imperfections within are all mine. There are songs and musicians referenced throughout these stories and, still, the blap-zomp-tonk is unsatisfactorily tracked and remains somewhat quiet and unlisted. I appreciate the musicians who interrupted and complemented these stories as well as the dozens of friends and colleagues who provided recommendations, shared songs and albums, and passed on playlists and car tapes (for the latter I am indebted to Cam McKittrick). These stories were, in part, supported by the Social Science and Humanities Research Council (Insight Development Grant and Insight Grant) as well as the Antipode Foundation.

D *ear Science and Other Stories* is a collection of ideas I have been gathering since about 2004.[1] The project began as a curiosity. I was originally interested in how race is attended to in feminist science and technology studies and how black feminists and black scholars work through the thorny racial privileges and biases that animate this field. My contribution to this conversation was to center black creatives (poets, musicians, visual artists) and think through how they attend to science in their work. I sat with June Jordan's kerosene and irradiation and phosphorescence.[2] I sat with the kerosene and irradiation and phosphorescence not to discount scientific racism and biological determinism, but to ask questions about how black worlds are not always wholly defined by scientific racism and biological determinism. I sought to draw attention to how black creatives work with scientific concepts in innovative and humanizing ways—attentive to racism, yes, but not understanding scientific racism as the only way to define black life.[3] This was complemented

---

The title of this story, "My Heart Makes My Head Swim," is from Frantz Fanon's *Black Skin, White Masks*, trans. Charles Lam Markmann (1952; rpt., New York: Grove, 1967), 140.

1. The title of this collection of stories, *Dear Science*, is borrowed from TV on the Radio, *Dear Science*, Interscope, 2008.

2. June Jordan, "Inaugural Rose," in *Directed by Desire: The Collected Poems of June Jordan*, ed. Jan Heller Levi and Sara Miles (Port Townsend, WA: Copper Canyon Press, 2007), 297.

3. I shy away from black science fiction and Afrofuturism and, for the most part—when addressing science specifically—settle on exploring the ways black creatives engage science outside these genres. Although this list is a too-small sample of the expansive work in black science fiction, black speculative fiction, and Afrofuturism, see Kodwo Eshun, "Further Considerations of Afrofuturism," CR: *The New Centennial Review* 3, no. 2 (Summer 2003):

by ongoing research on Sylvia Wynter's "demonic model," which she discusses in her essay "Beyond Miranda's Meanings," and the concepts of "autopoiesis" and "science of the word," which she takes up in a number of her essays. The demonic model, taken from physics, is used by Wynter to think about the intellectual and conceptual ground through which Caribbean women recalibrate the meaning of humanity. "Autopoiesis" is a term developed by biologists Humberto Maturana and Francisco Varela. It is used by Wynter to show that we invest in our present normative mode of existence in order to keep the living-system—our environmental and existential world—*as is*. This is a recursive logic; it depicts our presently ecocidal and genocidal world as normal and unalterable. Our work is to notice this logic and breach it. Wynter's extension of Aimé Césaire's "science of the word," speaks to interdisciplinarity, dislodging our biocentric system of knowledge, and showing that the natural sciences, the humanities, and the social sciences are, when thought together, generative sites of inquiry.[4] In using concepts such as these—scientific terms that are not cast as purely and objectively scientific yet retain within them traces of the hard sciences—Wynter theorizes race outside raciology and positions blackness and black studies as an analytics of invention. My curiosity led me to think about the humanizing work black creatives illuminate in their scientifically creative and creatively scientific artworlds, while also drawing attention to the disruptive work that black feminists and black schol-

387–402; André M. Carrington, *Speculative Blackness: The Future of Race in Science Fiction* (Minneapolis: University of Minnesota Press, 2016); and Sami Schalk, *Bodyminds Reimagined: (Dis)ability, Race, and Gender in Black Women's Speculative Fiction* (Durham, NC: Duke University, 2018).

4. Sylvia Wynter, "Beyond Miranda's Meanings: Un/Silencing the 'Demonic Ground' of Caliban's 'Woman,'" in *Out of the Kumbla: Caribbean Women and Literature*, ed. Carole Boyce Davies and Elaine Savory Fido (Trenton, NJ: Africa World Press, 1990), 355–372; Sylvia Wynter and Katherine McKittrick, "Unparalleled Catastrophe for Our Species? Or, to Give Humanness a Different Future: Conversations," in *Sylvia Wynter: On Being Human as Praxis*, ed. Katherine McKittrick (Durham, NC: Duke University Press, 2015), 9–89. See also Aimé Césaire, "Poetry and Knowledge," in *Lyric and Dramatic Poetry*, trans. Clayton Eshleman and Annette Smith (Charlottesville: University Press of Virginia, 1990), xlii–lvi. A biocentric system of knowledge that assumes we are, totally and completely and purely, biological beings, beholden to evolution and its attendant teleological temporalities, rather than humans who are physiological-story-makers, both bios *and* mythoi, who produce fictive evolutionary stories about our biological selves. "Biocentric" is defined numerous times throughout this text, although the explanation in the story "(Zong) Bad Made Measure" is the most comprehensive.

ars do (as they breach the recursive field of feminist science and technology studies and other disciplines).

I share *Dear Science* not as a project that describes science, particularly black science, through (or as) scientific racism, but as a study of how we come to know black life through asymmetrically connected knowledge systems. Science is present—it is tied to the curiosities noted above—but it is restless and uncomfortably situated and multifarious rather than definitive and downward-pressing.[5] This is a book about black livingness and ways of knowing. This shift—from studying science to studying ways of knowing—has allowed me to work out where and how black thinkers imagine and practice liberation as they are weighed down by what I can only describe as biocentrically induced accumulation by dispossession. The weight is important here, because it signals not simply a monumental system of knowledge that is fueled by colonial and plantocratic logics, but the weight that bears down on all black people, inside and outside the academy, and puts pressure on their physiological and psychic and political well-being. *Dear Science* takes into account how black intellectual life is tied to corporeal and affective labor (flesh and brains and blood and bones, hearts, souls) by noticing the physiological work of black liberation. These labors are, however, impossible to track and capture with precision. In noticing the physiological work of black liberation, I am asking for a mode of recognition that does not itemize-commodify black liberation and black embodied knowledge. Indeed, tracking down (quantifying and/or endlessly describing) black corporeal and affective and physiological labor belies the kinds of black studies these stories tell. For this reason, affective-physiological-corporeal-intellectual labor, within this text, is momentary and somewhat erratic; I imperfectly draw attention to how seeking liberation, and reinventing the terms of black life outside normatively negative conceptions of blackness, is onerous, joyful, and difficult, yet unmeasured and unmeasurable. Mnemonic black livingness. My heart makes my head swim.[6]

5. *Dear Science* works with scientia (knowledge) in its most general sense. Science (biology, math, physics, and so on) animates scientia, but science (testable materials, systematic methods that result in explanation, experiments and predictions and discoveries) is not the central preoccupation of *Dear Science*. Science is a shadow, a story, a friendship. Science reveals failed attachments.

6. Fanon, *Black Skin, White Masks*, 140.

Within, I share a series of interdisciplinary stories that are indebted to anticolonial thought and black studies. *Dear Science* argues that black people have always used interdisciplinary methodologies to explain, explore, and story the world, because thinking and writing and imagining across a range of texts, disciplines, histories, and genres unsettles suffocating and dismal and insular racial logics. By employing interdisciplinary methodologies and living interdisciplinary worlds, black people bring together various sources and texts and narratives to challenge racism. Or, black people bring together various sources and texts and narratives not to capture something or someone, but to question the analytical work of capturing, and the desire to capture, something or someone. The stories think through how racism and other forms of oppression underpin the political economy of academic and nonacademic disciplinary thinking (the demand to gather and live with seemingly transparent data, in a range of sectors; living with data [policies, reports, cards and carding] that ostensibly prove that those communities living outside normalcy are verifiably outside normalcy; giving over the data in exchange for capital). Within black studies and anticolonial studies, one can observe an ongoing method of gathering multifariously textured tales, narratives, fictions, whispers, songs, grooves. The textures offer one way to challenge the primacy of evidentiary and insular normalcies, because they are allegedly incongruous. In assembling ideas that are seemingly disconnected and uneven (the seabird and the epilogue, the song and the soil, the punch clock and the ecosystem, the streetlight and the kick-on-beat), the logic of knowing-to-prove is unsustainable because incongruity appears to be offering atypical thinking. Yet curiosity thrives. The industry punch clock calibrates and recalibrates the ecosystem (water . . . rich in corrosive chemicals purged from the factories of its industrial past) and . . .[7] She asks: What happens when our blood falls to the soil and seeps in? She wonders: What happens to our conception of land when it is an absorbent receptacle for black people's erythrocytes, leukocytes, thrombocytes? She answers: Strange fruit.[8]

7. Malini Ranganathan, "Thinking with Flint: Racial Liberalism and the Roots of an American Water Tragedy," *Capitalism Nature Socialism* 27, no. 3 (2016): 18.

8. Danyel Haughton, your question still sits with me. See also Katherine McKittrick, "Plantation Futures," *Small Axe* 17, no. 3 (November 2013): 1–15; Billie Holiday, "Strange Fruit," Commodore, 1939.

Agony. Also, assembling ideas that are seemingly connected (the weight and the measure, the cloth and the silk, the road and the vehicle) fuse and break apart how we know, because we seek out continuities and ruptures. And curiosity thrives. The weight (pull of gravity) and measure (calculation) are overlapping and different (uncommon weight/uncommon weight/new weight . . . water parts) and . . .[9] What is meaningful, then, are the ways in which black people are interdisciplinary actors, continually entangling and disentangling varying narratives and tempos and hues that, together, invent and reinvent knowledge. This interdisciplinary innovation illuminates, to borrow from Mark V. Campbell, multiple skills and ways of knowing that privilege collaboration and bring into view unorthodox practices of belonging that discredit ethnic absolutism and its attendant geographic fictions.[10]

This is a way of living, and an analytical frame, that is curious and sustained by wonder (the desire to know). This is a method that demands openness and is unsatisfied with questions that result in descriptive-data-induced answers. Black studies and anticolonial thought offer methodological practices wherein we read, live, hear, groove, create, and write across a range of temporalities, places, texts, and ideas that build on existing liberatory practices and pursue ways of living the world that are uncomfortably generous and provisional and practical and, as well, imprecise and unrealized.[11] The method is rigorous, too. Wonder is study. Curiosity is attentive. Black method is therefore not continuously and absolutely undisciplined (invariably without precision, invariably undone).[12] Black method is precise, detailed, coded, long, and forever. The practice of bringing together multiple texts, stories, songs, and places involves the difficult work of thinking and learning across many sites, and thus coming to know, generously, varying and shifting worlds and ideas.

9. M. NourbeSe Philip, *Zong!* (Toronto: Mercury Press, 2008), 55–56, 59.

10. Mark V. Campbell, "Everything's Connected: A Relationality Remix, a Praxis," *C. L. R. James Journal* 20, no. 1 (2014): 97–114. See also Paul Gilroy, *The Black Atlantic: Modernity and Double Consciousness* (Cambridge, MA: Harvard University Press, 1993).

11. Ruth Wilson Gilmore, "Abolition Geography and the Problem of Innocence," in *Futures of Black Radicalism*, ed. Gaye Theresa Johnson and Alex Lubin (New York: Verson, 2017), 225–240; AbdouMaliq Simone, *Improvised Lives* (Cambridge, MA: Polity, 2019).

12. To be totally undisciplined can perhaps undermine the intellectual labor of black people who rigorously and generously share and build and remember stories and lessons that we collectively utilize as we move through this world. We are not always undone. Our undoing is practiced, patient, focused.

Sometimes this is awful because we are gathering dense texts and uncomfortable ideas that wear us out. Sometimes this is awful because we are aware we cannot know forever, yet we are committed to the everlasting effort of figuring out how we might, together, fashion liberation. We have no time. This rigor is animated by diasporic literacy, VèVè Clark's wonderfully useful reading practice that investigates and shows how we already do, or can, illuminate and connect existing and emerging diasporic codes and tempos and stories and narratives and themes. Clark shows how diasporic literacy is structured through "recognized references sharing a wealth of connotations."[13] She theorizes Mayotte Capécia, Mahalia Jackson, Jomo Kenyatta, food, furnishings, and laughter as grammars, figures, and practices that are written into creative-intellectual texts as prompts.[14] These literacies function to expand the text outside itself (the prompt opens a door). Kenyatta and laughter are not endlessly explained and unpacked; instead, they cue what does not need explanation but requires imagination and memory and study. Diasporic literacy signals ways of being and ways of living (memories, imaginations, mnemonics), that we know and share in order to collectively struggle against suffocating racial logics. Like sorrow songs. Like freedom dreams. Like erotic. Like flying cheek-bones.[15]

STORY

The ideas and curiosities gathered in *Dear Science* are bundled and presented as stories. Telling, sharing, listening to, and hearing stories are relational and interdisciplinary acts that are animated by all sorts of people, places, narrative devices, theoretical queries, plots. The process is sustained by invention and wonder. The story has no answers. The stories offer an aesthetic relationality that relies on the dynamics of creating-narrating-listening-hearing-reading-and-sometimes-unhearing. The sto-

13. VèVè Clark, "Developing Diaspora Literacy: Allusion in Maryse Condé's *Hérémakhonon*," in *Out of the Kumbla: Caribbean Women and Literature*, ed. Carole Boyce Davies and Elaine Savory Fido (Trenton, NJ: Africa World Press, 1990), 308–309.

14. Clark, "Developing Diaspora Literacy," 308–309.

15. W. E. B. Du Bois, *The Souls of Black Folk* (1903; rpt., New York: Vintage, 1990); Robin D. G. Kelley, *Freedom Dreams: The Black Radical Imagination* (Boston: Beacon, 2002); Audre Lorde, "Uses of the Erotic: The Erotic as Power," in *Sister Outsider* (Berkeley, CA: Crossing Press, 1984), 53–59; M. NourbeSe Philip, *She Tries Her Tongue, Her Silence Softly Breaks* (Charlottetown, Canada: Ragweed Press, 1989), 51–53.

ries do not offer lucid tales or answers; rather, they signal ways of living in a world that denies black humanity (or, more aptly, the stories signal ways of black livingness).[16] The story-text itself, read aloud or quietly, is an imprint of black life and livingness that tells of the wreckage and the lists and the dance floors and the loss and the love and the rumors and the lessons and the heartbreak. It prompts. The story does not simply describe, it demands representation outside itself. Indeed, the story cannot tell itself without our willingness to imagine what it cannot tell. The story asks that we live with what cannot be explained and live with unexplained cues and diasporic literacies, rather than reams of positivist evidence. The story opens the door to curiosity; the reams of evidence dissipate as we tell the world differently, with a creative precision. The story asks that we live with the difficult and frustrating ways of knowing differentially. (And some things we can keep to ourselves. They cannot have everything. Stop her autopsy.) They cannot have everything.

I present *Dear Science* as a series of stories as a way to hold on to the rebellious methodological work of sharing ideas in an unkind world. Sharing can be uneasy and terrifying, but our stories of black worlds and black ways of being can, in part, breach the heavy weight of dispossession and loss. Our shared stories of black worlds and black ways of being breach the heavy weight of dispossession and loss because these narratives (songs, poems, conversations, theories, debates, memories, arts, prompts, curiosities) are embedded with all sorts of liberatory clues and resistances (PFUnk/f.u.n.k.).[17] Sharing, therefore, is not understood as an act of disclosure but instead signals collaboration and collaborative ways to enact and engender struggle. As a collection of stories, too, *Dear Science* understands theory as a form of storytelling. Stories and storytelling signal the fictive work of theory. I hope this move, at least momentarily, exposes

16. Barbara Christian writes: "I am inclined to say that our theorizing (and I intentionally use the verb rather than the noun) is often in narrative forms, in the stories we create, in riddles and proverbs, in the play with language, because dynamic rather than fixed ideas seem more to our liking. How else have we managed to survive with such spiritedness the assault on our bodies, social institutions, countries, our very humanity?" Barbara Christian, "The Race for Theory," *Feminist Studies* 14, no. 1 (Spring 1998): 68. See also Saidiya Hartman on "critical fabulation," in "Venus in Two Acts," *Small Axe* 12, no. 2 (June 2008): 1–14. Hazel V. Carby's *Imperial Intimacies: A Tale of Two Islands* (London: Verson, 2019) is, for me, a beautiful and creative work that offers a mode of storytelling that captures and bends disciplined-interdisciplined genres.

17. Listen to Prince, "F.U.N.K.," NPG Digital, 2007.

the intricacies of academic work where fact-finding, experimentation, analysis, study, are recognized as narrative, plot, tale, and incomplete inventions, rather than impartial treatises. As story, theory is cast as fictive knowledge and insists that the black imagination is necessary to analytical curiosity and study. Story is theoretical, dance, poem, sound, song, geography, affect, photograph, painting, sculpture, and more. Maybe the story is one way to express and fall in love with black life. Maybe the story disguises our fall.

Kevin Young offers a rich analysis of black stories, storying, storytelling, and story-making. He outlines how black stories can be acts of keeping something or someone or somewhere hidden (desire, love, half of the story, where it's at, kin). He also addresses how the practice of twisting stories and narratives (lying, counterfeiting, remapping, recoding, forging) subverts, refuses, and resists racism.[18] Thus, the work of telling and the story itself enmesh, to offer not a descriptive tale but a strategic lesson in and for black life. With this in mind: the content of the story is a lesson (you, we, recode and forge and invent, this is how we live, I will keep your secret); the act of teaching and telling the story is collaborative (I will share this with you, coauthor this with you, and live this life with you, I will tell you my secret); the contents of the story are multifarious and interdisciplinary (characters, plots, twists, metaphors, unexplained codes, places, secrets, connotations, structure the lesson and telling). The lesson, the telling, the contents, are ways of life (ways of being). The story, too, Dina Georgis writes, has the capacity to affectively move us and, at the same time, incite a listening practice that is "neither disengaged nor wanting to master what it sees and hears."[19] If the function of the story is to invite the reader-viewer-interlocutor-listener to feel, respond, and be moved, it also, Ruth Wilson Gilmore reminds us, establishes powerful alignments (provisional and not) that are put to work with and for loved ones.[20] Gilmore shows how utilizing various narrative devices and reading across materials (photocopies, pamphlets, newsletters, scripture, statistics, drawings, announcements, charts, legal documents and cases, theories) engenders practices of solidarity and collaboration that

18. Kevin Young, *The Grey Album: On the Blackness of Blackness* (Minneapolis: Graywolf, 2012).

19. Dina Georgis, *The Better Story: Queer Affects from the Middle East* (New York: SUNY Press, 2013), 1, 18.

20. Ruth Wilson Gilmore, *Golden Gulag: Prisons, Surplus, Crisis, and Opposition in Globalizing California* (Berkeley: University of California Press, 2007).

work within existing, and imagine new, geographies of liberation.[21] The story, as interdisciplinary method, is thus tasked with immense and hopeful possibilities. The story is the practice of black life. With and for love. In this way, and as an interdisciplinary methodology, the story—theoretical, creative, groovy, skilled, action-based, secreted, shared—is a verb-activity that invites engagement, curiosity, collaboration.

SIMULTANEITY

Sylvia Wynter writes that we are a "storytelling species," while also observing that our stories—especially our origin stories—have an impact on our neurobiological and physiological behaviors.[22] Her observations draw attention to the natural sciences as well as interdisciplinarity, emphasizing a dynamic connection between narrative and biology (stories have the capacity to move us). In addition to contesting a teleological-biocentric genre of the human, the dynamism between biology and narrative affirms the black methodologies noted above: science and story are not discrete; rather, we know, read, create, and feel science and story simultaneously.[23] Or, we tell and feel stories (in our hearts), and this telling-feeling tells-feels the empirics of black life. Reading across our curiosities, the story and imagination are testimonies grounded in the material expression of black life. The story has physiological components. And stories make place.[24] This means the metaphoric, allegorical, symbolic, and other devices that shape stories also move us and make place. These narrative devices, so thick and complicated in black studies, demand thinking about the interdisciplinary underpinnings of black studies beyond an additive model.[25] Conceptualizing stories and attendant narrative de-

21. Gilmore, *Golden Gulag*, 182, 212–248.

22. Sylvia Wynter, "Towards the Sociogenic Principle: Fanon, Identity, the Puzzle of Conscious Experience, and What It Is Like to Be 'Black,'" in *National Identities and Sociopolitical Changes in Latin America*, ed. Mercedes F. Durán-Cogan and Antonio Gómez-Moriana (New York: Routledge, 2001), 30–66.

23. "I burst apart." Fanon, *Black Skin, White Masks*, 109.

24. "I hurried back to Eatonville because I knew the town was full of material and that I could get it without hurt, harm or danger." Zora Neale Hurston, *Mules and Men* (1935; rpt., New York: HarperCollins, 1990), 2.

25. Kimberlé Williams Crenshaw, "Mapping the Margins: Intersectionality, Identity Politics, and Violence against Women of Color," *Stanford Law Review* 43, no. 6 (1991): 1241–1299; Patricia Hill Collins, *Black Feminist Thought: Knowledge, Consciousness, and the Politics of Empowerment* (1990; rpt., New York: Routledge, 2000), 18.

vices as *tied to* extraliterary sites (place, body, home, for example) is an interdisciplinary-intersectional reading practice that interlaces the material and the metaphoric. Here the work of Neil Smith and Cindi Katz is useful.[26] They ask us to think about the ways different kinds and types of geographic terms—space, location, position, mapping, and so on—are often utilized without attending to the politics that underwrite these terms. Specifically, the material, concrete, and grounded work of physical-material space goes missing in some theories that draw on space and spatial concepts. A research statement such as "I am going to map the feelings of racialized domestic workers and discover their spaces of containment" clearly demonstrates troubling spatial metaphors that emerge from and embrace colonial reasoning. Conceptualizing certain geographic terms in this way also reifies the absoluteness of space and casts it as an empty container, thus naturalizing uneven geographies and their attendant social inequities. Leaning heavily on metaphoric concepts risks fixing social identities in place because it ostensibly puts forth a "floating world of ideas" that are simply hovering around us.[27] This kind of outlook removes social actors from the production of space and other infrastructures. This is not a call to disregard metaphor but, instead, a plea to take seriously how metaphors are necessarily illuminating, and are indeed structured by and through, the complex groundedness of black life—as extraliterary-storied-material-metaphoric-interdisciplinary-dynamic-curious-scientifically-creative (feeling). Rather than disregard metaphor, we sit with metaphor.

Thinking through the interdisciplinary interplay between narrative and material worlds is especially useful in black studies, because our analytical sites, and our selfhood, are often reduced to metaphor, analogy, trope, and symbol. To borrow from Hortense Spillers, black people are, in many instances, conceived through "mythical prepossession."[28] What happens when we, black people, are read or analyzed as pure metaphor? And what kind of metaphors are we? I suspect, in some cases, we are metaphor-

---

26. Neil Smith and Cindi Katz, "Grounding Metaphor: Towards a Spatialized Politics," in *Place and the Politics of Identity*, ed. Michael Keith and Steve Pile (New York: Routledge, 1993), 67–83.

27. Smith and Katz, "Grounding Metaphor," 80.

28. Rhetorical wealth, telegraphic coding, overdetermined normative properties. Hortense Spillers, "Mama's Baby, Papa's Maybe: An American Grammar Book," in *Black, White, and in Color: Essays on American Literature and Culture* (Chicago: University of Chicago Press, 2003), 203.

ically unliving. In terms of geography, our sense of place is often preconceptualized as dead and dying and this lifelessness extends outward, from that death and deadliness, toward extinction.[29] The dead spaces are inextricably linked to the dehumanizing scripts—they require one another: one cannot have (and dispose of) the welfare queen without (loathing and pushing her out of) the objectionable infrastructures that surround her. At the same time, black geographies are often described through metaphor: postslave black geographies are described as fugitive, underground, maroon; past-present black geographies are described as nonexistent, margin, tomb, womb, aquatic, hidden, zones-of-nonbeing. Often (not always!) these metaphors are delinked from their material underpinnings or histories, which means racial violence risks being cast and/or read as figurative (the geographic idea is abstracted from its material and experiential and embodied underpinnings: the escape is abstracted from the material and intellectual conditions that incited each *different* form of flight when the past flight equals [exactly anticipates] present escape). Particularly sinister are the redoubled workings of death and/as metaphor—which destroys all we are and annihilates our sense of place. This is precisely why paying close attention to the materiality of the black story matters. We cannot politicize ourselves collectively unless we address how the racist trope and absolute space are corelatedly working against black life. Part of our intellectual task is, then, to perhaps get in touch with the materiality of our analytical worlds. Part of our task is to read carefully and, when necessary, reckon with materiality of metaphor.[30] It is worth repeating, then, that this is not a request to abandon metaphors. We need metaphors! Metaphors offer an (entwined material and imagined) future that has not arrived and the future we live and have already lived through.[31]

29. Katherine McKittrick, "On Plantations, Prisons, and a Black Sense of Place," *Journal of Social and Cultural Geography* 12, no. 8 (2011): 947–963.

30. We cannot risk exclusively and solely relying on metaphors or analogies or symbols as literary devices that advance our argument about blackness. We cannot drop blackness into the realm of motif, and depart, disguising the difficult and complicated and extraliterary worlds that animate and are relational to black life.

31. Katherine McKittrick, *Demonic Grounds: Black Women and the Cartographies of Struggle* (Minneapolis: University of Minnesota Press, 2006), 16–19; Tanya Titchkosky, "Life with Dead Metaphors: Impairment Rhetoric in Social Justice Praxis," *Journal of Literary and Cultural Disability Studies* 9, no. 1 (2015): 1–18. Read, too, Toni Morrison on metaphor in her "Disturbing Nurses and the Kindness of Sharks," from *Playing in the Dark: Whiteness and the Literary Imagination* (New York: Random House, 1990), 62–91.

Metaphors are "observational scaffolding."[32] Metaphors function to radically map existing useable (entwined material and imagined) sites of struggle and liberation and joy! Metaphors move us. Metaphors are not just metaphoric, though. They are concretized. This means—if we believe the stories we tell and share—that the metaphoric devices we use to think through black life are signaling practices of liberation (tangible, theoretical, imaginary) that are otherwise-possible and already here (and over there).

COLLAPSE

The task is, I believe, to get in touch with the materiality of our analytical worlds, draw attention to how black studies thinks across a range of places, times, genres, texts, shadows, grooves that are punctuated with diasporic literacy, and collectively think-know-live black life as curious, studied, and grounded. The analytics, as story, allows us to learn and share, and get in touch, without knowing totally. Thus, as we grieve long-standing racial violences, as we are punched by memories of those we have lost, as we archive the most brutal of punishments, as we are weighed down by losing her, them, over and over and we know her and we do not know her and we did not know their name until it happened (we did not know his name until he was gone, I did not know his name, I cannot know, I found the name, I came across her after she was gone) and we feel heartbreak and we see it again and again, as we study the severity of plantation temporalities (then-now), as we are weighed down, and the loss is there beside us, as we grieve and collapse, we do not know absolutely. Still. Losing her. *Dear Science* seeks to tell and live and generate an ethical distance. I hope to write an ethical distance while recognizing that our collective histories of racial violence put pressure on how we live, now.[33] I found her picture. I hope to write an ethical distance and grieve what I, we, cannot know without industry-of-objecthood enveloping her. I kept your secret.

32. Teju Cole, "Double Negative," in *Known and Strange Things* (New York: Random House, 2016), 71.

33. Simone Browne, *Dark Matters: On the Surveillance of Blackness* (Durham, NC: Duke University Press, 2015); Dionne Brand, *A Map to the Door of No Return: Notes to Belonging* (Toronto: Vintage, 2002).

In *Dear Science*, I write and study stories about algorithms, lists, science, footnotes (references, citations), plantations, consciousness, grooves and beats, poetry, geography, methodology, and theory. The stories are inter-disciplinary narratives that use and amend the academic form to wade through complexities of black intellectual life. This project shares what I have learned from friends, colleagues, students, musicians, writers, and poets, and it also includes some photos of texts, images, stories, and songs that have helped me work out what I have and have not learned. This book is very much indebted to the writings of Édouard Glissant and Sylvia Wynter—two very different thinkers who have inspired me (many of us) to keep reading and sharing and wondering. The stories are connected but can be read in any order. These are stories about black life. The stories begin from the premise that liberation is an already existing and unfinished and unmet possibility, laced with creative labor, that emerges from the ongoing collaborative expression of black humanity and black livingness.

....

FOOTNOTES (BOOKS AND PAPERS SCATTERED ABOUT THE FLOOR)

....

*I*n 2015, I began scrolling images at my public talks. The image slides are on a continuous loop. The images are of ideas (in text, song, visual art, maps and places, objects, people) that have shaped my thinking. I started doing this because I was finding it difficult to track, within the context of a public talk, how I know what I know, where I know from, who I know from, and what I cannot possibly know. I try to make a new slideshow or film for each public talk, so I remember to revisit ideas before I give a presentation and think about them in a new context. I include these images because while I feel I know my research fields intimately, how I came to know these fields is fading, so I revisit and recontextualize. At the same time, this history, my memory, is overlaid by newer research questions, texts, images, events, places, people. Confidently and in my own specific and scattered way—to give an obvious example—I know well the tensions between modernity and race and gender and blackness. I found my way to this confidence by reading and rereading those who have studied and written about race, capitalism, and modernity. I found my way by sharing, talking, and writing about writers, scholars, and cultural producers I love to teach, read, reread, and read again. I found my way by reading and rereading work I do not agree with and by making my way through books and ideas I dislike. I sometimes show texts, such as images of music (scores, album cover art, musicians), because I adore music and it structures my life and work, but these ideas are not represented satisfactorily in my research. *The nonwordness of sounds.*[1]

The subtitle of this story, "Books and Papers Scattered about the Floor," is from Nella Larsen, *Quicksand* (New York: Penguin, 1928), 13.

    1. Alexander G. Weheliye, *Phonographies: Grooves in Sonic Afro-Modernity* (Durham, NC: Duke University Press, 2005), 101.

I show the images because I have increasingly noticed that some labor—specifically the exertion that lies within studying and writing and making and grooving—somehow seems to disappear after issuance. The exertion disappears.[2] The images are on a loop, and I add to this loop frequently. The images are not intended to carry clear meaning. They are looped, and the loop represents what I and what we cannot say or hear or see or remember just as it establishes a repetitive, circuitous, and circular but also inaccurate representation of coming to know. The loop is not intended to be meaning-making; the loop can only show fragments and moments of knowing. Shadows: *the interstices of the invisible and visible/ residual elements may be articulated by and within new social practices, in effect, as a "new" emergent formation.*[3] I show the images because I want to be as honest as I can about my intellectual history while also recognizing my dishonest memory. I show the images because I want to be honest about where my ideas come from while recognizing that this is also a process of forgetting. *My sadness sits around me.*[4] So I read in-and-with black studies to honor those who have shared their intellectual and political energy with me—their effort—in myriad infrastructures, feelings, texts, stories, exchanges.[5]

This short story is about citations, endnotes, footnotes, notes, references, bibliographies, texts, narratives, parentheses, sources, and pages. It is a story, one of many, about what we do with books and ideas. It is a story about how we arrange and effectuate the ideas that make ideas. By observing how arranging, rearranging, and collecting ideas outside ourselves are processes that make our ideas our *own*, I think about how our ideas are bound up in stories, research, inquiries, that we do not (or should not claim we) own. This leads me to work through the ways black studies and academic research and writing—when we are doing our very best work—acknowledges the shared and collaborative intellectual praxis that

2. I have thought about this, often. The exertion she puts into her intellectual projects is ineffable. Her intellectual work cannot be tracked on the page. What she does to get there requires tremendous physiological and intellectual effort.

3. Avery Gordon, *Ghostly Matters: Haunting and the Sociological Imagination* (Minneapolis: University of Minnesota Press, 1997), 24; Lisa Lowe, *The Intimacies of Four Continents* (Durham, NC: Duke University Press, 2015), 19.

4. June Jordan, "My Sadness Sits around Me," in *The Black Poets*, ed. Dudley Randall (New York: Bantam, 1971), 248.

5. I do not know everywhere. My privilege is gaping. My geographic bias is obvious and objectionable. I will do better. I add slides weekly, monthly. I keep reading. I am ashamed. Adding more slides is shameful. Vulgar. This note, all notes, are vulgar.

makes our research what it is. This is, for me, especially important because our ideas, on the page or in the presentation, might suggest otherwise; sometimes our ideas imply that we arrived there, in that page or presentation, on our own, as the sole owners of our own ideas. *A property interest.*[6]

Risking the sovereignty of our own stories.[7] What if the practice of referencing, sourcing, and crediting is always bursting with intellectual life and takes us outside ourselves? What if we read outside ourselves not *for* ourselves but to actively unknow ourselves, to unhinge, and thus come to know each other, intellectually, inside and outside the academy, as collaborators of collective and generous and capacious stories?[8] Unknowing ourselves. The unhinging opens up a different conversation about why we do what we do, here, in this place, that despises us—not focusing on reparation of the self, alone, but instead sharing information and stories and resources to build the capacity for social change.[9] *Alternative outcomes.*[10] The unhinging, unknowing ourselves, opens up learning processes that are uninterested in a self that is economized by citations. And still, displacing the self, unknowing who we are, is awful: it is indeterminate and unpredictable and lonely. Togetherness can be difficult and lonely, too.[11]

6. Cheryl I. Harris, "Whiteness as Property," *Harvard Law Review* 106, no. 8 (June 1993): 1715.

7. Dina Georgis, *A Better Story: Queer Affects from the Middle East* (New York: SUNY Press, 2013), 73.

8. Here we can also reference referencing in black musics: See, for example, Betty Davis's "They Say I'm Different," from *They Say I'm Different* (Seattle: Light in the Attic Records, 1974): "I'm talkin' bout Big Momma Thornton / Lightning Hopkins / Howling Wolf / Albert King / Chuck Berry / Chuck Berry / Chuck Berry." See also Stevie Wonder, "Sir Duke," from *Songs in the Key of Life* (Detroit: Tamla, 1976). On referencing place, see Murray Forman, "'Represent': Race, Space and Place in Rap Music," in *That's the Joint! The Hip-Hop Studies Reader,* 2nd ed., ed. Murray Forman and Mark Anthony Neal (New York: Routledge, 2011), 247–269. On referencing place, see Mark V. Campbell, "Connect the T. Dots—Remix Multiculturalism: After Caribbean-Canadian, Social Possibilities for Living Difference," in *Ebony Roots, Northern Soil: Perspectives on Blackness in Canada,* ed. Charmaine Nelson (Cambridge, MA: Cambridge Scholars Publishing, 2010), 254–276. On referencing, sampling, and mentions in hip-hop (thank you Mark Campbell for sharing this article), see Justin A. Williams, "Theoretical Approaches to Quotation in Hip-Hop Recordings," *Contemporary Music Review* 33, no. 2 (2014): 188–209.

9. Ruth Wilson Gilmore, *Golden Gulag: Prisons, Surplus, Crisis, and Opposition in Globalizing California* (Berkeley: University of California Press, 2007), 28–29.

10. Gilmore, *Golden Gulag,* 28.

11. "If she wants to meet me that's fine if she doesn't / that is also fine." Jackie Kay, "Chapter Five: The Tweed Hat Dream," in *The Adoption Papers* (Newcastle upon Tyne, UK: Bloodaxe Books, 1991), 19.

The awfulness, though, opens up a conversation about why we do what we do and offers methods for living, here, in this place, that despises us. The unknowing brings together unexpected intellectual conversations that, together, resist dehumanization. The unknowing risks reading what we cannot bear and what we love too much. Unknowing ourselves.[12] Unknowing does not seek or provide answers: the steady focus is, instead, on working out how to share ideas relationally. Perhaps the function of communication, referencing, citation, is not to master knowing and centralize our knowingness, but to share *how we know*, and share how we came to know imperfect and sometimes unintelligible but always hopeful and practical ways to live this world as black.[13] *The text passes from a dreamed-of transparency to the opacity produced in words.*[14] The parentheses enfold and convey, the notes buttress, and they leave shadows.[15] Citing is not easy. Referencing is hard.[16]

12. "In a way, the ethics and methodologies of encounters, anecdotes, conversations and storytelling I am invoking through radical vulnerability, strive to achieve in the realm of research praxis, a politics of indeterminacy, or a politics without guarantees." Richa Nagar, *Muddying the Waters: Coauthoring Feminisms across Scholarship and Activism* (Urbana: University of Illinois Press, 2014), 13.

13. "Mastery is never complete.... We are always living in excess of what we know about our motives, our actions, and what we say we value." Dina Georgis, *The Better Story: Queer Affects from the Middle East* (New York: SUNY Press, 2013), 106. "The different subjectivities and material conditions of those who produce and exchange knowledge continue to be erased under the sign of mastery. Yet these different conditions have everything to do with what knowledge is produced and how it is handled." Cindi Katz, "Towards Minor Theory," *Environment and Planning D: Society and Space* 14 (August 1996): 497.

14. Édouard Glissant, *Poetics of Relation*, trans. Betsy Wing (1990; rpt., Ann Arbor: University of Michigan Press, 1997), 115.

15. See also Kobena Mercer, "Decolonization and Disappointment: Reading Fanon's Sexual Politics," in *The Fact of Blackness: Frantz Fanon and Visual Representation*, ed. Alan Read (Seattle: Bay Press, 1996), 114–130.

16. In childhood development studies, referencing signals social engagement; it is a specific developmental milestone (typically achieved by neurotypical children when they are between eight and fourteen months old). The interaction is between a child and a parent/adult and an object (e.g., a ball): the parent shows interest in the ball and encourages the child to observe and to do the same; the reference is the child's nonverbal look to the adult, who is talking about, pointing to, providing information about the ball; the nonverbal look (the reference, which shows shared interest in the ball) and other cues (referencing the ball by following the finger that is pointing to the ball, or perhaps referencing by mimicking and also pointing to the ball) indicates that the child is watching and learning about the world. The adult will perhaps reinforce the interaction and referencing by narrating the activity ("Look! a ball!"). The child is referencing the adult/parent and learning

This is a story, one of many, about how we know, how we come to knowing, and how we share what we know. I am interested in how references, citations, and bibliographies are central to the project of black studies. I am also curious about effectuated and effectuating ideas and learning and knowing. I believe that bibliographies and endnotes and references and sources are alternative stories that can, in the most generous sense, centralize the practice of sharing ideas about liberation and resistance and writing against racial and sexual violence. *Alternative outcomes.*

---

about the world by showing an interest in what the adult/parent is interested in; the interaction is joined. The focus is not on the child, per se, but on the child receiving social and emotional attention from the interaction and learning from that attention (such as the adult's voice of encouragement or facial expressions); referencing is acknowledging the ball-as-a-shared-site-of-interest and, at the same time, recognizing that the social relationship (the connection between the parent and child) is meaningful and garners social and emotional attention. When a child does not reference, the assumption is that they are slower at developing social skills and/or are not "information seeking." Neuroatypical children—who do not reference in the same way as neurotypical children—may find normative referencing very difficult. This does not mean, in my view, that these children are not adept at information seeking; rather, it means that they are seeking information (normative and nonnormative information) differently! The level of social engagement referencing demands is high; it takes some neuroatypical children outside of themselves, requiring they step onto a normative path (a path they may consider nonnormative), which is laborious. Some working in the field that studies autism spectrum disorders might say, then: referencing does *not* come *naturally* to neuroatypical kids . . . in the way it comes *so naturally* to normal kids. This developmental-milestone-skill perspective on referencing, for me, opens up an important challenge: what does it mean, and to whom are we signaling, when referencing (citation practices) comes *easy*? I am not, to be sure, conflating (neurotypical-neuroatypical) social referencing with academic citation practices; rather, I am underscoring how the term "referencing" carries in it the clinical normalization of referencing practices (developmental milestones, which are tracked biological, psychological, and emotional changes in children) that can provide a way for us to notice that, for some people inhabiting our worlds, referencing is tough and awfully hard. If we rotate the script, and understand the hardness not as unusual but as a way of living and a way of being and navigating our messed-up world that rewards all kinds of normativities, then we can learn that engaging with the materials we read to show *how we know* can be (ideally, I would argue) a painful undoing of who we think we are and, as well, how we come to share what we know differently. The neurotypical are *not*, throughout the referencing process, *becoming* neuroatypical or autistic of course; rather this example gives us a way to notice and engender conditions of relation wherein we refuse normative authenticating processes. Lauren Cornew, Karen R. Dobkins, Natacha Akshoomoff, Joseph P. McCleery, and Leslie J. Carver, "Atypical Social Referencing in Infant Siblings of Children with Autism Spectrum Disorders," *Journal of Autism and Developmental Disorders* 42, no. 12 (December 2012): 2611–2621; Erin Manning, *The Minor Gesture* (Durham, NC: Duke University Press, 2016); Jonathan Alderson, *Challenging the Myths of Autism* (Toronto: HarperCollins, 2011).

I am indebted to the endnotes and footnotes prepared by the motley crew Richard Iton, Lisa Lowe, Sylvia Wynter, Vladimir Nabokov, and David Foster Wallace.[17] The notes these authors include in their works, like many others, not only show the labor and effort that underpins research and writing; they also signal stories of other stories that direct you to a story and place connected to, but not of, the story you began. *Pale Fire*.

This is not, explicitly, a story about the metrics of citation practices or impact factors. I am, as I note below, cognizant of this important critique of white and patriarchal citation practices and how they can "justify ongoing forms of domination."[18] I am more interested in how referencing works in black studies and how this referencing uncovers a lesson that cannot be contained within the main text.[19] What if citations offer advice? What if citations are suggestions for living differently?[20] What if some citations counsel how to refuse what they think we are?

17. Vladimir Nabokov, *Pale Fire* (New York: Vintage, 1989); David Foster Wallace, *Infinite Jest: A Novel* (Boston: Little, Brown, 1996); Lisa Lowe, *The Intimacies of Four Continents* (Durham, NC: Duke University Press, 2015); Richard Iton, *In Search of the Black Fantastic* (Oxford: Oxford University Press, 2008); on Sylvia Wynter, see n. 25 in this story. See also Anthony Grafton, *The Footnote: A Curious History* (Cambridge, MA: Harvard University Press, 1999).

18. Carrie Mott and Daniel Cockayne, "Citation Matters: Mobilizing the Politics of Citation toward a Practice of 'Conscientious Engagement,'" *Gender, Place and Culture: A Journal of Feminist Geography* 24, no. 7 (2017): 954–973; Lauren Berlant, *The Female Complaint: The Unfinished Business of Sentimentality in American Culture* (Durham, NC: Duke University Press, 2008), 40–41.

19. "In this respect, it is always interesting to carefully read Fanon's footnotes. To begin with, *Black Skin, White Masks* contains more footnotes than any of Fanon's later texts. Some of those footnotes run two or three pages. In *Black Skin, White Masks*'s footnotes, Fanon often engages himself in a conversation with an imagined opponent or appeals to personal memories and thus reveals more about his thoughts than he does in the text. Fanon's footnotes are like the repressed, unconscious foundations of his text. Or, in the words of Gayatri Spivak, they are the marginalia of Fanon's texts, his way of separating his public from his private self." Françoise Vergès, "Creole Skin, Black Mask: Fanon and Disavowal," *Critical Inquiry* 23, no. 3 (Spring 1997): 582–583.

20. Worn Down (Fall 2017). NourbeSe Philip's long-cycle-poem *Zong!* (2011) swirled in my head. I was alerted to the award-winning art installation by Rana Hamadeh (*The Ten Murders of Josephine and On Proxy Bodies: A Script in Progress*, Rotterdam, 2017), a piece that attends to the *Zong* massacre—specifically the *Gregson v. Gilbert* case—and ongoing (historically present) racial violences. I was curious about the ways in which the work of Philip was, for the most part, not present in the images, ideas, and theories Hamadeh used in her work (those I could access from afar, to be clear). From what I understand, Philip's *Zong!* is given a nod within the exhibition (as "phonic substance") and is also noted to be an "inspiration." Reviewing the exhibition from afar, I wondered about how the intellectual effort of a

Sara Ahmed makes the very smart observation that citation practices are gendered and racialized. Citation decisions are a political project for Ahmed because, she argues, absenting white men (from our bibliographies, references, footnotes) reorganizes our feminist knowledge worlds. By excluding white men from her (our) bibliographies she (we) can gen-

---

black woman poet undergirds *The Ten Murders* yet is also, for the most part, removed from the visual and textual work that is presented. What is the work of citation here? And uncitation?

A scanning of an exhibition review, along with an interview, would lead one to think that perhaps the legal archives from the *Zong* massacre were sought out, reviewed, and studied by Hamadeh and then visually built into her installation. However, a trip to the archives is not required. *Gregson v. Gilbert* can be found within Philip's *Zong!* itself: it serves as the narrative through which her poetics emerges; the case is also reproduced within the book and is retold in the "Notanda." The legal case anchors Philip's 2008 long-cycle-poem and is intensified by the creative work she did with and to those legal narratives to produce *Zong!* in order to poetically express her political obligation to the black-unnamed who were murdered. In *Zong!* the fragments of the legal archive are reworded to reconceptualize the weight of unremembered loss. In *Zong!* the unnamed and the forgotten are named in trace. In *Zong!* poetics are the analytics of black life. With *Zong!* we learn to unread and reread unspeakability.

In 2017, just six weeks before the exhibition was launched, Hamadeh contacted Philip and requested permission and blessings to use *Zong!* in her installation. In addition to detailing how *Zong!* would be presented and archived in the exhibition, Hamadeh wrote to Philip explaining that the book, long in her hands, was "a daily ritual that grew slowly throughout my working process into becoming an important theoretical and affective scaffolding within the work." The artist intended to use Philip's work and ideas in the exhibition (and perhaps the work and ideas were already integrated before permission was requested, given that Philip was contacted only six weeks before the launch . . . of course, tracking time is always unhelpfully awful).

Philip did not provide permission. She did not agree with the conditions under which her work would be used and, as well, made clear that she was also very busy and worn out. Her sister was dying and needed care.

Without permission and sweeping aside Philip's care-work and mourning, it seems Hamadeh reimagined the work of *Zong* with scraps of *Zong!* The nod to Philip within the exhibition itself is coupled to the kind of documents many, in theory, have access to (e.g., the legal archives from the original case, *Gregson v. Gilbert*, available in *Zong!* as noted above). But in some ways this coupling—the nod and the archive that is already there—establishes a kind of alibi for rewriting and forgetting the creative-intellectual work Philip expresses in *Zong!* In one interview Hamadeh presents her engagement with the *Zong* massacre as her own intellectual work and theoretical intervention—Philip is not mentioned. Instead, she explains: "This archive of horror shall not be understood as the trace of the massacre, but rather as the fragmentary, unspoken, and unspeakable phonic materiality that is captured and trapped within the trace—that subsists *because of* and *despite of* that trace" and "I treat the *Gregson vs. Gilbert* document in the exhibition as a primary document that defines the notion of documentality as a whole." Hamadeh also includes her own poetics in her exhibition:

erate new ideas and chip away at, and possibly break down, the walls of patriarchy that have excluded and refuse feminist ways of knowing.[21] Decentering the citations, and thus the experiences, of white men unmakes a scholarly system that champions and normalizes white patriarchal scholarly traditions. I struggle with the outcome of this citation project. I wonder

---

For, thought is made in the mouth. / Let's talk about the voice / of the record / as the record / Not of the captured, but of capture / Not of weight, but the modality of measure / The voice of the killer

The records, the mouth, the weights and measures, the voice. Bad made measure. Curious. It seems to me—from afar—that Hamadeh is, at least in part, working with and reworking the long-cycle-poem (not necessarily the original archival documents): scratching it out and scraping it up and remaking it into something else. In the process of rewriting, the creative labor of Philip—the intellectual effort of her monumental rehumanizing black studies project, *Zong!*—wears down.

I will not reproduce all of *Zong!* in order to provide textual proof of Hamadeh's rewording and revising of Philip's long-cycle-poem. I view this from afar. How Hamadeh understands and writes the *Zong* massacre is on her shoulders, as is Philip's clear, exhausted, unwillingness to be a part of the project. I ask, though, that we dwell on the politics of permission. I ask that we dwell on the politics of permission in relation to black women. And, I want to underscore and centralize and illuminate the effort Philip put into the long-cycle-poem. I was told to cite black women. We are told to cite black women. Sometimes the words and ideas of black women, when cited, become something else. Sometimes the ideas of black women wear out and wear down even though these narratives provide the clues and instructions to imagine the world anew. Often the words and ideas and brilliance of black women remain unread. The words and ideas of black women go uncited. The intellectual effort is unnoticed and stepped over and swept aside. Worn down, sometimes the intellectual work of black women is unmentionable. We must continue to cite their words and ideas well. We must read them well. I cite and site *Zong!* and NourbeSe Philip as brilliant intellectual effort. I want to engage this text as labor. It is not a nod, gesture, signal, or inspiration. It is poetic infrastructure—black women's work—that radically repoliticizes black life.

I viewed images of the exhibition that were shared by a colleague who saw it in Rotterdam in 2017. See https://frieze.com/article/rana-hamadeh and http://moussemagazine.it /rana-hamadeh-carolina-rito-2017. Other quotations are from an email correspondence between Philip and Hamadeh (emphasis in the original and permission granted by Philip) and my personal email communication with Philip (permission granted); "Bad made measure" is from M. NourbeSe Philip, *Zong!* (Toronto: Mercury Press, 2008), 5. See also Katherine McKittrick, "Diachronic Loops/Deadweight Tonnage/Bad Made Measure," *Cultural Geographies* (December 2015): 1–16.

21. Sara Ahmed, "White Men," *Feminist Killjoys* (blog), November 4, 2014, https://feminist killjoys.com/2014/11/04/white-men/. In the above blog post, Ahmed is thoughtful about her citation practices before *Living a Feminist Life* (Durham, NC: Duke University Press, 2017), noting her referential relationships with scholars such as Immanuel Kant, G. W. F. Hegel, Edmund Husserl, and Maurice Merleau-Ponty.

how it inadvertently turns on impossible foreclosures: What does it mean to read Jacques Derrida and abandon Derrida and retain Derrida's spirit (or specter!)? Do we unlearn whom we do not cite? And what of our teaching practice? Do we teach refusal? Can we not teach our students to engage with various authors and narratives, critically, while also asking them to raise up the work of black women and other scholars, writers, artists, interviewees, teachers, who go unrecognized? How do we teach each other to read (disapprove, evaluate, critique, use, forget, abandon, remember) "white men" or other powerful scholars? Or is the critique (uncitation) to enact erasure? The project of erasure, too, often unfolds as an affirmation of racial privilege: here I recall (mostly white) feminists sparklingly shouting with a kind of breathy desperation that they, too, have been overciting and venerating white male scholarship, and that Ahmed has discovered a brand-new way to recognize and credit and legitimize the ideas of the marginalized; this leads these breathy speakers to hail the work of—mostly nonblack, mostly white feminist, mostly academic—privileged scholars![22] That aside, Ahmed's citation project matters to me because it asks that we think about the epistemological grounds through which we theorize and imagine and name liberation in our referencing practices.

Citation points to method and how we come to write what we know. Citation is important because it frames and supports (legitimizes) our

22. Where and when do we cut those purveyors of dreadful feminism? When do we refuse to cite the bourgeois feminists, or the left-leaning feminists, or the Western feminists who write about Third World "culture" or who adore a two-sex system or who despise and abuse their black administrative assistants or who fail their black students or who publicly humiliate and threaten nonwhite women and men? How do we cite those who stole and steal our work, our ideas? When do we refuse to engage those feminist scholars who despise those who clean their homes and tend their gardens and care for their children? When do we refuse to cite or read or talk about dreadful awful brutal feminism? How do we cite the feminists who call other feminists "terrorists"? Where and when do we stop citing the nonwhite, including black, patriarchal scholars who, heckle, cut down, plagiarize, kick about, ignore, talk over, interrupt, demote, demean black women? (Suddenly, the unraveling: out with the nonwhite capitalists who smartly write of ecofeminism, out with the boring female identified white liberals who write of political theory and the saccharine promises of equality, be gone nonradical nonqueer nonanarchist nonfeminist women who write of community gardens.) "Dominant forms of feminism that fail to address the rapacious qualities of corporate capital or 'predatory capitalism' can be legitimately criticized for ideological limitations that render some feminisms complicit in dehumanizing systems and in mystifying the convergence of corporate wealth and repressive state policies." Joy James, *Shadowboxing: Representations of Black Feminist Politics* (New York: Palgrave, 1999), 182.

argument. This also shows that if we *begin* with Michel Foucault as our primary methodological and theoretical frame—if Foucault is our referential scaffolding—*we will, most certainly, draw Foucauldian conclusions*. There is nothing at all wrong with a Foucauldian project and Foucauldian conclusions, of course—to suggest so would be remiss and skirt around the work of citations I am seeking to address. This example simply centralizes the importance of how referential beginnings and referential scaffoldings shape conclusions.

Theory is absence, obscure and propitious.[23] Working with scholars like Sylvia Wynter, Édouard Glissant, and Frantz Fanon, I read and re-read their work, to observe their complex analytical and methodological worlds. These scholars, it seems to me, are much more interested in *how* we know, and how we come to know, than in *who* we know. They tell us that there is no beginning through which firm conclusions can be made. They tell us beginnings-to-ends and questions with knowable answers are ineffective analytical equations. They tell us that liberation cannot, in any way, be a formulated *answer* to how we resolve the troubling awful world we inhabit *if it is posed as a subsequent counterreaction to that troubling awful world*—for that end-answer all too often demands a beginning-question framed within the perimeters of, and thus invested in the systemic replication of, our awful world. *Anxiety to convey meaning often results in overemphasis, and emphasis as a way of conveying meaning means that you are unconsciously holding on to meaning and limiting it*.[24]

Sylvia Wynter taught me to recognize how radical theory-making takes place outside existing systems of knowledge. Sylvia Wynter taught me that radical theory-making takes place outside existing systems of knowledge. Sylvia Wynter taught me that radical theory-making takes place outside existing systems of knowledge and that this place, outside (demonic grounds), is inhabited by those who are brilliantly and intimately aware of existing systems of knowledge. Sylvia Wynter taught me that radical theory-making takes place outside existing systems of knowledge and that this place, outside (demonic grounds), is inhabited by those who are brilliantly and intimately aware of existing systems of knowledge (as self-replicating). Sylvia Wynter taught me that radical theory-making takes place outside existing systems of knowledge and that this place,

---

23. Glissant, *Poetics of Relation*, 129.

24. M. NourbeSe Philip, "Lessons for the Voice (1)," in *She Tries Her Tongue, Her Silence Softly Breaks* (Charlottetown, Canada: Ragweed Press, 1989), 72.

outside (demonic grounds), is inhabited by those who are brilliantly and intimately aware of and connected to existing systems of knowledge (as self-replicating) and that this awareness provides theoretical insights and projections of humanity that imagine a totally new way of being. Sylvia Wynter taught me that radical theory-making takes place outside existing systems of knowledge and that this place, outside (demonic grounds), is inhabited by those who are brilliantly and intimately aware of and connected to existing systems of knowledge (as self-replicating) and that this awareness provides theoretical insights and projections of humanity that imagine a totally new way of being that observes how our present mode of being functions unjustly and cannot sustain itself ethically.[25] Sylvia Wyn-

25. Sylvia Wynter, "1492: A New World View," in *Race, Discourse, and the Origin of the Americas: A New World View*, ed. Vera Lawrence Hyatt and Rex Nettleford (Washington, DC: Smithsonian Institution Press, 1995), 5–57; Sylvia Wynter, "Africa, the West and the Analogy of Culture: The Cinematic Text after Man," in *Symbolic Narratives/African Cinema: Audiences, Theory and the Moving Image*, ed. June Givanni (London: British Film Institute, 2000), 25–76; Sylvia Wynter, "Beyond Miranda's Meanings: Un/Silencing the 'Demonic Ground' of Caliban's 'Woman,'" in *Out of the Kumbla: Caribbean Women and Literature*, ed. Carole Boyce Davies and Elaine Savory Fido (Trenton, NJ: Africa World Press, 1990), 355–372; Sylvia Wynter, "Beyond the Categories of the Master Conception: The Counter-doctrine of the Jamesian Poiesis," in *C. L. R. James's Caribbean*, ed. Paget Henry and Paul Buhle (Durham, NC: Duke University Press, 1992), 63–91; Sylvia Wynter, "Beyond the Word of Man: Glissant and the New Discourse of the Antilles," *World Literature Today* 63, no. 4 (Autumn 1989): 637–647; Sylvia Wynter, "Ethno or Socio Poetics," *Alcheringa/Ethnopoetics* 2, no. 2 (1976): 78–94; Sylvia Wynter, "New Seville and the Conversion Experience of Bartolomé de Las Casas: Part One," *Jamaica Journal* 17, no. 2 (May 1984): 25–32; Sylvia Wynter, "New Seville and the Conversion Experience of Bartolomé de Las Casas: Part Two," *Jamaica Journal* 17, no. 3 (August–October 1984): 46–55; Sylvia Wynter, "Novel and History, Plot and Plantation," *Savacou* 5 (1971): 95–102; Sylvia Wynter, "On Disenchanting Discourse: 'Minority' Literary Criticism and Beyond," in *The Nature and Context of Minority Discourse*, ed. Abdul R. JanMohamed and David Lloyd (New York: Oxford University Press, 1990), 432–469; Sylvia Wynter, "Rethinking 'Aesthetics': Notes towards a Deciphering Practice," in *Ex-iles: Essays on Caribbean Cinema*, ed. Mbye Cham (Trenton, NJ: Africa World Press, 1992), 238–279; Sylvia Wynter, "The Ceremony Must Be Found: After Humanism," *boundary 2* 12, no. 3, and 13, no. 1 (Spring/Fall 1984): 19–70; Sylvia Wynter, "The Eye of the Other," in *Blacks in Hispanic Literature: Critical Essays*, ed. Miriam DeCosta (New York: Kennikat, 1977), 8–19; Sylvia Wynter, "The Pope Must Have Been Drunk, the King of Castile a Madman: Culture as Actuality and the Caribbean Rethinking of Modernity," in *Reordering of Culture: Latin America, the Caribbean and Canada in the Hood*, ed. Alvina Ruprecht and Cecilia Taiana (Ottawa: Carleton University Press, 1995), 17–41; Sylvia Wynter, "Towards the Sociogenic Principle: Fanon, Identity, the Puzzle of Conscious Experience," in *National*

ter taught me that black women are radical theory makers and that black women inhabit demonic ground.[26]

The sharing of ideas (no beginnings, no ends) enables a terrain of struggle, through which different futures are imagined. In this instance, we must ask how the cited works of some black scholars enable a new humanism, planetary humanism, radical theories of liberation, poetics of relation, a new worldview, and therefore refuse the crude capital economization of collated names standing in as ideas.[27] I do not believe that ci-

Identities and Sociopolitical Changes in Latin America, ed. Mercedes F. Durán-Cogan and Antonio Gómez-Moriana (New York: Routledge, 2001), 30–66; Sylvia Wynter, "Unsettling the Coloniality of Being/Power/Truth/Freedom: Towards the Human, after Man, Its Overrepresentation—an Argument," CR: *The New Centennial Review* 3, no. 3 (Fall 2003): 257–337.

26. Wynter, "Beyond Miranda's Meanings," 365.

27. As well and at the same time some citation practices show how black intellectuals and other social theorists are differentially sourced (through erasure, through quick and fast and understudied referencing, through detailed and thorough engagements, and so on) in the (economic and otherwise) production of academic knowledge. Excised from, and despised within. The academy needs the figure of the black: we are the analytical sites, the data, the experiment, the security guards, the cleaners, the administrative assistants, the nonnormative teachers, through which so much scholarship moves. In books and articles, the figure of the black moves in tandem with citations that are, at times, animated by desperation: if I/we cite Claudia Rankin, if I/we cite Frantz Fanon, if I/we cite James (C. L. R., Joy, Baldwin . . .), I/we are, theoretically, "doing" race and blackness.

The desperation, exasperated, often goes sideways.
To do race I will cite . . .

~~Gloria Anzuldua~~.
~~Toni Morrison~~.
~~Zadie Smith~~.
~~Buchi Emecheta~~.
Donna Haraway on situated knowledge ~~which is built on the words of Buchi Emecheta~~.
~~Gilles Deleuze and Félix Guattari~~.
Borderlands.

The bookend to this is citation advice. Pages and pages. I have noticed that each year our graduate students present their thesis proposals, during the question and answer period, only the black students are asked if they have read *x* or *y* or *z*. The nonblack students are asked about their research and the black students are given reading lists. This happens to me, this happens to us, too. Have you read [insert name of theorist] on animals? Oh! You must. You need this. Your project on black things will suffer if you have not read what I have read. Here is a list of what I have read and what I *know* you have not read. Here is a list of what

tation, as a practice that includes or excludes, is useful. I am not interested in citations as quotable value.[28] I want to reference other possibilities such as, citations as learning, as counsel, as sharing. I say this because, after many years of thinking about referencing practices, I am pretty certain that much of the work in black studies does not cite books and articles and ideas and music and art in order to quickly and uncritically authorize the author's project. Much of black studies is not written for the impact factor. Much of black studies baffles the scientometric index. I believe, instead, that referencing in black studies is a lesson in living. To put it another way, referencing and citation in black studies are what Carmen Kynard calls "vernacular insurrections": narratives that are "not only counterhege-

---

you do not know. Here is a list of what I am reading for you and your book on black things. Look! Look!

De temps à autre, on a envie de s'arrêter.
From time to time you feel like giving up.
From time to time one would like to stop.

Sometimes citation practices do not take the time to feel and recognize liberation. Sometimes referencing signals allusion rather than study. "Doing race" is not the same as undoing racism. Citations are economized. Some citations are unfreeing. Some citations objectify black people. Works cited are not always about the work in which the works cited appears.

See Frantz Fanon, Peau noire, masques blancs (Paris: Les Éditions du Seuil, 1952), 145; Frantz Fanon, Black Skin, White Masks, trans. Richard Philcox (1952; rpt., New York: Grove, 2008), 116, 136. Many thanks to Yasmine Djerbal for assistance with translations (English-toward-French and French-toward-English).

See also Analogue University, "Control, Resistance, and the 'Data University': Towards a Third Wave Critique," Antipode Interventions, March 31, 2017, https://antipodefoundation .org/2017/03/31/control-resistance-and-the-data-university/.

"But suddenly racism and 'women of colour' appear as phrases or topics thrown into books as chapters, producing tight little breathless paragraphs or footnotes . . . " Himani Bannerji, "Returning the Gaze: An Introduction," in Returning the Gaze: Essays on Racism, Feminism, and Politics, ed. Himani Bannerji (Toronto: Sister Vision, 1993), xiv. Thank you, Ellyn Walker.

See also Katherine McKittrick, "bell hooks," in Key Contemporary Theorists on Space and Place, ed. Phil Hubbard, Rob Kitchin, and Gill Valentine (London: Sage, 2004), 189–194; and Katherine McKittrick, Demonic Grounds: Black Women and the Cartographies of Struggle (Minneapolis: University of Minnesota Press, 2006), 154, 146.

28. "Did you ever read my words, or did you merely finger through them for quotations which you thought might valuably support an already conceived idea concerning some old and distorted connection between us?" Audre Lorde, "Letter to Mary Daly," in Sister Outsider: Essays and Speeches (1984; rpt., Berkeley: Crossing Press, 2007), 68.

monic, but also affirmative of new, constantly mutating languages, identities, political methodologies, and social understandings that communities form in and of themselves both inwardly and outwardly . . . not merely the bits and pieces chipped off or chipping away at dominant culture, but a whole new emergence."[29] The notes, the citations, the books, the references have, to borrow again from Kynard, "black freedom-inspired purpose."[30]

Ahmed—to get back on track—*incompletely continues* the work of many black feminists and black scholars. Black thinkers have always turned to each other to generate ideas and develop a body of scholarship that calls out and responds to the overarching biocentric and colonial knowledge system that cannot, in any way, honor black intellectual life. Ida B. Wells. *Red Record*.[31] Turning to each other is not, though, an inward-looking project that requires exclusion.[32] This scholarship delineates worldviews outside and across white supremacist and colonial ways of knowing. Part of this work has involved subverting and rehistoricizing existing knowledge systems by sharing black ways of knowing and living. Black ways of knowing and living. *Red Record. Southern Horrors.* This sharing practice—passing on what we know and how we know it and how to read, reread, and unread—reorganizes our knowledge worlds by providing textual and methodological (verbal, nonverbal, written, unwritten) confirmations of black life as struggle. Citation could, then, perhaps be considered one fulcrum of black studies: in a world that despises blackness the bibliography—written or sung or whispered or remembered or dreamed or forgotten—ushers in, or initiates, or teaches, or affirms. This is the praxis of being black and human as struggle. This cites and sites a genre of humanness that emerged from but is *not solely* defined by plantocratic logics of dispossession: the works cited, what we tell each other about what we know and how to know, contain *how to* refuse practices of

29. Carmen Kynard, *Vernacular Insurrections: Race, Black Protest, and the New Century in Composition-Literacies Studies* (Albany: SUNY Press, 2013), 10–11.

30. Kynard, *Vernacular Insurrections*, 18.

31. Jacqueline Jones Royster, ed., *Southern Horrors and Other Writings: The Anti-lynching Campaign of Ida B. Wells, 1892–1900* (Boston: Bedford/St. Martins, 1996).

32. "The intellectual and cultural achievements of the black Atlantic populations exist partly inside and not always against the grand narrative of Enlightenment and its operational principals." Paul Gilroy, *The Black Atlantic: Modernity and Double Consciousness* (Cambridge, MA: Harvard University Press, 1993), 48.

dehumanization.[33] The works cited untangle systems of oppression and talk about resisting racist violence. The works cited are many and various divergent and overlapping texts, images, songs, and ideas that may not normally be read together.[34] The works cited, all of them, when understood as *in conversation* with each other, demonstrate an interconnected story that resists oppression. We do not have to agree with all the works in the works cited. We do not have to like all of the works in the works cited. We do have to trust that the works in the works cited are helping us understand and talk about and theorize how to know the world differently. The praxis, then, is not about who belongs and who does not belong in the index or the endnotes; rather, it is about how we, collectively, are working against racial apartheid and different kinds and types of violence.[35]

While many black scholars certainly cite white men, when we read their work closely we can notice that they are anticipating and, a priori, politically moving beyond Ahmed's project by producing intellectual narratives that envision renewed liberatory infrastructures that are stitched together *not* by specific names, but by the *practice of sharing ideas* about how we might and can resist multiscalar injustices. Hortense Spillers. Carole Boyce Davies. Joy James. Maya Angelou. Zora Neale Hurston. Barbara Christian. Barbara Smith. Paula Giddings. *When and Where I Enter.* Thus, we might recognize black studies not as a citational project of naming and unnaming, but instead as sharing ideas about how to struggle against oppression. This has less to do with white men as embodied knowers and more to do with *doing the work of liberation.* This is not, to be clear, a refutation of the politics of naming (#sayhername) but noticing that naming and citing black life (#sayhername) is *not* simply an act

33. "And where the words of women are crying to be heard, we must each of us recognize our responsibility to seek those words out, to read them and share them and examine them in their pertinence to our lives. That we not hide behind the mockeries of separations that have been imposed upon us and which so often we accept as our own. For instance, 'I can't possibly teach Black women's writing—their experience is so different from mine.' Yet how many years have you spent teaching Plato and Shakespeare and Proust? Or another: 'She's a white woman and what could she possibly have to say to me?' Or, 'She's a lesbian what would my husband say, or my chairman?' Or again: 'This woman writes of her sons and I have no children.' And all the other endless ways we rob ourselves of ourselves and each other." Audre Lorde, *Sister Outsider: Essays and Speeches* (Berkeley, CA: Crossing Press, 1984), 44.

34. "No matter how many studies and references we accumulate (though it is our profession to carry out such things), we will never reach the end of such a volume; knowing this in advance makes it possible for us to dwell there." Glissant, *Poetics of Relation*, 154.

35. Listen to Ella Fitzgerald, "My Happiness," Brunswick, 1958.

of identification-designation but also a code for sharing one method that helps us, collectively, understand and navigate and perhaps undo the wrongness of the world. How do we notice that the named and unnamed can, together, teach us about liberation? How do our questions change if we are not interested in exclusion? Makeda Silvera. *Silenced.*[36] The work of citation, for black feminists specifically, has always been one of compiling and sharing bibliographies and syllabi and stories and memories that map long-standing conversations about how we know what we know and how we share our livingness.[37] Rememory. Recall the headings on pages 221–378 of *But Some of Us Are Brave.* The headings are: bibliographies, bibliographic essays, nonprint material, *doing the work*, selected course syllabi.

Sonia Sanchez.
The Black Woman.
University of Massachusetts, Amherst.
Black Studies.
Spring 1975.[38]

While I brokenheartedly abandoned feminism many years ago, I did not abandon black feminist thought. What is important about Ahmed's refusal of white male citations, for me, is that it inadvertently historicizes the citational politics that have *always* informed black feminist thought and black studies. The groundbreaking work by black women intellectuals, inside and outside the academy, provided and continues to provide an outlook wherein *doing the work* necessitates—has always necessitated— what VèVè Clark calls "diaspora literacy": the ability to read and comprehend multifarious and overlapping discourses of the black diaspora from an informed and learned perspective.[39] What Clark so brilliantly shows is that black intellectual life has always required highly skilled citation

36. Makeda Silvera, *Silenced: Talks with Working Class West Indian Women about Their Lives and Struggles as Domestic Workers in Canada* (Toronto: Sister Vision Press, 1989).

37. I will not attempt to list all the syllabi for freedom produced from about 2012 onward. Teaching Trayvon; Ferguson Syllabus; Discussion Guide: Justice for Colten Boushie; Waller County Syllabus . . .

38. Gloria T. Hull, Patricia Bell Scott, and Barbara Smith, eds., *All the Women Are White, All the Blacks Are Men, but Some of Us Are Brave* (New York: Feminist Press, 1982), 349.

39. VèVè Clark, "Developing Diaspora Literacy: Allusion in Maryse Condé's *Hérémakhonon*," in *Out of the Kumbla: Caribbean Women and Literature*, ed. Carole Boyce Davies and Elaine Savory Fido (Trenton, NJ: Africa World Press, 1990), 303–319.

knowledge and citation practices. Bigger Thomas. We all know Bigger Thomas. If we do not know Bigger Thomas and someone mentions Bigger Thomas, we go research Bigger Thomas and read and reread *Native Son* and read those essays on *Native Son* and then we read James Baldwin's take and also *White Man Listen!*, *Eight Men*, *Black Boy*, after which we maybe look over a few of those essays on Bigger Thomas and Biggie Smalls. We then ask everyone we know about Bigger Thomas—what they like, what they don't like, what they thought of Wright's portrayal of masculinity, political economy, racism. *He walked home with a mounting feeling of fear.*[40] We know who Bigger Thomas is. Gayl Jones. Queen Bee. *Eva's Man*. Work It. Queen B. We know. Walking through the perfumed things honeybees loved. She was stretched on her back beneath the pear tree soaking in the alto chant of the visiting bees, the gold of the sun and the panting breath of the breeze . . .[41] Charmaine Lurch's giant wire bees. The wires hold exoskeletons and chitin together. The wires cast shadow. Wire hymenoptera, wrapped.[42] Charmaine's wires.

I am suggesting, then, that many black citation practices are not about inclusion and exclusion; this approach is wrongheaded because, in my view, it derails what Angela Y. Davis calls the "serious theory of black liberation" and what is clearly and succinctly stated in *But Some of Us Are Brave* as "doing the work."[43] Black studies engenders, shares, and demands diasporic literacy; black studies theorizes black liberation not through categories (identity) but from the perspective of struggle (struggle is entangled with identities-places-embodiments-infrastructures-narratives-feeling). In this sense, citations are tasked to resist racial and gendered violence through the sharing of ideas. To repeat, this does not mean names do not matter; it means, instead, that naming is enveloped in the practice of sharing how we live this world and live this world differently (#sayhername is an *unfolding method* of struggling against racial violence, #sayhername punctuates hu-

40. Richard Wright, *Native Son* (New York: Signet, 1940), 37.

41. Toni Morrison, *Beloved* (New York: Plume, 1987), 226; Gayl Jones, *Eva's Man* (Boston: Beacon, 1976); Missy Elliott, "Work It (Official Video)," YouTube video, 4:25, posted October 26, 2009, https://www.youtube.com/watch?v=cjIvu7e6Wq8; Lil' Kim, "Big Momma Thang," *Hard Core*, Big Beat/Atlantic, 1996; Zora Neale Hurston, *Their Eyes Were Watching God* (1937; rpt., New York: Perennial, 1990), 11. "Picnics swarmed those summers as fervidly as bees": John Keene, *Annotations* (New York: New Directions, 1995), 25.

42. Charmaine Lurch, *Through the Material Landscape*, art exhibition at Daniels Spectrum Gallery, February 8–March 12, 2017.

43. Angela Y. Davis, *Women, Race, and Class* (New York: Vintage, 1982), 152.

man being as praxis).[44] These references are not so much about who is or who is not relevant to the work we do as about how we radically reimagine liberation collectively. *Playing in the Dark*. Naming demands that we ask about the unnamed and honor the unnameable.

> Books and papers scattered about the floor, fragile stockings and underthings and the startling green and gold negligee . . . [45]

> Once you have approached the mountains of cases in order to mine the books from them and bring them into the light of day—or, rather, of night—what memories crowd upon you![46]

She Tries Her Tongue, Her Silence Softly Breaks.
June Jordan.
Patternmaster. Again.
The Wretched of the Earth.

Demeure faite de défaites
demeure faite de carènes vives
demeure faite de passiflore
demeure cent fois faite et défaite . . . [47]

Song of Solomon. Inventory. Édouard Glissant.
Out of the Kumbla. The Black Fantastic.

Relation. I spend the final portion of this story returning to a comment I made earlier: when we are doing our very best work, we are acknowledging the shared and collaborative intellectual praxis that makes our research what it is. Here I turn to Édouard Glissant to figure through how books and sources and footnotes and referencing generate textual narratives that are at once opaque and liberatory. As we know, *Poetics of Rela-*

44. Sylvia Wynter and Katherine McKittrick, "Unparalleled Catastrophe for Our Species? Or, to Give Humanness a Different Future: Conversations," in *Sylvia Wynter: On Being Human as Praxis*, ed. Katherine McKittrick (Durham, NC: Duke University Press, 2015).

45. Nella Larsen, *Quicksand* (New York: Penguin, 1928), 13.

46. Walter Benjamin, "Unpacking My Library," in *Walter Benjamin: Illuminations*, ed. Hannah Arendt, trans. Harry Zohn (New York: Schocken Books, 1968), 59–67. See also Dionne Brand, *Inventory* (Toronto: McClelland & Stewart, 2006); Dionne Brand, *Ossuaries: Poems* (Toronto: McClelland & Stewart, 2010); Dionne Brand, *Land to Light On* (Toronto: McClelland & Stewart, 1997).

47. Aimé Césaire, "Demeure I," from *Solar Throat Slashed*, ed. and trans. A. James Arnold and Clayton Eshleman (Middletown, CT: Wesleyan University Press, 2011), 36.

tion begins with the slave ship and the chapter titled "The Open Boat": the cramped suffocating space, the mess of vomit and lice, the weight of death, the vertigo and the dizziness.[48] *Whenever a fleet of ships gave chase to slave ships, it was easiest just to lighten the boat by throwing cargo overboard.*[49] My sadness sits around me.[50] Glissant's text is, for me, brilliant for the way it offers us the nonworld as one (but perhaps not *the only*) beginning of blackness. In *Poetics of Relation* the Middle Passage forecloses the normative ties between identity and place, the blood and land. Filial geographies are unkind and harmful. Filial geographies are unkind. Black geographies are unhinged from territory and its attendant juridical requirements. The Middle Passage is rupture. The Middle Passage annihilates land claims. The Middle Passage is unspeakable. The Middle Passage is a nonworld. The nonworld is too awful to pass on but it does not expire. The nonworld produces a set of restless geographic knowledges that "cannot be 'proved' . . . but can be imagined, conceivable, in transport of thought."[51] Suspended, undifferentiated identity, removed, not-yet, without names, nowhere at all, unmade, unknown, unclaimed richness of possibility.[52]

Glissant refuses all modes of geographic belonging that are tied to racist and colonial knowledge systems. Glissant shows that one of the most brutal of racial geographies—the Middle Passage—produces conditions of black defiance and disobedience.[53] He uproots and discards ancestry. He gives us unconscious fugitive memories and errantry and relation and opacity.[54] The enslaved, including those lost on the Middle Passage, are tasked to inhabit the world differently. Enslaved and postslave subjects are tasked to imagine and live the world differently. Glissant's analytical move is, in my view, profound. The consequences of the Middle Passage

48. Glissant, *Poetics of Relation*, 5–6.

49. Glissant, *Poetics of Relation*, 6.

50. June Jordan, "My Sadness Sits around Me," in *The Black Poets*, ed. Dudley Randall (New York: Bantam, 1971), 248.

51. Glissant, *Poetics of Relation*, 174.

52. Hortense Spillers, "Mama's Baby, Papa's Maybe: An American Grammar Book," *Diacritics*, 17, no. 2 (Summer 1987): 72.

53. Glissant, *Poetics of Relation*, 8.

54. Glissant, *Poetics of Relation*, 7. Is this boat sailing into eternity toward the edges of a nonworld that no ancestor will haunt . . . "Je te salue, vieil Ocean!" You still preserve on your crests the silent boat of our births, your chasms are our own unconscious, furrowed with fugitive memories.

rupture, the outcome of annihilation, is a way of knowing and belonging capaciously and generously. The nonworld and its inhabitants are not beholden to the taxonomic proof that swirls around them, defines them, objectifies them. We are not beholden to the taxonomic proof that swirls around us. Instead, the nonworld engenders the urgent praxis of unwriting racial taxonomies and its attendant spatial violences. This is the referential work of black studies. The nonworld produces a referential knowledge system that is committed to sharing black ways of knowing and living. The nonworld produces a knowledge system that cannot be proved. The nonworld produces a lesson that cannot be contained in the main text.

One important key to think about is, of course, geography: colonial and positivist geographies necessitate authentication, and authentication authenticates belonging on colonial and positivist terms. Knowledge systems that value transparency authenticate these geographies. The purveyors of colonial and positivist geographies, those empowered by racial capitalism, authenticate these spaces by valuing and economizing normative reading-citation practices that require racial subordination. Derek Gregory draws attention to the ways the production of space is tied to "the materiality of intellectual inquiry."[55] Avery Gordon, in a slightly different way, thinks about "the materiality of institutional storytelling."[56] We can thus acknowledge that references and citations are concretized, that colonialism and positivism have referential consequences, that references concretize inequity, and that referencing is a spatial project. The reference notes are like map legends and cartographic keys that further explain how we read the plot, the cartogram, the borders, the diagrammatic data. We can also notice, at the same time, that citations in black studies—when cast as doing the work of liberation rather than calculating names (whether through studied excision or crunching numbers)—provide concrete clues about how to live this world differently. The materiality of intellectual inquiry—the ideas we share, the counsel we give each other—is an ongoing referential conversation about black humanity. The materiality of intellectual inquiry is a conversation that knows and believes in and does not have to be convinced of black humanity. The materiality of intellectual inquiry—the ideas we share—is a referential conversation that begins from black livingness.

55. Derek Gregory, *Geographical Imaginations* (Oxford: Blackwell, 1994), 14.
56. Gordon, *Ghostly Matters*, 40.

A referential beginning (of colonial and plantocratic geographies) that is driven by a logic of accumulation, dispossession, exclusion, and dehumanization cannot, therefore, capture a black sense of place. Glissant, keenly aware of these constraining and brutal processes, turns geography on its head by refusing the lawlike systems that underwrite the production of space; instead he argues that the production of space, for black subjects, holds in it the possibility of a nonworld that unravels, in postslave contexts, as a totally different system of geographic knowledge that cannot replicate subordination precisely because it is born of and holds on to the unknowable. He gives us, to return to my earlier point, unknowing as a way of being, and, perhaps most importantly, as we wade through *Poetics of Relation*, he shows us that the citational politics are inexhaustible enunciations of ideas that cannot be systematized yet resonate together. He reads James Joyce beside Bob Marley beside the architecture of Chicago beside the shantytown.[57] Glissant gives us everything and nothing all at once: diasporic literacy emerges from our collective (opaque relational) knowledge of the open boat; the open boat necessitates black freedom-inspired purpose as a lesson; the lessons cite and site how we might live black outside the taxonomies that swirl around us. Referencing is hard: we share our lessons of unknowing ourselves and, in this, refuse what they want us to be; we risk reading what we cannot bear and what we love too much and then we let it go, revise, and read it again.

57. Glissant, *Poetics of Relation*, 93.

THE SMALLEST CELL REMEMBERS A SOUND

*T*his story is about methods and methodologies.[1] It thinks about methodology as an act of disobedience and rebellion and focuses on how black studies scholars have used and can use method to engender radical scholarly praxis. The story understands, in advance, that the commitment to disciplinary thought is thick and wide-ranging. Discipline is the act of relentless categorization.[2] In many academic worlds categories are organizational tools; categories are often conceptualized as discrete from each other. Categories are things, places, people, species, genres, themes, and more, that are grouped together because they are ostensibly similar. Categories are classified and ranked and sometimes divided into subcategories (genus). Academic disciplines make knowledge into categories and subcategories; methodology and method make discipline and knowledge about categories. Canons and canonization are very clear and obvious examples of this.[3] The weight of discipline is evidenced

The title of this story, "The Smallest Cell Remembers a Sound," is from M. NourbeSe Philip, *She Tries Her Tongue, Her Silence Softly Breaks* (Charlottetown, Canada: Ragweed Press, 1989), 63.

1. For an extended, overlapping, and different story, see Chela Sandoval, *Methodology of the Oppressed* (Minneapolis: University of Minnesota Press, 2000).

2. In this story I discuss discipline, disciplinarity, disciplined thought, as academic *areas* of study. Thus, I am not referring to the *practice and work* of study. In much of black studies this work is very disciplined. It is a practice of rigor, care, monumental effort. This work takes time, and has psychic and economic costs. It is enveloped in long lists of books, extensive notes and songs, and layers of intellectual histories and theories by black and nonblack thinkers (the work, the practice, is disobedient not undisciplined).

3. Harold Bloom, *The Western Canon: The Books and School of the Ages* (New York: Harcourt Brace, 1994).

by the density of disciplinarity and the method of making disciplined categorization happen: around every corner, at every turn, disciplinary practitioners provide disciplined narratives that confirm the solidity of disciplinary knowledge and its categorical difference from other ways of knowing.[4] The canon, the lists, the dictionaries, the key thinkers, the keywords, the core courses, the required courses, the anthologies, the qualifying exams, the comprehensive exams, the core textbooks, the tests, the grading schemes and rubrics, the institutes, the journals, the readers. Core.[5] Learning outcomes.[6] The demonstrated knowledge of Jürgen Habermas texts requires the refusal of W. E. B. Du Bois and can in no way imagine—even in refusal—Ida B. Wells. (The breadth and depth of the answer demonstrates the scholars' substantive and comprehensive knowledge of . . .) Disciplines are coded and presented as disconnected from experiential knowledge; experiential knowledge is an expression of data (The objective census numbers factually show that the poor living here experience . . .). Disciplines stack and bifurcate seemingly disconnected categories and geographies; disciplines differentiate, split, and create fictive distances between us.

Discipline is empire. Sylvia Wynter's essay "On How We Mistook the Map for the Territory, and Re-imprisoned Ourselves in Our Unbearable Wrongness of Being, of *Désêtre*" provides a very useful critique of discipline. In this piece, Wynter dwells on black studies—the black arts movement, the interventions of Frantz Fanon and Aimé Césaire, anticolonial

4. Barbara Christian, "The Race for Theory," *Feminist Studies* 14, no. 1 (Spring 1998): 67–79.

5. Core: the central or most important part of something.

6. "Learning outcomes are statements of what a learner is expected to understand, value, or demonstrate after completion of a process of learning. The Learning Outcomes are measurable, and communicate expectations to learners about the skills, attitudes and behaviors they are expected to achieve after successful completion of a course, program or degree. Accurate assessment of learning outcomes is an essential component of competency-based education. This project aligns well with the academic plan . . . which emphasizes the development of fundamental academic skills, transferable skills that span a range of disciplines and are essential for professional practice. . . . The aims of the project are: to quantify student achievement of transferable learning outcomes; to develop reliable and sustainable means of assessing student learning; to encourage faculty to develop and assess transferable skills in their courses and programs; and to build a foundation for a wider rollout of this type of assessment across faculties and programs over the next few years." See Queen's University, "Queen's Learning Outcomes Assessment," accessed March 20, 2018, http://www.queensu.ca/qloa/home.

movements in the Caribbean and South Africa, the post-1960s institutionalization of Africana-African-Afro-American Studies, and more. She thinks about these moments and movements in black studies as layered, although very different, political responses to a regime of truth—upheld by capitalism and its multiscalar fallout—that is propelled by racism and racial violence. She delineates the revolutionary potential of black studies and shows this potential to be couched in global black and nonblack activist and anticolonial struggles and a "network of extracurricular institutions" (read: extra-academic). She also remarks on the "penetrating insights" that emerged from "globally subordinated peoples moving out of their Western assigned places and calling into question what was, in effect, the structures of a global world system."[7] She then breaks down how this radical and collective questioning of place, by the world's most marginalized, was incorporated into the "consumer horizon of expectation of the generic class."[8] Her breakdown is detailed. What I observe here are the links Wynter makes between biocentricity, racism, and the institutionalization of what I am going to crudely call "identity-disciplines" (women's studies, feminist studies, ethnic studies, queer studies, African American studies, and so on). Using black and African American studies as her focus, Wynter addresses the tensions between liberatory thought and generic institutionalized politics. One of her analytical threads explores race as a key concept that shapes a range of knowledge systems; she teases out how racism and self-alienation are part of a larger self-replicating system that, within the context of capitalism, profits from maintaining a biocentric order wherein the figure of the black is assigned the status of less-than-human. This order is, all at once, breached and disrupted and resisted by and through black intellectual thought (scholarly contributions, creative texts, and so on); absorbed by a range of people across racial identifications; profitable. The analytical thread Wynter offers allows us to think about how systems and practitioners of disciplinary knowledge (even in subdisciplines, such as posthumanist thought or Marxist theory, and/or "identity-disciplines" such as ethnic studies or women's studies, all of which appear to "counter" the normative disciplines and canons),

7. Sylvia Wynter, "On How We Mistook the Map for the Territory, and Re-imprisoned Ourselves in Our Unbearable Wrongness of Being, of Désêtre," in Not Only the Master's Tools: African American Studies in Theory and Practice, ed. Lewis R. Gordon and Jane Anna Gordon (London: Paradigm, 2006), 108, 112.

8. Wynter, "On How We Mistook the Map for the Territory," 158.

are invested (experientially and economically and psychically) in sustaining our present system of knowledge (which venerates *Homo oeconomicus*). The rigid and restrictive underpinnings of disciplinary thinking become apparent when we notice that categorization—*specifically the method and methodology of sustaining knowledge categories*—is an economized emulation of positivist classificatory thinking (thinking that is produced in the shadows of biological determinism and colonialism).[9] Generic. Genus. The learning system and its attendant methodology produce an ungenerous taxonomy that segregates kinds and types of knowledge as well as the spaces where ideas are generated. The taxonomy is ranked and funded accordingly. In this learning system, the (fictive) differences between humans swell.[10]

The splitting and differentiation of ways of knowing is in part, Edward Said reminds us, the function of empire.[11] Discipline is empire.[12] This is exemplified when, for example, we notice that "studying black people" and "studying indigenous people" is an intricate Malthusian project of bifurcating each racial history according to different identity markers and genealogies (which shadow biocentric and colonial logics); describing black and indigenous politics as only and always and authentically emerging from blood-identity; refusing to notice or acknowledge the many black and indigenous communities that have always, together (even if not always under the same stars), been fighting against colonialism, racism, capitalism, empire, nation, and their attendant sexedgendered brutalities; unseeing black-indigenous intimacies and love and friendships; documenting and reporting that indigenous people are singular *objects* of study that are only and always poor, oppressed, abject,

9. William Clark's *Academic Charisma and the Origins of the Research University* (Chicago: University of Chicago Press, 2006) tracks academic disciplines and practices and figures (faculty, students, department heads, and so on) from juridicio-ecclesiastical to politico-economic, thus offering a genealogy of how tradition, rationality, discipline, hierarchy, and specialization get embedded within the university learning system and increasingly economized. See also Craig Steven Wilder, *Ebony and Ivy: Race, Slavery, and the Troubled History of America's Universities* (New York: Bloomsbury, 2013); and Abigail Boggs and Nick Mitchell, "Critical University Studies and the Crisis Consensus," *Feminist Studies* 44, no. 2 (2018): 432–463. Thank you, Adam Bledsoe, for sending me *Ebony and Ivy*.

10. Richard Herrnstein and Charles Murray, *The Bell Curve: Intelligence and Class Structure in American Life* (New York: Free Press, 1994).

11. Edward W. Said, *Culture and Imperialism* (New York: Vintage, 1993).

12. Listen to Jimmy Cliff, "Many Rivers to Cross," *The Harder They Come*, Island Records, 1972.

dead, extinct; documenting and reporting that black people are singular *objects* of study that are only and always poor, oppressed, abject, dead, extinct; ignoring the capaciousness of theories of liberation (Frantz Fanon) that are repetitively used and reused and worked with and worked over and worn down, by all sorts of people, across racial identifications (people who might otherwise understand themselves as inhabiting very different racial-geographic histories than Fanon himself); academically profiting from racial differentiations and differences that are affirmed by descriptions, documentations, reports, and data; locating these differentiations within taxonomic affective geographies.[13] With this example in mind, disciplinary thinking disciplines how we study identity as though identity is anachronistically and biologically fixed to corporeal matter, splitting (split genera) otherwise collective black and indigenous struggles against empire, while also financially and geographically organizing studies of race by putting a merit-value on *differentiated descriptions* of premature death and misery that, inadvertently or explicitly, reify a system of knowledge that cannot bear black and indigenous life (and black and indigenous relationality). Conversations between split genera are strongly discouraged. The financial requirements are to participate in this system or be pushed out of it. Population control is academically lucrative. Discipline is empire. Description is not liberation.

The incorporation of "identity" into disciplined learning systems—the *institutionalization* of identity within the context of the university—has resulted in a grim reification of a biocentric order.[14] Identity is often conflated with flesh. Identity has biologic traces. Identity is corporeal. Studying identity so often involves demonstrating that biology is socially constructed, *not displacing biology* but, rather, empowering biology—the flesh—as the primary way to study identity. Race (including whiteness) galvanizes the biologics of identity.[15] In academic settings, identity-

13. Read with Michelle Daigle, "The Spectacle of Reconciliation: On (the) Unsettling Responsibilities to Indigenous Peoples in the Academy," *Environment and Planning D: Society and Space* (January 2019): 1–19.

14. Roderick Ferguson, *The Reorder of Things: The University and Its Pedagogies of Minority Difference* (Minneapolis: University of Minnesota Press, 2012); Kandice Chuh, *Imagine Otherwise: On Asian Americanist Critique* (Durham, NC: Duke University Press, 2003).

15. Paul Gilroy, *Against Race: Imagining Political Culture beyond the Color Line* (Cambridge, MA: Harvard University Press, 2000). The resistance to *Against Race*, particularly (but not only) from black US scholars, has always been curious to me—so much so that I

disciplines—just like the discipline of English literature—are canonized and economized: there are good identities and bad identities; there are good women, good queers, good people of color, and there are bad women, bad queers, bad people of color. There are good books and bad books. This does not mean, however, that English literature or history or mathematics are more ethical disciplines because they do not immediately seethe identity and its attendant corporeal matter; rather, it means that in academic settings, identity-disciplines function to uphold misery and empire and the segregation of ideas and idea makers precisely because *all* disciplines are *differently* enfleshed and classified and hierarchized.[16] If identity is biologic—or, to be more specific, narratively biologized—are the identities that make and produce and uphold disciplining categories not, also, biologizing disciplines? If so, *all* disciplinary thinking is laden with colonial logics and all disciplines are enfleshed (as gendered, raced, sexed, and so on). Identity-disciplines—*those areas of study that were set up to research and work to undo oppression and are so often kept afloat and administered by hardworking queer-black-indigenous-people-of-color!*—are particularly poignant examples of how academic institutions colonize the production of knowledge by defining, policing, determining, financing, what categories (genus, studies) should live and die.[17] For disciplines

---

thought I was misreading the book, or that my copy was missing a chapter. It is as though the title for the US edition of the book—*Against Race*—is some kind of template implying that Gilroy is, himself, "against race" and that the text is a refusal of black studies. The discussion of fascism is hard, the journey into black conservatism is hard too, as are the discussions of corporeal authenticities . . . but this book is not a negation of race, blackness, or black studies. It is a monumental critique of race thinking and ultranationalism. The European edition of this book is titled *Between Camps: Nations, Cultures and the Allure of Race* (London: Allen Lane, 2000).

16. See Alexander G. Weheliye, *Habeas Viscus: Racializing Assemblages, Biopolitics, and Black Feminist Theories of the Human* (Durham, NC: Duke University Press, 2014). Enfleshment—and here I am paraphrasing Weheliye—is the process through which racial codes get attached to (un)gendered bodies, which then symbolically and materially dwell in—and navigate as enfleshed *persons*—the fallout of racial capitalism and colonialism. Remember, too, that this process is dynamic: (un)gendering is a fundamental part of how racial codes get worked out as narrative and theory. So, enfleshment is the process through which we come to know the gendered workings of humanity within the context of prevailing racial codes.

17. Malinda Smith's research on equity in universities delineates this clearly: white women faculty evidence otherness and diversity in the academy, thus fulfilling equity requirements and policies; whiteness outlives blackness, indigeneity, and other nonwhite

under duress—almost always identity-disciplines!—there are redoubled costs to doing anticolonial and decolonial work: participate in the existing system, love and study the categories as they are, or be harmed. Participate in the existing system, which objectifies black people and dehumanizes black scholars, love and study and describe, incessantly, the abject and downtrodden and objectified black, live with racism and the awfulness you walk through every day—and economize it—or get out.[18]

Method-making. This story is not meant to eschew academic institutions. As I note below, black methodology and method-making (which are academic and extra-academic), offer rebellious and disobedient and promising ways of undoing discipline. And those of us who work in these places that weigh us down can carve out surprising and generous spaces that challenge existing political visions, allow us to fight against inequity and racism, work against racial violence, and collaborate. These spaces, of course, were studied, named, lived, and revolutionized by figures like Claudia Jones (in a global sense)—freedom spaces (that are sometimes right there within and in excess of the mess of the academy).[19]

The moment Wynter notices—when globally subordinated peoples moved out of their Western assigned places and called into question the structures of a global world system—is, I want to argue, a rebellious methodological moment that enunciates black life outside of crude biologized identity claims. To put it another way, Wynter *methodologizes* the unfinished possibilities of collective struggle. Here, I want to make really clear, is one of Wynter's uniquely urgent contributions to black studies and studies of liberation: she does not have a specific object of inquiry; nor does she have a specific question (What is black studies? Where is liberation? Why are we dying?). Indeed, with this in mind I would argue (boldly!)

identifications. Malinda Smith, "Gender, Whiteness, and the 'Other Others' in the Academy," in *States of Race: Critical Race Feminism for the 21st Century*, ed. Sherene Razack, Malinda Smith, and Sunera Thobani (Toronto: Between the Lines Press, 2010), 37–58.

18. "The best university scholars are characterized as entrepreneurial and investment savvy, not simply by obtaining grants or fellowships, but by generating new projects from old research, calculating publication and presentation venues, and circulating themselves and their work according to what will enhance their value." Wendy Brown, *Undoing the Demos: Neoliberalism's Stealth Revolution* (New York: Zone Books, 2015), 36–37. Thank you, Jamie Peck.

19. Carole Boyce Davies, *Left of Karl Marx: The Political Life of Black Communist Claudia Jones* (Durham, NC: Duke University Press, 2007).

that describing her work as invested in "the human" (as an object of analysis) is perhaps misguided; such a description often privileges *Homo oeconomicus* (the figure of Man2 in her work) as the human we must undo and, at the same time, undermines her ongoing argument that the human is not singular (or even the doubly entwined Man1-Man2) but, rather, is *a manifestation of new ways of living with each other* that emerges from an interspecies-interecological schema. A preoccupation with only-the-human also privileges and centers the very human she (and we) seek to challenge by disregarding or marginalizing the perspectives of Man's human others and Wynter's ongoing insistence on a species perspective that is tied to our ecological worlds (plot-and-plantation, drought, desertification, global warming and climate change, and so on). If our analyses of Wynter's work are preoccupied with the figure of the human, we risk only talking about and writing about and describing the human we already know. In reducing her ideas to a singular fictive figure, we will lose our way.[20]

20. Some readings of Wynter's "human" center or recenter the scholars themselves, because they use this category-figure to conflate a range of human experiences and histories. The argument is, often, that Wynter's reconceptualization of the human (beyond or after Man) is capaciously "everyone," which the scholar reads as a singular slot that collapses us all (a collective we) into one stable human category. At the same time, this conceptual move reifies the human they are claiming to undo by attaching an analytical currency to a singular enfleshed identity (the scholar as describer of collective humanity). And . . . for the white antiracist scholar doing work on black and indigenous worlds, the fictive singular slot of "all humans"—*seemingly* endorsed by an anticolonial scholar, Wynter—is the perfect antiracist opening to claim and center white humanity. Curious. This, too, rushes past Wynter's reading of black intellectuals and creatives as providing the intellectual infrastructure for a version of humanity that cannot be contained by enfleshed monohumanism and its colonial wreckage; it also rushes past her studies of uneven human experiences. For this reason, I find that Wynter's call to think through "who and what we are" (in an extra-philosophical sense) a much more refined—yet analytically generous—rendering of how she imagines our interspecies-interecological struggles. This phrase exemplifies how her work does not dwell on singular human (or the category of human), per se, but knotted processes of knowing which lead to us to grapple with (not settle on or describe) the question of who and what we are (extra-philosophically): "The Argument proposes that the new master code of the bourgeoisie and of its ethnoclass conception of the human—that is, the code of selected by Evolution/dysselected by Evolution—was now to be mapped and anchored on the only available 'objective set of facts' that remained. This was the set of environmentally, climatically determined phenotypical differences between human hereditary variations as these had developed in the wake of the human diaspora both across and out of the continent of Africa; that is, as a set of (so to speak) totemic differences, which were now harnessed to the task of projecting the Color Line drawn institutionally and discursively between whites/ nonwhites—and at its most extreme between the Caucasoid physiognomy (as symbolic life,

Wynter is offering a way to read radically. A small slice of her project, then, is not to provide us with a problem (Man1-Man2) followed by a solution (replace Man1-Man2), but to, first, encourage us to read differently (from a third perspective, from the perspective of struggle, from demonic ground) and observe how our present system of knowledge, a biocentric system of knowledge upheld by capitalist financing, is a self-referential system that profits from recursive normalization; and, second, to read and notice the conditions through which self-replicating knowledge systems are breached and liberation is made possible. Black intellectuals engender a perspective of struggle, the demonic ground, and other heretical interruptions. Across her writings, Wynter illuminates the ways in which the

---

the name of what is good, the idea that some humans can be selected by Evolution) and the Negroid physiognomy (as symbolic death, the 'name of what is evil,' the idea that some humans can be dysselected by Evolution)—as the new extrahuman line, or projection of genetic nonhomogeneity that would now be made to function, analogically, as the status-ordering principle based upon ostensibly differential degrees of evolutionary selectedness/ eugenicity and/or dysselectedness/dysgenicity. Differential degrees, as between the classes (middle and lower and, by extrapolation, between capital and labor) as well as between men and women, and between the heterosexual and homosexual erotic preference—and, even more centrally, as between Breadwinner (jobholding middle and working classes) and the jobless and criminalized Poor, with this rearticulated at the global level as between Sartre's 'Men' and Natives . . . before the end of politico-military colonialism, then postcolonially as between the 'developed' First World, on the one hand, and the 'underdeveloped' Third and Fourth Worlds on the other. The Color Line was now projected as the new 'space of Otherness' principle of nonhomogeneity, made to reoccupy the earlier places of the motion-filled heavens/non-moving Earth, rational humans/irrational animal lines, and to recode in new terms their ostensible extrahumanly determined differences of ontological substance. While, if the earlier two had been indispensable to the production and reproduction of their respective genres of being human, of their descriptive statements (i.e., as Christian and as Man1), and of the overall order in whose field of interrelationships, social hierarchies, system of role allocations, and divisions of labors each such genre of the human could alone realize itself—and with each such descriptive statement therefore being rigorously conserved by the 'learning system' and order of knowledge as articulated in the institutional structure of each order—this was to be no less the case with respect to the projected 'space of Otherness' of the Color Line. With respect, that is, to its indispensability to the production and reproduction of our present genre of the human Man2, together with the overall global/national bourgeois order of things and its specific mode of economic production, alone able to provide the material conditions of existence for the production and reproduction of the ethno-class or Western-bourgeois answer *that we now give to the question of the who and what we are."* Sylvia Wynter, "Unsettling the Coloniality of Being/Power/Truth/Freedom: Towards the Human, after Man, Its Overrepresentation—an Argument," CR: *The New Centennial Review* 3, no. 3 (Fall 2003): 315–317 (emphasis added).

history of blackness provides the conditions to learn and live and love our world differently. Reading anticolonially is deciphering practice.[21] As a methodology (rather than simply a time past that is over and done with) the 1960s *questioning* of the global world system that Wynter highlights is productively unfinished. Positioned as an open *questioning*, method and methodology are unhinged from the stasis of noun, and thrown into the less predictable work of verb.

Method-making. I theorize Wynter's insights on the rebellious potential of 1960s—what she describes as the *groundwork* for the realization of a new order of being human—as long-standing and unfinished method-making.[22] This kind of analytical maneuvering marks black rebellion as method-making; this is one way to signal and think about the praxis of black life and livingness. The maneuvering, ideally, dwells on and thinks about the questioning and overturning of normative systems of knowledge, and thus what it means to be human, by situating the *process* of inquiry as the analytical framework through which to study. Method-making compulsively moves with curiosity (even in frustration) rather than applying a set of techniques to an object of study and generating unsurprising findings and outcomes. Methodology is disobedient (rogue, rebellious, black).[23]

Description is not liberation. Methodology that is relational, intertextual, interdisciplinary, interhuman, and multidisciplinary honors black studies. Methodology that is relational, intertextual, interdisciplinary, interhuman, and multidisciplinary provides an intellectual framework through which the study of black life cannot be reduced to authentic biological data (biologized-identity-discipline) that emanates some kind of truth about racial oppression (black people are abject) and a solution to repair that truth (we must fix [correct], fix [designate and detain], and get rid of the abject). As I note above, discipline operates to reify biocentric and colonial categories; if the study of black people gets caught up in the disciplined projects of empire, black humanity is unthinkable. Indeed, so trusted and commonsense are studies that begin with black dehumanization and/or social death and accompanying methods of proving ab-

21. Sylvia Wynter, "Rethinking 'Aesthetics': Notes towards a Deciphering Practice," in *Ex-iles: Essays on Caribbean Cinema*, ed. Mbye Cham (Trenton, NJ: Africa World Press, 1992), 237–279.

22. Wynter, "On How We Mistook the Map for the Territory," 163.

23. Thank you, Lisa Lowe.

jection or saving the objectified figure that any burst of rebellion against that assigned place is almost (not totally) obliterated. Description is not liberation.

With this in mind, it is also important to observe how black knowledge is continually cast as biological knowledge. Even as some scholarly questions understand "the social construction of race" to be undoing scientific racism and biological determinism (by rightly naming them racist fictions), the central orienting concept in social constructionist arguments is biology. Biology can overwhelm, sneaking in with its "social construction" or "identity" (feminist) alibi (problem: the sexed-raced body is socially constructed). This problem seemingly displaces biology, but in fact consolidates gendered-racial categories by positioning them as concrete analytical foci (cores!) and, in the end, determining and finalizing how we seek to explain injustice (answer: biological determinism is wrong). Consolidation. If the problem and the answer are framed through a biocentric learning system (biologized identity-disciplines) the figure of the black is guaranteed the consummate slot of nonhuman precisely because blackness, in this specific learning system, is, a priori, expressing descriptive (socially produced) abjectness ("a hemorrhage that splattered my whole body with black blood").[24] What we observe is a self-replicating learning system that realizes itself through sustaining biocentric categories. Description is not liberation.

If we are committed to anticolonial thought, our starting point must be one of disobedient relationality that always questions, and thus is not beholden to, normative academic logics. This means our method-making may not necessarily take us where we want to go, but it will take us, as Glissant writes, to "an unknown that does not terrify."[25] Doing anticolonial work in the academy and talking about race in relation to discipline and interdiscipline can be enriched by thinking across texts and places. If, as I have suggested above, the discipline of thought stabilizes and restricts the category of race, we must recognize that the project of academically attending to race (as enfleshed by discipline and categorized by genus) cannot always bear black life. Indeed, the work of discipline, so neatly and so quietly tied to the biocentric infrastructures of empire, forbids a

24. Frantz Fanon, *Black Skin, White Masks,* trans. Charles Lam Markmann (1952; rpt., New York: Grove, 1967), 112.

25. Édouard Glissant, *Poetics of Relation,* trans. Betsy Wing (Ann Arbor: University of Michigan Press, 1997), 9.

genre of blackness that is *not* solely and absolutely defined by and through abjection, subjection, and objectification. The project of making discipline overwhelmingly only gives us two options for the study of black people—to describe racism and resist racism; these options rarely have any noise or curiosity or questions about black life interrupting them. Discipline, even identity-discipline, cannot adequately attend to blackness precisely because black life is absent from the disciplinary question. Or, discipline describes black death and degradation as legitimate scholarly findings.

Method-making is the enactment of black life and bursts through disciplined abjection. Method-making is relation.

> We are just barely beginning to conceive of this immense friction. The more it works in favour of an oppressive order, the more it calls for disorder as well. The more it produces exclusion, the more it generates attraction. It standardizes—but at every node of Relation we will find callouses of resistance. Relation is learning more and more to go beyond judgements into the unexpected dark of art's upsurgings. Its beauty springs from the stable and the unstable, from the deviance of many particular poetics and the clairvoyance of a relational poetics. The more things it standardizes into a state of lethargy, the more rebellious consciousness it arouses.[26]

Method-making acknowledges and despises and critiques degradation without sourcing it as the only way to know black people. Method-making knows black people know. We know more than the abjectness that is projected upon us. We are not obsequious. We are not abject. We know more. We know. We know ourselves.

Method-making. Black scholars, artists, writers rely on a variety of sources (music, math, sociology, science, geography, history, fine art, dance, and everything in between and beyond) in order to study, convey, and talk about race and racism. In a range of texts—*The Souls of Black Folk, Poetics of Relation, American Civilization, Women, Race, and Class, Black Feminist Thought, A Genealogy of Resistance, Development Arrested, In the Break, The Black Atlantic, Blues People, Golden Gulag, Dropping Anchor, Setting Sail, Dark Matters, Solidarity Blues,* and so on—the work stands across-with-outside-within-against disciplinary boundar-

26. Glissant, *Poetics of Relation*, 138–139.

ies.[27] *Jazz*. *Race Men*.[28] Indeed, as we read and read and reread, we notice we cannot seem to study otherwise.[29] Betty Davis.

Method-making is the generating and gathering of ideas—across-with-outside-within-against normative disciplines—that seek out liberation within our present system of knowledge. The goal is not to *find*

27. W. E. B. Du Bois, *The Souls of Black Folk* (New York: Vintage, 1903, 1990); Édouard Glissant, *Poetics of Relation*, trans. Betsy Wing (1990; rpt., Ann Arbor: University of Michigan Press, 1997); C. L. R. James, *American Civilization* (Oxford: Blackwell, 1992); Angela Davis, *Women, Race, and Class* (New York: Vintage, 1982); Patricia Hill Collins, *Black Feminist Thought: Knowledge, Consciousness, and the Politics of Empowerment* (1990; rpt., New York: Routledge, 2000); M. NourbeSe Philip, *A Genealogy of Resistance: And Other Essays* (Toronto: Mercury Press, 1997); Clyde Woods, *Development Arrested: The Blues and Plantation Power in the Mississippi Delta* (London: Verso, 1998); Fred Moten, *In the Break: The Aesthetics of the Black Radical Tradition* (Minneapolis: University of Minnesota Press, 2003); Paul Gilroy, *The Black Atlantic: Modernity and Double Consciousness* (Cambridge, MA: Harvard University Press, 1993); Amiri Baraka, *Blues People: Negro Music in White America* (New York: W. Morrow, 1963); Ruth Wilson Gilmore, *Golden Gulag: Prisons, Surplus, Crisis, and Opposition in Globalizing California* (Berkeley: University of California Press, 2007); Jacqueline Nassy Brown, *Dropping Anchor, Setting Sail: Geographies of Race in Black Liverpool* (Princeton, NJ: Princeton University Press, 2009); Richard Iton, *Solidarity Blues: Race, Culture, and the American Left* (Chapel Hill: University of North Carolina Press, 2000).

28. Toni Morrison, *Jazz* (New York: Alfred A. Knopf, 1992); Hazel Carby, *Race Men* (Cambridge, MA: Harvard University Press, 1998).

29. Here I recall Jacqueline Nassy Brown's insightful presentation on Stuart Hall. Brown writes: "In 1985, Hall published in a journal called *Critical Studies in Mass Communication*. The article is called, 'Signification, Representation, Ideology: Althusser and the Post-structuralist Debates.' Just as the title promises, we're entering the realm of High Theory. Toward the end of the article, and with barely a transition, he moves into the realm of autobiography—toward the important theoretical goal of showing how 'some of the things I have said about Althusser's general concept of ideology allow us to think about particular ideological formations.' He continues, 'I want to think about that particular complex of discourses that implicates ideologies of identity, place, ethnicity and social formation generated around the term 'black''' (108). From there he offers a narrative that is alternately poignant and funny—for example, saying that once, when he returned to Jamaica for a visit, his mother told him, 'I hope they don't mistake you over there for one of those immigrants!'" Brown writes that Hall continually inserted himself, and blackness, in places where you would least expect them to appear. Her decision to focus on Hall's interruption of the scholarly journal narrative is especially meaningful, as she shows how Hall both works within and refuses normative systems of academic knowledge, while also figuring "black" as an open-ended Althusserian intellectual inquiry. Jacqueline Nassy Brown, "Stuart Hall's Geographic Refusals: A Response to Katherine McKittrick," paper presented at the conference *Stuart Hall: Geographies of Resistance*, CUNY GC, New York, March 26, 2015. Thank you, JNB, for

liberation, but to seek it out. The process of seeking will, ideally, be persistently unsatisfied with ideas that are and were constructed alongside the "ambivalent legacy of emancipation and the undeniably truncated opportunities available to the freed."[30] The process of seeking is one of inquiry and curiosity. While I am only addressing how a sliver of black liberation is enacted—through the praxis of method-making—I hope this story provides us, as academics and thinkers who compulsively seek out liberation, with the intellectual mechanisms to do this work in a variety of university settings that, as we know, were not built to honor the lives of black and other marginalized communities. Seeking liberation is rebellious.

Connections. Reading across a range of texts and ideas and narratives —academic and nonacademic—encourages multifarious ways of thinking through the possibilities of liberation and provides clues about living through the unmet promises of modernity; method-making undercuts the profitable standardization of racial authenticities and disciplining practices.[31] These processes, in turn, hopefully challenge two bothersome analytical habits. The first, which has been continually inserting itself into this story, is the tendency to seek out and find marginalized subjects, who then serve as academic data and provide authentic knowledge about oppression.[32] The second is the tendency to privilege some theoretical or academic work as the methodological and intellectual frame through

---

sharing a hardcopy of your presentation. See also Stuart Hall, "Signification, Representation, Ideology: Althusser and the Post-structuralist Debates," *Critical Studies in Mass Communication* 2, no. 2 (1985): 91–114.

30. Saidiya Hartman, *Scenes of Subjection: Terror, Slavery, and Self-making in Nineteenth-Century America* (London: Oxford University Press, 1997), 12.

31. A note on interdisciplinarity: normally, interdisciplinary method asks the scholar to bring together two or more academic disciplines, in order to hopefully broaden and refine our approach to any given subject; interdisciplinary work seeks to breach the barriers between prescribed and sanctioned knowledge bases as a way to challenge how we understand the production of knowledge. As I see it, though, this is more than bringing together texts; interdisciplinary methods must always insist that nonwhite academic and nonacademic voices be understood in relation to, rather than outside of, dominant disciplinary academic debates and theories in order to continually unsettle what we think we know. I say this, too, because the production and protection of disciplinary knowledge—including "interdisciplines" like gender studies or other identity studies—is a racialized and protectionist knowledge project.

32. Keguro Macharia, "On Being Area-Studied: A Litany of Complaint," GLQ: *A Journal of Lesbian and Gay Studies* 22, no. 2 (2016): 183–189.

which to analyze the data (so we apply Karl Marx or a Marxist frame, say, to sites or communities of oppression). Both of these approaches objectify the data (insert the figure of the black), by assuming black objecthood is only and primarily an analytical site. Studies that focus on resistance may counter objecthood while still assuming objecthood as cosmogony of black existence. This is not just an occurrence in the social sciences; it also occurs in the humanities, when the data is creatively based (applying Judith Butler to, say, Toni Morrison, as though Morrison's creative text is not an intellectual narrative but, rather, data that, for example, illuminates performativity. What has Morrison taught Butler?! *Something*, I hope!).[33] So the conundrum is soldered to our analytical sites, specifically when blackness is conceptualized, a priori, as a site that signifies dispossession or emerges out of dispossession. The data-of-dispossession, like the enfleshed identity-discipline, is mobilized to advance feminist or related antioppression projects, only to dispossess the marginalized by presupposing that their political vision is teleological, moving, say, from oppressed to free. All too often this process *describes* black objecthood. Description does not question the generic class. It is not curious or uncomfortably and persistently open. If the rebellions and resistances that question our present system of knowledge are authenticated and read as *only* oppositional to objecthood, rebelliousness fades. As method of liberation and life, rebellion sustains.

Can the preoccupation with the black body—whether that involves liberating it from scientific racism or honoring it as a site of resistance—perhaps conceal a range of black knowledge formations that, while certainly embodied, are not reduced to the biologic? This is an urgent analytical problem because so often black knowledge is analytically posited, in advance, as biologic (an oppressed body that body-knowledge emanates from) and is therefore already marginal or excluded or outside to how we *know*. These places *of and for* blackness and black thought, laden with lingering racisms, can, we well know, seep into analyses too: disciplining, through the production of academic space *and* through the racial codification of scholarly rules, often determines how race is lived, debated,

---

33. For Butler on Morrison see Judith Butler, "After Loss: What Then?," in *Loss: The Politics of Mourning*, ed. David L. Eng and David Kazanjian (Los Angeles: University of California Press, 2003), 467–474; Judith Butler, *Excitable Speech: A Politics of the Performative* (New York: Routledge, 2013). See also Ernesto Javier Martínez, "On Butler on Morrison on Language," *Signs* 35, no. 4 (Summer 2010): 821–842.

departmentalized, interdepartmentalized, and mapped out in university settings. The disciplining of thought (the process of habitually delimiting what we know about blackness through honoring colonial perimeters) stabilizes race and perpetuates racism. More specifically, the biocentric logic of race, which sorts and assesses bodies according to phenotype and attendant evolutionary scripts, is part of a larger commonsense belief system that seemingly *knows* and thus *stabilizes* the biological data that validates unevolved black deviance; this belief system thus *knows*, in advance, who should live and who should survive and who should die and who is naturally selected and who is naturally not-selected. Indeed, this biocentric belief system is steadily carried forward, not articulating itself in the same way over time and space, but certainly shaping what we think we know about, and how we know, black people. Part of our intellectual task, then, is to work out how different kinds and types of voices *relate to each other* and open up unexpected and surprising ways to think about liberation, knowledge, history, race, gender, narrative, and blackness.[34] As we see from the work of many scholars of black studies, the liberatory task is not to measure and assess the unfree—and seek consolation in naming violence—but to posit that many divergent and different and relational voices of unfreedom are analytical and intellectual sites that can tell us something new about our academic concerns and our anticolonial futures.

I am especially interested in how black life and livingness are tied to creative, intellectual, physiological, and neurological labor. This emerges from noticing the physical cost of practicing a range of black studies. I am not abandoning the body or the biologic—we are, after all, flesh and muscle, bones and blood and water. Instead, I want to approach the biologic as relational to black intellectual life and creative praxis. Perhaps this will, if only for a moment, honor black life in ways that do not require beginning with, and then saving, the violated black body. In their narrative, poetic, visual, psychic, and physiological responses to racism, black cultural producers reconfigure normative and biologically determinist understandings of race by producing works that are in tandem with, yet imagine our past-present-future outside, colonial logics. Many black musical texts, to give an obvious example, are lyrical and sonic critiques of

34. For example: Mark V. Campbell, "Sonic Intimacies: On DJing Better Futures," *Decolonization: Indigeneity, Education and Society*, March 25, 2015, https://decolonization.word press.com/2015/03/25/sonic-intimacies-on-djing-better-futures/.

colonialism, racism, structural inequalities, and other forms of violence. What one can also take from black music, importantly, are the ways these counter-narratives to colonialism and racist violence are psychic and physiological experiences. Black creative texts are therefore narratively oppositional, but something else is going on that cannot be easily captured by an analytic of oppression/resistance. As studies on neurobiology and creativity show, the act of making and listening to and engaging creative texts—music, visual arts, and so on—brings neurological, affective, physiological pleasure, sadness, and reparative possibilities.[35] Black creative work is, I put forth, all at once, resistance, critique, method-making, praxis, and a site of neurological and physiological experience. The bundling of narrative, praxis, and corporeal feeling repositions blackness: the biologics of race are not a location of a priori oppression; instead, we glimpse how the creative and intellectual physiologies of black life are relational.

Black texts and narratives require reading practices that reckon with black life as scientifically creative; this is a way of being where black is not just signifying blackness but is living and resisting—psychically, physiologically, narratively—the brutal fictions of race (we do not just signify). Reading black this way demands a different analytical frame, a scientifically creative frame, that unfolds into a different future; this is a future that honors black creative praxis—the practice of making black life through, in, and as creative text.

The creative text does not have to be good or artful or aesthetically pleasing or popular. What the creative text *is*, does not matter as much as what it *does*. And one thing black creative text and black creative praxes do is illuminate narratives of black life and humanity and, at the same time, create conditions through which relationality, rebellion, conversation, interdisciplinarity, and disobedience are fostered. Thus, the text is not simply a representation; the text is bound up in acts of psychic and physiological rebellion and disobedience that continually unveil the limits of casting black knowledge as only emerging from the violated body. Part of our task, part of creative praxis, is to also honor the creative text as a

35. Oliver Sacks, *Musicophilia: Tales of Music and the Brain* (New York: Knopf, 2012); Daniel J. Levitin, *This Is Your Brain on Music: The Science of a Human Obsession* (New York: Plume, 2007); Aniruddh D. Patel, *Music, Language, and the Brain* (Oxford: Oxford University Press, 2010); Sally McKay, "On the Brain," *Canadian Art* 35, no. 4 (Winter 2018): 62–63.

theoretical text. If we are committed to relationality and interhuman dialogue, if we are committed to academic practices that disobey disciplines, then the song, the groove, the poem, the novel, the painting, the sculpture must be relational to theory and praxis. These kinds of strategies—reimagining the black biologic as creative knowledge, disobeying the disciplines, viewing black texts as verbs rather than nouns, engendering interhuman relationalities, asking the groove and the poem for theoretical insight—provide intellectual spaces that define black humanity outside colonial scripts.

Drexciya, an electronica band from Detroit, produced a series of concept albums between 1992 and 2002. The albums, it has been argued, musicalized the black Atlantic.[36] The band was a duo: James Stinson and Gerald Donald. Stinson died in 2002. The narratives and stories surrounding Drexciya are numerous: Stinson is said to have mostly worked alone, although the few early writings about the band and their music always include reference to Donald. They did not play their music to live audiences and both Stinson and Donald were involved in various other collaborative projects using their real or alternative names (the most recognizable is their affiliation with the Underground Resistance techno collective from Detroit).[37] Reading about Drexciya, one always comes across their secreted and complicated identities: anonymity was central to their work and identifications, and the band members' identities were not unearthed until Stinson's death. Anonymity was maintained because "the music is more urgent than the organizers of it and should take a place of primary importance. . . . It does not matter if one is known or not known directly."[38] Personality, they note, deflects from the creative

36. Kodwo Eshun, "Further Considerations on Afrofuturism," CR: The New Centennial Review 3, no. 2 (2003): 287–302.

37. A. J. Samuels, "Master Organism: A. J. Samuels Interviews Gerald Donald," Telekom Electronic Beats, June 2013, http://www.electronicbeats.net/gerald-donald-interview/. Tom Magic Feet, "James Stinson, 1969–2002: An Appreciation," Spannered, September 6, 2002, http://www.spannered.org/music/774/; Jason Birchmeier, "Artist Biography: James Stinson," All Music, accessed January 8, 2017, https://www.allmusic.com/artist/james-marcel-stinson-mn0001315741/biography.

38. Stephen Rennicks, "The Primer," Wire 321 (November 2010): 32; Matthew Bennett, "Drexciya Interview: The Anonymous Protagonists of Detroit Electro," Clash Music, May 12, 2012, http://www.clashmusic.com/features/drexciya-interview; Samuels, "Master Organism."

project.[39] Drexciya offers anonymity as method and critique, providing a moment of relief. More clearly, anonymity—not knowing (racial) personalities in advance and centering music and concept—briefly destabilizes the various surveillance systems that mark and make and weigh down black life while also questioning the authenticating workings of identity

39. Bennett, "Drexciya Interview"; Samuels, "Master Organism: A. J. Samuels Interviews Gerald Donald." Pushing personality aside. I gave a version of this paper at the American Studies Association (2014) emphasizing how Drexciya invited consideration of storms (real and metaphoric), harnessing the storm (after the Drexciya album *Harnessed the Storm*), and the storming and undoing-unleashing of black embodied-identity. Within the paper climate, climate change, atmosphere (nitrogen, oxygen, carbon dioxide, argon), were meant to displace race-embodiment-personality, and open up a way to think through blackness, ecology, liberation, and interdisciplinarity. That presentation and conversation led me to wonder about the push to temporally locate Drexciyans as Afrofuturist in Afrofuture time—particularly given how the story of the Middle Passage they offer leads to a present future (not necessarily a far future). In addition, the recent turn to visually depict Drexciyans raises a number of important questions that rest on representation. Specifically, the visual depiction of Drexciyans opens up how the fictive peoples are gendered, ungendered, degendered, transgendered, and outside gender altogether. Drexciyans, as represented by Ellen Gallagher, are beautifully relational (Gallagher storms us!). In her imagining of Drexciya, we see humanoid faces embedded within the leaves of sea plants; she draws attention to underwater life (plants, shells, seaweed, scales, watery circles) that are relational to the few almost-humanoids she details in her work. The human form is not central to her work; her undersea Drexciyans are constituted by, part of, within, fused with, and relational to nonhuman underwater life-forms. Indeed, for me, Gallagher's creative work is provocative for the way she decenters humanoid corporeality, black superhumanity, and Afrofuture time. For long moments, she offers Drexciyans as plant life. Other representations of Drexciyans are the widely circulated images of an undersea species that can be likened to scuba people (who are gendered masculine, feminine, or represented as genderless, depending on perspective). The graphic work of Abdullah Haqq works across, inside, and outside a humanoid-mermaid-merman frame while also settling on sexed-gendered forms of masculinity and femininity: we see smooth buxom muscled black feminized sea people, smooth top-heavy muscled black masculinized sea people, as well as other figures that move across these genders; most of Haqq's representations are anchored to a contemporary superhero comportment and thus imagine black futures (and therefore our present!) as a "hyperhuman hybrid": muscled underwater men and women, sea people who bear a corporeal resemblance to early twenty-first-century animated depictions of Batman, Aquaman, Spiderman, and Catwoman. See Ellen Gallagher, *Coral Cities* (London: Tate Publishing, 2007); Abdullah Haqq, "The Book of Drexciya, Volume One," accessed January 29, 2019, https://www.indiegogo.com/projects/the-book-of-drexciya-volume-one#/. On ungendering see also Weheliye, *Habeas Viscus*. The term "hyperhuman hybrid" is from Paul Gilroy, *Against Race: Imagining Political Culture beyond the Color Line* (Cambridge, MA: Harvard University Press, 2000), 347.

claims. As method-makers, Drexciya are "out of sight" and thus offer an analytic that speaks to long-standing resistances to racism.[40] At the same time, their unknowability asks that we listen, or try to listen, and perhaps wonder, what unidentified identifications bring to bear on how we engage creative texts. Possibility.

Even so, descriptors of Drexciya float and press. Their music and identities are described as cloistered, pugnacious, local, racial, exclusionary to the point of distraction, open, fresh, brooding, urgent.[41] The seeming anonymity is coupled with a more specific origin story. The liner notes of their 1997 album *The Quest* include the following cosmogony:

> Could it be possible for humans to breathe underwater? A foetus in its mother's womb is certainly alive in an aquatic environment.
>
> During the greatest holocaust the world has ever known, pregnant America-bound African slaves were thrown overboard by the thousands during labor for being sick and disruptive cargo. Is it possible that they could have given birth at sea to babies that never needed air?
>
> Recent experiments have shown mice able to breathe liquid oxygen. Even more shocking and conclusive was a recent instance of a premature infant saved from certain death by breathing liquid oxygen through its undeveloped lungs. These facts combined with reported sightings of Gillmen and swamp monsters in the coastal swamps of the South-Eastern United States make the slave trade theory startlingly feasible.
>
> Are Drexciyans water breathing, aquatically mutated descendants of those unfortunate victims of human greed? Have they been spared by God to teach us or terrorise us? Did they migrate from the Gulf of Mexico to the Mississippi river basin and on to the great lakes of Michigan?

40. Simone Browne, *Dark Matters: On the Surveillance of Blackness* (Durham, NC: Duke University Press, 2015), 21.

41. Andrew Gaerig, "Drexciya, *Journey of the Deep Sea Dweller II*," *Pitchfork*, May 31, 2012, http://pitchfork.com/reviews/albums/16678-journey-of-the-deep-sea-dweller-ii/; Antoin Lindsay, "Delving into the Drexciyan Deep: The Essential James Stinson," *Vice*, September 3, 2015, https://thump.vice.com/en_ca/article/8q7nnb/delving-into-the-drexciyan-deep -the-essential-james-stinson; Rennicks, "The Primer: Drexciya."

Do they walk among us? Are they more advanced than us and why do they make their strange music?

What is their Quest?

These are many of the questions that you don't know and never will.

The end of one thing . . . and the beginning of another.

Out

—The Unknown Writer[42]

Drexciya are often tagged as Afrofuturists.[43] The aquatopia that spatializes many of their albums promises a science fiction future that is shaped by and has learned from the violence of the Middle Passage. The cosmogony offered by Drexciya is seductive: it not only reminds us of funk and Sun Ra and Octavia Butler but also—perhaps more importantly—takes into account, and gives a regenerative future to, the violences that occurred on the Middle Passage. The killing of enslaved Africans on the Middle Passage was commonplace; the deliberate murdering aboard the slave ship *Zong* stands out as one of the more studied massacres.[44] According to Drexciya, the hundreds of enslaved people thrown overboard did not die; the enslaved, thrown overboard, gave and give us life.[45] But this reading, too, leans toward the narrative—for I think in Drexciya we seek, or at least I seek, something to cling to, something to know that is know-

42. The Unknown Writer, "Liner Notes from Drexciya," *Quest*, Submerge, 1997. For an extended discussion of the liner notes and the origin story see Nettrice R. Gaskins, "Deep Sea Dwellers: Drexciya and the Sonic Third Space," *Shima* 10, no. 2 (2016): 68–80.

43. Ytasha Womack, *Afrofuturism: The World of Black Sci-Fi and Fantasy Culture* (Chicago: Chicago Review Press, 2013), 70; Kodwo Eshun, "Further Considerations on Afrofuturism," *CR: The New Centennial Review* 3, no. 2 (2003): 287–302.

44. James Walvin, *The Zong: A Massacre, the Law, and the End of Slavery* (New Haven, CT: Yale University Press, 2011), 115; M. NourbeSe Philip, *Zong!* (Toronto: Mercury Press, 2008); Katherine McKittrick, "Diachronic Loops/Deadweight Tonnage/Bad Made Measure," *Cultural Geographies* (December 2015): 1–16.

45. See Gallagher, *Coral Cities*; Kate Forde, "Ellen Gallagher," *Frieze* 124 (June–August 2009): 189. Read with Dora Silva Santana, "Transitionings and Returnings: Experiments with the Poetics of Transatlantic Water," *TSQ* 4, no. 2 (May 2017): 181–190; LaMonda Stallings, *Funk the Erotic: Transaesthetics and Black Sexual Cultures* (Urbana: University of Illinois Press, 2015); Taunya Lovell Banks, "Still Drowning in Segregation: Limits of Law in Post–Civil Rights America," *Law and Inequality* 32, no. 2 (Summer 2014): 215–255.

able, and the cosmogony in the liner notes of *The Quest* provide a redoubled satisfaction: a legible neo–slave narrative that promises a future. But this future, as we know, has not arrived yet. We are still waiting.

While we wait, I turn to the music itself. I read Drexciya not as necessarily emerging from a narrative of the Middle Passage *toward* an Afrofuture aquatopia, but instead as collaborative sound-labor that draws attention to creative acts that disrupt disciplined ways of knowing. To begin, how might one describe lyricless Detroit techno? Andrew Gaerig describes the band's music as "short tracks of spackled, analog funk . . . offering occasional clues about Drexciya's sci-fi mystery. . . . Wild high-pass filters . . . provide plenty of twine for James Stinson and Gerald Donald to bind their clapping 808s. . . . Beautiful stylistic diversions. . . . A wily slab of electro."[46] On *Harnessed the Storm*, I hear fast tin beats atop heavy long-moving-long-shaking baselines that are animated by light green taps. On *Harnessed the Storm* I hear electronic hi-hats (*spa-spa-spa-spa-spa-spa*). I hear hollow echoes and deluge. On *Harnessed the Storm* I feel *bump-trap-boom* loss (trap). *Isk-isk-crash.*

These narratives—the Middle Passage cosmogony, the spackled analogue funk clapping 808s (*spa spa spa spa, zap, shhhh-isk,* loss), the anonymity of the band—can be thought about alongside creative labor. Working primarily with a synthesizer, the band generates and modifies sounds electronically; the synthesizer, as we know, can imitate different instruments: so, the moment of synthesization is about collaboration, borrowing, sharing, removing, and rewriting. With this, they use algorithms to create a signal with different sounds, thus taking waveforms, synthesizing them, to provide a soundtrack to the storm: they electronically harness the storm. Importantly, though, Drexciya also recorded all of their albums live. By this I mean they played live into a predigital analogue recorder. What we are given, as listeners, is synthesized improvisation. They harness the storm and then let it go. Improvisation demands practice and structure—it is not a natural process, it is practiced creative labor that is physiologically enacted. The labor of music, the work of making music, draws attention to acts of collaboration. The *work* of practice and practicing is, as well, always coupled with improvised sound—for one cannot improvise without practicing and arranging and rearranging memory patterns developed through partly unconscious repetition

46. Gaerig, "Drexciya."

and creative innovation. The brain and consciousness express, physiologically, creative labor that is then shared, passed on, collaboratively enjoined within a range of geographic contexts.

Drexciya gives us a different entry into theorizing and sharing black liberations by pushing us to think differently about how (and why) we gather knowledge: the band, their narratives, their anonymity and unintelligibility, and their lyricless improvised synthesized texts storm and explode identity-personality-embodiment, the moment we honor the creative labor that lies within and across these intertwining narratives. This is method-making. This is praxis. It is also a corelational interdisciplined lens through which we might read our human activities. Through this lens, black subjectivity is—in the Stuart Hall sense—becoming.[47] But I am also suggesting it is something else. Blackness here is work and it is a praxis of life: bringing human invention into existence and honoring this particular black story as evidence of the ongoing physiological and creative application of knowledge and skills that recode life. This is the praxis-practice that being thrown overboard demands. This is the praxis-practice engendered as we witness and live a script that delights in and profits from dehumanizing most of the world. And in terms of our intellectual work, this is a call to not only notice the voices that show us how "life is lived in a brutal and loveless society" but also to honor these voices as brilliant and intellectual and method-making.[48] Detroit electronica, black livingness, distracts the normative and positivist and disciplinary workings of knowledge and knowing, just as it demands new ways of being and new ways of listening that are invested in collaborative improvised liberations.

47. Stuart Hall, "Cultural Identity and Diaspora," in *Contemporary Postcolonial Theory: A Reader*, ed. Padmini Mongia (London: Arnold, 1996), 110–121.

48. Woods, *Development Arrested* (London: Verso, 1998), 288.

CONSCIOUSNESS (FEELING LIKE, FEELING LIKE THIS)

Separately and in tandem, blackness and the fantastic work to disrupt the bodily imperialisms of the colonial and corrupt the related, innocent representations of the modern. It is in this spirit that I might suggest that analyses of black politics, and by necessary extension the "generic" political, require that the exhaustion with politics itself that structures so much of contemporary discourse not delimit our own investigations of the ways certain things are kept together and others kept apart, and the capacity of the substances and processes associated with the cultural realm to deepen our understanding of these operations.

—Richard Iton, *In Search of the Black Fantastic*

ylvia Wynter's research on Frantz Fanon's sociogenic principle, race, and neurobiology shows how black consciousness can be understood in relation to liberation and cultural labor.[1] In her essay "Towards the Sociogenic Principle," Wynter works through how race and

"Feeling like, feeling like this" is from ESG, "Moody," *A South Bronx Story*, Universal Sound, 2000.

1. Encephalon. Sylvia Wynter's work on neurobiology and the brain (what is inside the head, the soft neural tissue, the synapses and their attendant chemicals and chemical signals) has led me think about the powerful weight of science-biology. Readers sometimes overdetermine brain in her work, rather than think about neurobiology alongside her overarching research program. By this I mean, when she writes of "neurobiology" or related terms (even a variation on what she describes as a "new *science* of human discourse" which can be found in a few of her essays) the reader often responds by suggesting that Wynter is singularly conceptualizing science-biology according to the exacting terms of colonial-modernity (which are bracketed by scientific racism or biological determinism). To put it differently, the reflexive response to "science" and "neurobiology" and the "brain" is to read these terms as falling under the category of "biological science," thus failing to consider how Wynter is conceptualizing "science" and "biology" outside the order of Man. For some reason, her work on the brain is not read in the same way as her work on music, film, intellectual leaps, slavery, religion,

racism inform the "puzzle of conscious experience."[2] While she explores these questions in a number of her writings, "Towards the Sociogenic Principle" offers a sustained discussion of the ways in which practices of

genre (as they are embedded in her wider thesis about blackness and humanity), and so on. The brain is removed by the reader, and then cast as *outside* her wider project. Wynter's research on neurobiology is thus read by some as a reification of the purely biological and thus a moment where the brain is a purely natural brain (that is *not* conditioned by extrahuman stories). This critique also suggests that she essentializes the brain by privileging its neuro*typicality*. While Wynter's work on neurobiology is by no means perfect—she is not a practicing neurobiologist, for example—across all of her writings the reader can observe the ways she seeks to illuminate the dangers of separating the natural sciences from the humanities and, as well and consequently, how she is conceptualizing science outside our present system of knowledge (which is a truth-making-positivist-biocentric system of knowledge). The brain, then, does not stand alone. I think it is important, therefore, to continually frame Wynter's research on neurobiology (indeed, all her research) through "science of the word," which means that the biological (in this case the brain) and the narrative (in this case how we story who and what we are) cannot be bifurcated. One way to challenge a biocentric reading of Wynter's insights on neurobiology is to notice how she engages science as a socially produced set of narratives that emerge *alongside* our human biologics (which means the soft neural tissue is not analytically privileged, nor is it analytically formed in advance of narrative). Notice too, importantly, that she is trying to work through and illuminate the *relationality* of brain-narrative-bios-mythoi. She is not suggesting that all brains are the same, all brains respond similarly to narrative, all brain synapses spark in the same way, good brains are normative, normative brains are typical and generic, brains, alone, are the path to freedom, bad brains are nonnormative, nonnormative brains are bad. Indeed, it is because the brain is structured by both the biological and narrative (bios-mythoi)—soft tissue existing and working *along-side* extrahuman scientific scripts that explain the function of the soft tissue differentially according to time and place—that we can work out how it is a site *where* neural differentiation takes place while also noticing the punishing limits of neurotypicality. It follows, of course, that all brains are *not* the same: here we can think about neuroatypical and nonneurotypical subjects as fully human *and* providing a pathway to a different way of knowing the bios-mythoi underpinnings of neurobiology while also stretching ourselves to consider how Wynter's theory of demonic ground is a *location* that provides the conditions to think outside normative systems and *cognitively* remap our inner and extrahuman worlds (repatterning how we know and what we know, how we know ourselves, to recast what they think we are). What if the alternative politics engendered on/in/with demonic grounds (and demonic ground) are theorized alongside neurobiology and neurological patterns?! What are the neurobiologics of the Fanonian leap? I must be science fiction. See Sylvia Wynter and Katherine McKittrick, "Unparalleled Catastrophe for Our Species? Or, to Give Humanness a Different Future: Conversations," in *Sylvia Wynter: On Being Human as Praxis*, ed. Katherine McKittrick (Durham, NC: Duke University Press, 2015), 9–89; Katherine McKittrick and Alexander Weheliye, "808s and Heartbreak," *Propter Nos* 2, no. 1 (Fall 2017): 13–43. Thank you, Alexander Weheliye, for encouraging me to think about and write out these curiosities.

2. Sylvia Wynter, "Towards the Sociogenic Principle: Fanon, Identity, the Puzzle of Conscious Experience, and What It Is Like to Be 'Black,'" in *National Identities and Sociopolitical*

racism are narratively connected to the physiological and neurobiological sciences. She argues that the larger symbolic belief system (the biocentric narrative or origin story of natural selection and accumulation by dispossession) of which racism is a part, is constitutive of, *not separate from*, the naturally scientific (what we might call flesh and blood and brain) aspects of humanness. The scientifically racist story of humanity shapes how we feel not just psychically, but physiologically too. Connecting prevailing belief systems to the physiological aspects of being human provides an analytical pathway to locate Fanonian black consciousness as a mode of *denaturalizing biocentricity and illuminating the neurobiological and physiological labor that underlies the praxis of liberation.* To put it differently, in focusing on the ways in which Fanon pinpoints and undoes the historioracial schema, Wynter highlights how he simultaneously knows and feels racism; her reading insists that *knowing is feeling is knowing* and therefore that consciousness, while still largely a mystery, helps us better understand the socio-neurobiological way of being black. She keeps us on track by highlighting the sparking synapses, the crumbling corporeal schema, the nausea, the biochemical stratum, that permeate Fanon's analysis and are knitted to knowing and feeling racism. Fanon shows that *"what* the brain *does* is itself culturally determined through the mediation of the *socialized sense of self,* as well as the 'social situation' in which this self is placed."[3] Wynter heretically argues that it is the New World black diasporic subject who provides a radical way to sort through consciousness because it is that collective group of people—geographically elsewhere and nowhere and also kept in place, I would add—who come to experience the *fictions* of race as a *lived* reality. The fictions of race are a lived reality. The contradictions of black life are painfully laborious: race is the fiction we must physiologically live with and through *as* racial violence just as it provides the conditions of being black that refuse our present system of knowledge. Black consciousness is the laborious and heretical aesthetics of freedom-making.

If Wynter is correct in her essay "Towards the Sociogenic Principle," and we can glimpse a sliver of consciousness through Frantz Fanon's insights, being black can be understood as an exertion of both liberation and life. I want to be careful here: I do not want to fall into a discussion about

Changes in Latin America, ed. Mercedes F. Durán-Cogan and Antonio Gómez-Moriana (New York: Routledge, 2001), 32.

3. Wynter, "Towards the Sociogenic Principle," 37 (emphasis in the original).

resilience—I am, we are, aware of the familiar story where black people are continually worked on and worked over yet seemingly never wear out. But I do want to honor that living blackness, living as black, is work, and that black people help us think through the ties between consciousness, labor, cultural production, and freedom seeking. The work of liberation does not seek a stable or knowable answer to a better future; rather, it recognizes the ongoing labor of aesthetically refusing unfreedom.[4] This aesthetic labor perhaps reveals, if only for a second and imperfectly, black consciousness.[5]

Dionne Brand begins: "There are maps to the Door of No Return. The physical door. They are well worn, gone over by cartographer by cartographer, refined from *Ptolemy's Geographia* to orbital photographs and magnetic field imaging satellites. But to the Door of No Return which is illuminated in the consciousness of Blacks in the diaspora there are no maps."[6] With this, Brand repudiates social death. The analytics she offers are not premised on (and then extend from) the obliteration of African and black life. Instead she begins with black consciousness: knowledge, mindfulness, notice, awareness, knowledge, (diasporic) literacy, thought, cognition, insight. Knowing. Illuminated. Here, at the beginning of *A Map to the Door of No Return*, we read of the generous nowhere of black life, alternative ways of being in the world and knowing the world that are not captured in *Ptolemy's Geographia*, orbital photographs, imaging satellites.[7] Illuminated in the consciousness of blacks. Esthesia. Brand writes black consciousness outside normative geographies and, in doing so, casts the most familiar and most mysterious aspects of black life as the work of psychically refusing the delimiting elapse of colonial space-time. Indeed, to begin with black consciousness in this way, as psychic anticolonial praxis, Brand signals that the brutal history we cannot totally know

4. We are not an impossibility.

5. Many thanks to Yaniya Lee for inspiring the format—chronological numbering—of this story. Following Lee, the numbering of paragraphs here plays with and questions the ledger, the archive, and the politics of accounting. See Yaniya Lee Lacharité, "When and Where We Enter: Situating the Absented Presence of Black Canadian Art," MA thesis, Queen's University (March 2019): 30–31. There are also numbered paragraphs throughout Dionne Brand's *A Map to the Door of No Return: Notes to Belonging* (Toronto: Vintage, 2001). See also Robin James' uses of numbers and letters in her *Resilience and Melancholy: Pop Music, Feminism, Neoliberalism* (Winchester and Washington: Zero Books, 2015).

6. Brand, *A Map to the Door of No Return*, 1.

7. Brand, *A Map to the Door of No Return*, 1.

but certainly feel in our hearts is always undoing itself. This is not a denial of the racial violence that accompanied transatlantic slavery (on the ship, on the Middle Passage, on the plantation, in the field, by the owners, in the quarters, on the roads, on the waterways, by the overseers in the kitchens, in the bedrooms, by the mistresses, in the shops, by the children, in the hallways) but instead an articulation of how one attends to that violence carefully. Indeed, if we read this brief excerpt ("There are maps to the Door of No Return. The physical door. They are well worn, gone over by cartographer by cartographer, refined from *Ptolemy's Geographia* to orbital photographs and magnetic field imaging satellites. But to the Door of No Return which is illuminated in the consciousness of Blacks in the diaspora there are no maps") as the ongoing labor of aesthetically critiquing unfreedom, it demands recognition (of past racial violences) with an ethical distance (this is a history we cannot fully know but certainly feel in our hearts). I identify this as the work of recognition and expanse. It is hard. I do not know what it was like there, then. I have never been. I cannot go. Some people go. They return to the infrastructures. Tours and visits.[8] Plantation tour. Plantation tours. One must not lose sight of *then* and one must notice how *now* means that you will necessarily lose sight of what was. Enter the text.

1. "I cannot bear the possibility of losing her."[9]
2. "We were not from the place where we lived and we could not remember where we were from or who we were."[10]
3. "I run each morning, two, three, sometimes four kilometers."[11]
4. "I think it was a Friday. As I said, I woke up ill. A headache blinding me like the sun across my eyes."[12]
5. "I am meeting him at the end of apartheid. . . . He is not weighed down; he is buoyant."[13]
6. "Everything far away is visible; everything close is viewed with distrust or disbelief."[14]

8. Perry Carter, David L. Butler, and Derek H. Alderman, "The House That Story Built: The Place of Slavery in Plantation Museum Narratives," *Professional Geographer* 66, no. 4 (2014): 547–557.

9. Dionne Brand, *A Map to the Door of No Return*, 154.

10. Brand, *A Map to the Door of No Return*, 5.

11. Brand, *A Map to the Door of No Return*, 98.

12. Brand, *A Map to the Door of No Return*, 158.

13. Brand, *A Map to the Door of No Return*, 97.

14. Brand, *A Map to the Door of No Return*, 101.

7. "How to describe this mix of utter, hopeless pain and elation leaning against this door?"[15]

8. "His wife and daughters always seemed washed with dread and exhaustion."[16]

9. Relief. These scraps of text are wearing me out. These scraps of text are mostly useless. They are useless but they provide a shadowy space for us to think: *A Map to the Door of No Return* is composed of notes threaded together by the analytical frame described above (black consciousness as the aesthetics of freedom-making, the work of freedom, the mindfulness of black life, the labor of recognition and expanse, those plantation futures where we witness the familiar brutality of racial violence [now] and we know it is not the same as that history that made us, race is the fiction we physiologically live with and through—all of which is informed by our ongoing refusal of what they want us to be); the notes are anticolonial stories; the notes are beautiful and sad and awful; the notes dwell on the black body, draw and undo maps, despise nation; the notes are love stories; the notes are creative text that are enunciated as sound, voice, place, punctuation, pause, quietly line by line, read aloud, with each other, alone. Love stories.

10. She writes, "Empire."[17] And the word punches you.

11. Relief: "Art, perhaps music, perhaps poetry, perhaps stories, perhaps aching constant movement—dance and speed—are the only comforts."[18]

12. What did it take to write this book? What is its sonic temporality? What labor went into the making of this? I read it, again. How do we hold on to what she offers—a different sense of place, an anticolonial way of being—and notice that the author is expressing the painful contradictions of black life? What is required to imagine, make, and live with and in excess of long-standing plantocratic and colonial logics?

13. These are the wrong questions. Again. It could be calendared, listed, monitored. The scraps of text are unsatisfying proof.

---

15. Brand, *A Map to the Door of No Return*, 41.
16. Brand, *A Map to the Door of No Return*, 9.
17. Brand, *A Map to the Door of No Return*, 75.
18. Brand, *A Map to the Door of No Return*, 26.

14. Perhaps, though, we are only meant to feel that punch and believe in those love stories.

15. Part of this story was to be about Donny Hathaway ("It's pretty special when an artist can create something that wipes them out").[19]

16. In *Development Arrested* Clyde Woods shows how black music observes, tracks, and resists injustice by exposing the inequities underpinning plantocratic political economies. By insisting that black freedom struggles are musical, he teaches us how to read black cultural production as an "unapologetic celebration of life" that is intimately linked to social change.[20]

17. Woods's concept, blues epistemology, works across three interlinked registers: to document black and other working-class resistances to long-standing plantocratic racisms; to call attention to how black intellectual-creative-community work engenders methodologies of thought and action; to explore a relational ethic of survival that emerged from, but exceeded and spatially challenges, plantation geographies.

18. Across these registers, we can notice that a large part of Woods's project is dedicated to exploring how we come to know black life through the production of space. The text itself, keenly aware of anthropological and sociological racial formations, pushes beyond socially scientific categories of blackness by offering a theory that relies heavily on what we cannot totally know but fall into love and into sadness with: song and its attendant soundscapes.[21] The move to centralize black song as

19. Edward Howard, liner notes for Donny Hathaway, *Extension of a Man*, Atco, 1973. Hathaway was diagnosed as paranoid schizophrenic and took his life in 1979. In the 2008 "Donny Hathaway" episode of the TV series *Unsung* (episode 104), it is explained that his mental health struggles led him to believe white people were going to, among other things, kill him. I stop.

20. Clyde Woods, *Development Arrested: The Blues and Plantation Power in the Mississippi Delta* (London: Verso, 1998), 20.

21. In his essay "Still Life," Richard Iton writes of love and love songs, asking the reader to consider how the ongoing legacies of transatlantic slavery and coloniality have, together, opened up affective registers that cannot be contained—or rendered legible—within our present racial logics. In identifying the struggle to write and sing about black life, Iton asks that we hold close—and in many ways take pleasure in—the uneasy tensions between black politics and "the love song stuff." Nile Rogers quoted in Iton, "Still Life," *Small Axe* 17, no. 1 (2013): 23. "Still Life" shows that the black love song "can be seen as one of the more familiar

expressive of black politics is not new; indeed, Woods's book is stacked with primary and secondary sources that support this argument. However, for me, the uniqueness of *Development Arrested* lies in the author's displacement of normative methodologies. As I read and reread this book, I wonder if Woods is perhaps asking us to hold onto and transgress a typical reading of black music (where songs describe bluesy experiences and/or illuminate resistance), while also gesturing to a third option: where songs demonstrate how knowing and feeling black music is corelational to being human. To put it differently, in this text the way of being black, or the way of black humanity, is to recognize music and soundscape as the way of, rather than external to, the self and the social world. In this sense *black is a sound is a way of being black and black being is an aurally aesthetic way of life.*

19. Music is, then, tied to ways of being. Woods often pairs music with the terms "consciousness" and, most often, "working-class consciousness." In doing so he tells us, over and over, that black

and available sites for the imagination of black political possibilities, radical and otherwise" (26). With this, Iton's essay also allows one to think carefully about the ways in which ongoing practices of racial violence both obscure and deny narratives of black love. As we learn to love and invest in loving black, we come to realize that this love, this act, is a confounding political option. Black love is/as/was strange and unexpected and bedazzling. Loving black people, Iton reminds us, discloses "the contending black thoughts defined by a differently gendered, chronologically disordered, and fundamentally reflexive spirit that is at times so exterior as to be beyond representation, registration, and recognition" (Iton, "Still Life," 31–32). Drawing on Iton's insights, we notice that black love is affectively and narratively and purposefully expressed as an assertion of black life; this assertion is a fantastic assertion, because it shows that the struggle to love and live black is bound up in, yet cannot be contained by, normative governmentalities that thrive on practices of racial, and specifically antiblack, violence. The love that emerges out of our plantation pasts, Du Boisian musical infrastructures of sorrow, cannot ethically end precisely because "the-end-of-love"—which is finding and grabbing a love that hates and despises blackness—defies the political work of black life. In Richard Iton's research and writing, then, the love song, the praxis of loving black, the set list of black life, lasts forever. Iton, "Still Life"; W. E. B. Du Bois, *The Souls of Black Folk* (1903; rpt., New York: Vintage, 1990); Katherine McKittrick, "Fantastic/Still/ Life: On Richard Iton (A Working Paper)," *Contemporary Political Theory* (February 2015): 24–32. Go and listen to Roberta Flack, "The First Time Ever I Saw Your Face," *First Take*, Atlantic, 1972; and Prince, "Love," *3121*, NPG/Universal, 2007; and Kanye West, "Hey Mama," *Late Registration*, Def Jam, 2005. Love is like the sky / you know it never stops. I knew our joy would fill the earth / and last until the end of time. No matter where you go / my love is true.

music is tied to labor and labor struggles and a kind of ephemeral mode of being.

20. Black music and the work of struggling for liberation are, together, ways of being and living black but this being and living are, depending on vantage point, and in Édouard Glissant's terms, opaque.[22] Indeed, if we focus on consciousness throughout *Development Arrested* we begin to see that black music and black consciousness are dynamic and that this dynamism understands the resistance to oppression to be open-ended and, Woods writes, "ever forward."[23]

21. According to *The Blackwell Companion to Consciousness*, "Anything that we are aware of at a given moment forms part of our consciousness, making conscious experience at once the most familiar and most mysterious aspect of our lives."[24] Anything that we are aware of.

22. What Woods gestures to is that part or all of the "anything we are aware of . . . the most familiar and the most mysterious" are those waveforms and grooves that are not easily contained or indexed by positivist epistemologies. Keeping in mind Ruth Wilson Gilmore's cautionary note in her introduction to the second edition of *Development Arrested*—that consciousness in this text is *not* reduced to experience—I read Woods's understanding of consciousness as a way of being and living black that yokes grounded political struggle to musical sentience.[25] Pair this with the too-brief and buried reference to the legacy of Steven Biko's black consciousness movement—at footnote 38 on page 335 in the original text—the music, the work, the struggle for liberation, emerge as sustained and sweeping dissent.[26] Consciousness in this text, I argue, consists of two redoubled and knotted modes of awareness: sonic perception and the work of

22. Édouard Glissant, *Poetics of Relation*, trans. Betsy Wing (Ann Arbor: University of Michigan Press, 1997).

23. Woods, *Development Arrested*, 140.

24. Susan Schneider and Max Velmans, "Introduction," in *The Blackwell Companion to Consciousness*, ed. Max Velmans and Susan Schneider (Oxford: Blackwell, 2007), 1.

25. Ruth Wilson Gilmore, "Introduction," in Clyde Woods, *Development Arrested: The Blues and Plantation Power in the Mississippi Delta*, 2nd ed. (1998; rpt., London: Verso, 2007), xiv.

26. Woods, *Development Arrested*, 335.

freedom. Or: black consciousness is the laborious and heretical aesthetics of freedom-making.

23. In knotting together music, labor, consciousness, and life, we have the conceptual grounding to read the songs and sounds that are within and exceed Woods's text as tangible commentaries on liberation. Steeped in labor and knotted to working-class consciousness, the political work of black music is not reduced to a metaphoric and "purely affective, implicit, sensuous experience."[27] Instead, music and music-making are concretized as implicit to struggle and hard work and, at the same time, are attached to that which we cannot totally know but love to hear.

24. This way of being black—what Richard Iton calls black fantastic—is uneasily situated within but necessarily disobeys colonial perimeters.[28]

25. While Woods does not spend a lot of time on acoustics, scores, and other musical temperaments, I want to run with his interlacing of black music and consciousness and work because it identifies the political contours of music-making and also provides an analytical foundation to think through what Marlon Bailey, riffing off of Robin Kelley, calls cultural labor: the tireless work of creating and expressing different forms of black life.[29] I turn to Bailey because his tracking of cultural work in *Butch Queens Up in Pumps* delineates not only laborious black gender performativity, but the quotidian and cooperative effort that is required to imagine, make, and live with and in excess of long-standing plantocratic and colonial logics.

26. Effort is everywhere. Effort is necessarily cooperative and everywhere. The analytical foundation is expansive and particular and casts liberation not as an achievement or the *object of effort*, but an expression of black life. In other words, if liberation cannot be accomplished within our present system of knowledge

27. Robin James, "Affective Resonance: On the Uses and Abuses of Music in and for Philosophy," *PhaenEx* 2 (Fall/Winter 2012): 59.

28. Richard Iton, *In Search of the Black Fantastic* (Oxford: Oxford University Press, 2008).

29. Marlon Bailey, *Butch Queens Up in Pumps: Gender, Performance, and Ballroom Culture in Detroit* (Ann Arbor: University of Michigan Press, 2013), 16–17; Robin D. G. Kelley, *Yo' Mama's Disfunktional! Fighting the Culture Wars in Urban America* (Boston: Beacon, 1997), 45.

(if the goal of freedom does not come from grasping for liberal accumulation and its attendant ways of knowing), then we can engender and honor already existing dense and complex political alternatives and radical ways of being and living that are "intensely personal and collective."[30] This allows us to understand, at least in part, how black consciousness is structured through but not determined by different kinds and types of oppression. Black consciousness navigates but is never the passive objectified receptacle of racism. Black consciousness is refusal. No. Black consciousness is the navigation of this world as a laborious aesthetics of freedom-making.[31]

27. We can then imagine these ways of being free as sutured: life-consciousness-work-effort-song. "Rebellious consciousness ... arouses."[32]

28. Song. Recalling Kara Keeling's wonderful book *The Witch's Flight*, we learn to pay special attention to the economy of song. Early in *The Witch's Flight*, Keeling mentions some of the tunes and lyrics that are excluded from her study because of high

30. Robin D. G. Kelley, *Freedom Dreams: The Black Radical Imagination* (Boston: Beacon, 2002), 35.

31. No. At times black thought is not always a refusal outright; it is not a denial or a rejection. Black thought is the intellectual praxis of living this world and seeking liberation; living this world and seeking liberation engages and disrupts this world and, importantly, allows us to gather and learn about ways of liberation that are already here, while imagining better futures. Sometimes refusals refuse too much. I, we, refuse what they want us to be while also gathering clues (notes, songs, grooves, memories, the forgotten) within and in excess of our present system of knowledge. The clues are insurgencies.

"Of course, refusal has its limits." AbdouMaliq Simone, *Improvised Lives* (Cambridge, MA: Polity, 2019), 23.

And ... "The Black Radical Tradition is a constantly evolving accumulation of structures of feeling whose individual and collective narrative arcs persistently tend toward freedom. It is a way of mindful action that is constantly renewed and refreshed over time but maintains strength, speed, stamina, agility, flexibility, balance. The great explosions and distortions of modernity put into motion—and constant interaction—already existing as well as novel understandings of difference, possession, dependence, abundance. As a result, the selection and reselection of ancestors is itself a part of the radical process of finding anywhere—if not everywhere—in political practice and analytical habit, lived expressions (including opacities) of unbounded participatory openness." Ruth Wilson Gilmore, "Abolition Geography and the Problem of Innocence," in *Futures of Black Radicalism*, ed. Gaye Theresa Johnson and Alex Lubin (New York: Verso, 2017), 237.

32. Glissant, *Poetics of Relation*, 138–139.

copyright fees. She describes the song "Smiling Faces Some-times," but does not reproduce the lyrics in print. The economy of reason, she suggests, demands something more of us, a different kind of effort: "Go listen to the song," she writes.[33] I go. I go and I listen. By listening, we enact a way of being with song outside market time. I wonder, then, how the interlacing of sound-waves and cultural work and consciousness asks us to pause, at least for a minute, and go listen to the song.

29. I read *Intimacies of Four Continents* out loud and then thought about *Vanity Fair, Beyond a Boundary* differently. I reread *Patternmaster*. The sound opens up a way of being black that ties consciousness to work, to liberation. The soundlessness does, too. What happens when we go listen to the song and listen outside of text as the text weighs us down? Do we listen as a way of working out who and what we are? Does listening to the song offer some relief? What if it doesn't? What if the experience is hard and awful? The labor of black life and black consciousness, the dailiness of black effort, and struggle, points to how wave-forms and soundscapes emerge from and move through, and then burst out of, ongoing plantocratic colonialisms. Listening changes the text.

30. Listening changes things. I cannot accurately explain black consciousness. I can only wonder and worry. I am not sure I offered a glimpse. I learned that black life is an expansive and open and cooperative aesthetics of struggling for liberation; I learned that black consciousness is an intimate, psychic, affective way of being that informs and unfolds into practical and cooperative modes of making liberation. Making liberation is weighed down by accumulation and dispossession and racism. Black people move through that weight.

31. In her study of C. L. R. James, Lisa Lowe discusses a moment of "passionate intensity" in which different people, across racial identifications, recalibrate their sense of community outside dismal colonial typologies. The passionate intensity (feeling like, feeling like) discloses a temporality outside colonial-plantocratic-market time. The passionate intensity signals

33. Kara Keeling, *The Witch's Flight: The Cinematic, the Black Femme, and the Image of Common Sense* (Durham, NC: Duke University Press, 2007), 6.

"where humanity is not yet, but will already have been . . . a conceptual space."[34] I learn that consciousness is a collaboration between sparking synapses and political struggle.[35] I learn that aesthetic labor—music, groove, text, poem, photo—provides the conditions to imagine and live who and what we are outside what they think we are. I learn that the song helps us think consciousness without being distracted by the demand for clarity. Song, story, invite "the ability to feel-with."[36] We feel-with.

34. Lisa Lowe, *The Intimacies of Four Continents* (Durham, NC: Duke University Press, 2015), 163–165.

35. "The interrelationship between the consciousness of the self and the emancipatory programme is of paramount importance. Blacks no longer seek to reform the system because doing so implies acceptance of the major points around which the system revolves." Steve Biko, "The Definition of Black Consciousness," in *I Write What I Like: Selected Writings* (1978; rpt., Chicago: University of Chicago Press, 2002), 49.

36. Sylvia Wynter quoted in Greg Thomas, "Yours in the Intellectual Struggle," in *The Caribbean Woman Writer as Scholar*, ed. Keshia N. Abraham (Coconut Creek, FL: Caribbean Studies Press, 2009), 47.

SOMETHING THAT EXCEEDS ALL EFFORTS

TO DEFINITIVELY PIN IT DOWN

*E*ach time I arrive at her home we stand in the doorway to catch up. I arrive and we catch up. It feels forever. We sit at her dining room table. I do not tire. We eat. We share the Haitian rum. Each time I leave I am weary and worn out.[1] A combination of speechlessness and fast thoughts and tireless sharing and stories that I can never remember fully and then I leave and I lose focus. Every time I leave "possibility" expresses itself affectively and physiologically. I feel possibility. I think this is what possibility feels like. It is not narrated textually. It is not an idea. I have always pushed myself and my students to think about how black liberation can be understood as a site of possibility and as a struggle that is ongoing but never resolved. This is the gift of black studies—a conceptual frame that draws attention to and critiques racism and other practices of discrimination but does not remain beholden to the system of knowledge that profits from oppression. I am committed to possibility analytically. But after each departure, I lose focus of the analytics. I feel unsteady. This is what possibility feels like. Maybe this is what possibility feels like. What she has generously offered me in our conversations is that doing this intellectual work, and indicting the system that misrepresents and obscures your creative-intellectual labor just as it thrives on racial violence, is a feeling too. I can only describe it as a kind of terrifying openness that promises a different future and this future is outside what we have been taught to recognize as liberation. The future, too, is here. I know this

"Something That Exceeds All Efforts to Pin It Down" is from AbdouMaliq Simone, *Improvised Lives* (Cambridge, MA: Polity, 2019), 5.

1. Each time I leave I feel as though I have been swimming for seven hours.

because I felt it in the doorway, at the table, and in the aftermath. Liberation is already there and here.

Rewind. Unparalleled catastrophe. We worked through the contents of the original document for seven years.[2] It is impossible to track exactly what went on in those seven years. It felt like endlessness moving very fast. The long conversation gave me a glimpse of the risky and rebellious project of undoing what we know, and making sense of the world in new ways; it required thinking big about the specificities of who and what we are in a world that denies black personhood. She draws attention to how race figures into genealogies that ask not only what it means to be human but also how we came to be who and what we are. In addition, she urges us to redefine the human through our racial attachments, for the sake of not just our collective selves but for the planet (and our environmental decline, climate change, is tied to the enslaved moving across the Middle Passage, a linear temporal-spatial logic of accumulation by dispossession and extraction that we still honor and replicate and resist, too).

The struggles against plantation and postplantation violences foster a range of interlocking perspectives that continually question and disobey geographic and intellectual practices that sequester, watch over, harm, and manage black diasporic peoples. This is an intellectual and physiological struggle. This is work. This is doing the work. In terms of the production of material and intellectual space, in my view, this (our) disobedience rarely replicates colonial-plantation geographic logics. Black expressive life cannot replicate these logics, and the task of nonreplication is exhausting. The disobedience sparks a stream of black texts and practices that continually imagine a way of being black as linked to landlessness and activity-based collaborative intellectual labor. In this, we share how we arrive at *struggle*; how we get there, what stories allow us get there, what stories disrupt what we know and what stories enable new ways of

2. Simple random sample of documents: draft Wynter interview, April 23, 2007; Sylvia Wynter, interview 2008; revised Wynter, May and June 2008; final Wynter draft, July 2010; Wynter March 21, 2011; Wynter, Marx section; Wynter new excerpt, new conclusion; Wynter, July part 1; Wynter, July part 2; Third Event 1; Third Event 2; Third Event 3; Third Event all; Wynter, Spring 2012, parts A B C D; In Closing/Coda/After/Word/The Third Event: Our Collective Drought/Desertification/Starvation/Accelerating Species Threat Catastrophe and Our Iconic Blombos Cave Type Initiation; Wynter McKittrick 1: Final: 2013; Wynter McKittrick 2: Final 2014; Wynter: revised ending 2014; Wynter_September and October Merged.

thinking about freedom. This is black life and its affective expression. Maybe this is what possibility feels like.

The question of stories and storytelling illuminate the method of collaboration I learned from working with her. I learned from her that sharing stories engenders creative rigorous radical theory. Wait. I learned from her that sharing stories *is* creative rigorous radical theory. The act of sharing stories *is* the theory and the methodology. The process is difficult to make sense of in terms of the process and praxis of collaboration as affective possibility. Every time we speak on the telephone, I have my pen in hand, but I do not always use it. We share ideas, and stories, and our histories, and part of this collaboration was her generously sharing ideas that I wrote down because I believed them with all my heart. And lucky for me, she believed me, too.[3] (We must believe each other; we must believe the stories we tell one another.) I guess what I am trying to write but cannot pinpoint is that the collaborative aspects of the work allowed us to share ideas in ways that I did not anticipate. The project is, then, not solely text; it is the unpublishable work of conversing over several years and continuing that conversation. I did not expect to be this patient. The conversation is forever and it is forever rewound very fast and then replayed: "The friendship itself, a form of life that cannot be totally capitalized on and is therefore slightly in excess of work as we know it. . . . Working in friendship could be a way to work outside of productivist demands."[4]

Friendship is hard freedom. Maybe friendships effectuate consciousness and liberation and possibility.

I remind myself, a lot, to be patient with ideas about race and oppression. I believe, with all my heart, that black life is rebellious and always incomplete. I understand why I feel that way when I depart. The sound of the conversation signals a loss that I cannot write it out. I cannot remember the words to the song. Her intellectual labor, and the intellectual labor of black peoples—creative-activist-scholarly-working peoples—and

3. Believing in black life and black livingness is radical generous political act. Believing each other and believing the stories we tell each other about what happened. Believing what we love and what we find hard. Believing our unsettling encounters which each other. Believing our experiences with racism and racist and sexist violence. Believing our broken hearts.

4. Avery Gordon and Céline Condorelli, "Conversation 1," in Avery Gordon, *The Hawthorn Archive: Letters from the Utopian Margins* (New York: Fordham University Press, 2018), 92–93.

the task of indicting our present system of knowledge, is exhausting. It is not profitable work. I think the most important thing that she observes is that while the undoing is hopefully exhausting, it must be done. Her work is asking us: What is to be done and what are we doing to reimagine how might we live the world differently? How has this world already been radically reimagined by and through black thought, and how do we share that knowledge with each other so that we might practice a humanism made to the measure of the world?[5] If we do not do this work, if we do not collaboratively call into question a system of knowledge that delights in accumulation by dispossession and profits from ecocidal and genocidal practices, if we do not produce and share stories that honor modes of humanness that cannot and will not replicate this system, we are doomed.

The collaboration and conversation have allowed me to work out where and how black people imagine and practice liberation as they are weighed down by biocentrically induced accumulation by dispossession. There is weight on their-our physiological and psychic well-being. The struggle against oppression is tied our flesh and brains and blood and bones and hearts and souls; there are underlying, often invisible, moments of black liberation. I remember that quantifying and endlessly describing black corporeal and affective and physiological labor belies what black studies offers. There are some things we can just keep for ourselves. Somethings they cannot have and know. We don't need to measure black life and its possibilities. What it feels like is good enough. Maybe we are not an impossibility. Maybe we are, in the words of Aimé Césaire, "poetically beautiful" and therefore possible outside the terms of what they think we are.[6]

5. Aimé Césaire, *Discourse on Colonialism*, trans. Joan Pinkham (1955; rpt., New York: Monthly Review Press, 2000), 73.

6. Aimé Césaire, "Poetry and Knowledge," in *Lyric and Dramatic Poetry*, trans. Clayton Eshleman and Annette Smith, xlii–lvi (Charlottesville: University Press of Virginia, 1990).

NO PLACE, UNKNOWN, UNDETERMINED

···································

Original source: Place of creation: No place, unknown, or undetermined. Credit: Ted Grant /
Library and Archives Canada / PA-170252. Restrictions on use: nil. Copyright assigned to
Library and Archives Canada by copyright owner Ted Grant.

NO PLACE, UNKNOWN, UNDETERMINED

Original source: Place of creation: No place, unknown, or undetermined. Credit: Ted Grant /
Library and Archives Canada / PA-170252. Restrictions on use: nil. Copyright assigned to
Library and Archives Canada by copyright owner Ted Grant.

....

Original source: W. E. B. Du Bois, *Black Reconstruction in America, 1860–1880* (1935; rpt., New York: Atheneum, 1992), 732–733.

NOTES

Original source: W. E. B. Du Bois, Black Reconstruction in America, 1860–1880 (1935; rpt., New York: Atheneum, 1992), 732–733.

d opinions in order to prove that
the North vengeful or deceived,

olution After Lincoln.
cious Minority.
er.
ade and Its Consequences. Four

ction and Its Results.
ia Politics, 1865-1902.
Slavery.
Carolina Under Negro Govern-

ained.
h Carolina, 1865-1877.
very, New York, 1863.

N S

the Negro.)

ress.
1865.

The Outcome of a Visit to the

n Reconstruction. Letters to *Le*

cumentary History of American

es.
ion, 1865-1912.
n Civil War.
orgia Plantation.
ns of a Half Century.
f the United States During Re-

n Lincoln.
e Spring and Summer of 1875.
e United States Since the Civil

aboard Slave States, 1856.
Varioloid, *Atlantic Monthly,*

Schurz, Carl, Remi
Sherman, John, Re
Simkins, Francis B
    construction.
Smedes, Susan Dab
Somers, Robert, Th

(These historian
pathetically about t

Bancroft, Frederic,
Beard, Augustus F
Birmingham, T. M
Bothune, Elizabeth
Brewster, James, Sl
Eaton, John, Grant
Lewinson, Paul, Ra
Reid, Whitelaw, A
    1866.
Russell, Charles E
Skaggs, W. H., Sou
Stewart, Lucy Shel
Tinker, Edward L
Wilson, Henry, Hi
    ica.

(These authors
most cases do not i

Ambler, G. H., Se
Ames, Herman V
    United States I
    Report of the A
Bancroft, Frederic A
    Carolina and N
Banks, Enoch M.,
Brooks, Robert P.,
Flack, Horace E.,
Fleming, Walter F
    tion of the Ra
—. The Freedn

BLACK ECOLOGIES. CORAL CITIES. CATCH A WAVE

....

Original source: Ellen Gallagher, *Coral Cities* (London: Tate, 2007). "Catch a Wave" is from Drexciya, "Wavejumper," *The Quest*, Submerge, 1997.

BLACK ECOLOGIES. CORAL CITIES. CATCH A WAVE

Original source: Ellen Gallagher, Coral Cities (London: Tate, 2007). "Catch a Wave" is from Drexciya, "Wavejumper," The Quest, Submerge, 1997.

Coral Cities

ELLEN
GALLA
GHER

Original Source: Charmaine Lurch's Studio, Toronto, Ontario, Canada. Photo by the author.

CHARMAINE'S WIRE

Original Source: Charmaine Lurch's Studio, Toronto, Ontario, Canada. Photo by the author.

POLYCARBONATE, ALUMINUM (GOLD), AND LACQUER

···

Original source: Betty Davis, *They Say I'm Different*, Light in the Attic Records, 1974.

POLYCARBONATE, ALUMINUM (GOLD), AND LACQUER

Original source: Betty Davis, They Say I'm Different, Light in the Attic Records, 1974.

BLACK CHILDREN

Original source: June Jordan, "The Test of Atlanta," in *Directed by Desire: The Collected Poems of June Jordan*, ed. Jan Heller Levi and Sara Miles (Port Townsend, WA: Copper Canyon Press, 2007), 390–391.

Original source: June Jordan, "The Test of Atlanta," in Directed by Desire: The Collected Poems of June Jordan, ed. Jan Heller Levi and Sara Miles (Port Townsend, WA: Copper Canyon Press, 2007), 390–391.

Eric Middlebrooks, 14 years old, de
Christopher Richardson, 14 years o
Aaron Wyche, 11 years old, de
LaTanya Wilson, 7 years old, d
Anthony B. Carter, 9 years old, d
Earl Lee Terrell, 10 years old, d
Clifford Jones, 13 years old, d
Aaron Jackson, Jr., 9 years old,
Patrick Rogers, 16 years old, dea
Charles Stevens, 12 years old, dea
Jeffrey Lamar Mathis, 10 years ol
Darron Glass, 10 years old, missi
Lubie "Chuck" Geter, 14 years ol

What kind of a person could kill a Black child
and then kill another Black child and then
kill another Black child and then kill another
Black child and then kill another
Black child and then kill another Black
child

and stay above suspicion?
What about the police?
What about somebody Black?
What sixteen year old would say no to a cop?
What seven year old would say no thanks to me?
What is an overreaction to murder?
What kind of a person could kill a Black
child and then kill a Black child
kill a Black

TELEPHONE LISTING

....

Original source: Sandra Brewster, *From Life 3*, 2015, mixed media on wood, 60 × 48 in.

TELEPHONE LISTING

Original source: Sandra Brewster, From Life 3, 2015, mixed media on wood, 60 × 48 in.

*I*n March 2014, *Harper's* published the report "Chronicle of a Death Foretold."[1] In this piece, Monte Reel describes a program implemented by Chicago schools in 2009 that would "determine exactly which of their 400,000 students would get shot."[2] The program became known alongside an initiative called "The Culture of Calm." Consultants from the Massachusetts Institute of Technology and the University of Chicago developed an algorithm that scanned juvenile detention and school attendance records, as well as test scores, and used these archives to prognosticate the preventable death of youths. When I first came across this report, I could not read past the first page: the report begins with Davonte Flennoy, a young man who was—to use an awkward nonword—"algorithmed." More specifically, data was pulled from Flennoy's archival file, and this led to interpretable paper scores; in the application of the algorithm, his well-being and his psychic and biologic life were rendered in excess of a deterministic set of discursive calculations. To put it simply, the algorithm mathematically refused all aspects of his livingness. Flennoy's archive—his records, his test scores—were culled and collated, and he was determined to be highly killable, or "ultra-high-risk."[3] Indeed, in

The subtitle of this story, "My Head Was Full of Misty Fumes of Doubt," is from Zora Neale Hurston, *Dust Tracks on a Road* (1942; rpt., New York: HarperCollins, 1991), 195.

1. Monte Reel, "Chronicle of a Death Foretold: Predicting Murder on Chicago's South Side," *Harper's*, March 2014, 43–51.

2. Reel, "Chronicle of a Death Foretold," 43.

3. Reel, "Chronicle of a Death Foretold," 46. On risk thinking see Nikolas Rose, "At Risk of Madness," in *Embracing Risk: The Changing Culture of Insurance and Responsibility*, ed. Tom Baker and Jonathan Simon (Chicago: University of Chicago Press, 2002), 209–237.

many ways his life only enters the mathematical equation as death. The algorithm was granted more energy and vitality—through the act of application—than Flennoy (the object and outcome of the mathematical analysis). After the predictive system algorithmically anticipated his death, and measures were taken to prevent his death, Flennoy was killed in June 2012. This report sat on my desk for just over two years, and I read the first page over and over. I could not fully integrate into my psyche the idea of an algorithm that was manufactured to assume, anticipate, predetermine, and foretell deadly violence; at the same time, I did not want to consume, yet again, what I and we already know. I read that first page over and over for about two years, noticing that the compulsion to repeat put me in a state, to borrow from Dina Georgis, "of simultaneously not wanting to forget and not wanting to know."[4]

When I returned to the report and completed reading it, I learned that the predictable algorithmic model saw both funding cuts and ineffectual results: the key to the program was to run the algorithm, identify ultra-high-risk people, and prevent their deaths by providing them with mentors who would support, teach, counsel youths. The cost was about $15,000 per student, annually, and the funding model was unsustainable; as well, gunshot victimization did not decrease among the algorithmed.[5] Soon after, a similar predictable-analytics formula was adopted by the Chicago Police Department—one we are all familiar with and referred to as the predictive policing model: this algorithm identifies a series of "hot spots" and "hot lists" that single out criminals and their attendant geographies.

I begin this story with the *Harper's* report not because what is uncovered is new or astonishing but because it shows how blackness and race are implicit to mathematical codes, discourses, and problems. The report, without reserve, situates black youths in the midst of what Bernard Harcourt calls "actuarial predictions."[6] The predictions—the hot spots,

4. Dina Georgis, *The Better Story: Queer Affects from the Middle East* (Albany: SUNY Press, 2013), 47.

5. Rachel Levenstein, Sue Sporte, and Elaine Allensworth, "Findings from an Investigation into the Culture of Calm Initiative," *University of Chicago Consortium on School Research*, October 2011, https://consortium.uchicago.edu/publications/findings-investigation-culture-calm-initiative. Dana Chandler, Steven D. Levitt, and John A. List, "Predicting and Preventing Shootings among At-Risk Youth," *American Economic Review: Papers and Proceedings* 101, no. 3 (2011): 288–292. Thank you, Nik Theodore.

6. Bernard Harcourt, *Against Prediction: Profiling, Policing, and Punishment in an Actuarial Age* (Chicago: University of Chicago Press, 2007), 2.

the ultra-high-risk youths, for example—emerge from the "mechanical combining of information for classification purposes."[7] The question of why or how or under what conditions premature death is predictable is not asked. Instead, death is an analytical and methodological variable in the overall equation. Even the underfunded and defunded program, which was intended to save black life and engender mentorship, grimly assumed loss (the vulnerable were not given life, they were given foreseeable death).

For the two years the report sat on my desk, unread, I thought about the mathematics of black life. I wrote an essay where I wanted to centralize black life rather than preventable and premature death; that essay argues, in a less-than-straightforward way, that one way to imagine black life differently is to rethink the mathematics that underwrite slave archives.[8] Following Saidiya Hartman's "Venus in Two Acts," I explore how archives document and institutionalize sexist and racist practices. I argue that because the archives primarily document instances of violence toward and the death of black enslaved people, racism acts as an eerie origin story that can steer us, analytically, toward death. What the archive tells us is what we already know and what we resist, but it can also structure and frame how we enter into the present and future in our writing: Middle Passage and plantation systems formalized and made ubiquitously mundane, in writing and practice, violence against black people, black subordination, and racism, and we sometimes use this as a blueprint to understand and struggle against oppression. Anything in excess of violence, racism, and subordination—black life, black joy, the practice of loving, for example— is either absent or perversely tied to the dehumanizing logics of white supremacy. My central questions for that essay were: If the archive is a knowledge network that records and normalizes black subordination, how do we understand this network outside of itself? What happens to our understanding of black humanity when our analytical frames do not emerge from a broad swathe of numbing racial violence but, instead, from multiple and untracked enunciations of black life?

What I want to think about in this story, in a similar but different way, is how black life is absent from the classificatory algorithms that are applied to statistically organize our world. This absence affirms how the

7. Paul Meehl quoted in Harcourt, *Against Prediction*, 16–17.
8. Katherine McKittrick, "Mathematics Black Life," *Black Scholar* 44, no. 2 (Summer 2014): 16–28.

premature death of black people, and, more broadly, the acute marginalization of the world's most vulnerable communities, are entrenched in algorithmic equations. What I am struggling to work out, then, is twofold: that premature death is an algorithmic variable; that black life is outside algorithmic logics altogether.[9] It follows that coded infrastructures and patterns that are instituted to name and/or resolve social problems are bound up in biocentric thinking and, as well, that we are already grasping an alternative knowledge system when we analytically privilege black life. I am not, I want to underline, suggesting that we replace the dead with the living; I am not seeking to dismiss our losses. I want, instead, to reimagine blackness—as life and living memory and whatever is in between—as emerging from a black sense of place. My concern is therefore, broadly, methodological: How do we come to and formulate answers and what do we want from these solutions, politically? How might a black sense of place rethink the demand to fix and repair black humanity by lifting black folks up, from subhuman to a genre of human that cannot bear black life? What if black life opens up question marks and unanswerable curiosities?

A black sense of place draws attention to geographic processes that emerged from plantation slavery and its attendant racial violences yet cannot be contained by the logics of white supremacy. A black sense of place is not a standpoint or a situated knowledge; it is a location of difficult encounter and relationality. A black sense of place is not individualized knowledge—it is collaborative praxis. It assumes that our collective assertions of life are always in tandem with other ways of being (including those ways of being we cannot bear). A black sense of place always calls into question, struggles against, critiques, undoes, prevailing racist scripts. A black sense of place is a diasporic-plantocratic-black geography

9. If a nonuniform problem enters the data processes machine, it generates a noncomputable form and the output may not be predictable or calculable. The process of working with and working out the equation might: result in infinite calculation; or, alternatively (depending on the mechanics underpinning the working with and working out), the data processing machine might be offered a different set of rules through which to accommodate the nonuniform problem and resolve it. Gualtiero Piccinini, "Alan Turing and the Mathematical Objection," *Minds and Machines* 13 (2003): 23–48. If black life is the nonuniform problem, we might sit with this and its attendant noncomputability. If entered (recorded, logged), within the context of computation, black life might offer us multiple ways to unthink the problematic enfleshment of algorithms because it is an irresolvable variable; if entered (recorded, logged) into the equation, and within the working with and working out stages, the unsolvable also provides the opportunity to sit with unpredictability-entropy as this relates to the potential, not only the death-dealing, technologies of human life.

that reframes what we know by reorienting and honoring *where* we know from.[10] This is a place where, to borrow from Édouard Glissant, "analytic thought is led to construct unities whose interdependent variances jointly piece together the interactive totality."[11] A black sense of place is a methodology and an analytical frame that believes in and believes black humanity. So I ask: What does a black sense of place *do* to algorithms that presume, in advance, black premature death? How might we shift our methodological questions so that we do not end up in an analytical bind that affirms rather than undoes racial violence?

A black sense of place draws attention to uncomfortable relationalities yet understands these as a method through which we can wade through the horrific uneasiness of black death that is, as we know, posited as an easy resolution to a vast range of social problems. What I also want to signal, as I move through this story, is how some geographies get called up as answers to problems. To put it simply, solving crimes often involves surveying and marking black and/or impoverished geographies and claiming that this is not profiling because places, rather than people, are being targeted. In other words, social problems are resolved through producing calculations, equations, and problem-solving operations; these problems (black people) are translated into cartographically itemized racial codes.[12] Part of our task, then, is to notice how algorithms have a place and take place and produce place and how blackness—*where* we know

10. Katherine McKittrick, "On Plantations, Prisons, and a Black Sense of Place," *Social and Cultural Geography* 12, no. 8 (2011): 947–963.

11. Édouard Glissant, *Poetics of Relation*, trans. Betsy Wing (1990; rpt., Ann Arbor: University of Michigan Press, 1997), 92.

12. These problem-solving operations can be imagined in relation to the Du Boisian question "How does it feel to be a problem?" In this case, the calculations and other mathematical operations require the uneasy embodiment of racial and racist designation and resultant structures of feeling (how does it feel to be?). The mathematics seek to resolve (solve, find an answer to) us. We are the repository of the mathematical operations. The affective work Du Bois points to is taxing. We know that problems are trouble. Problems are harmful and problems get in the way. Problems need to be resolved. Problem is dilemma, nightmare, mess. How does it feel to be a problem? It feels oppressive. It feels worrying. It feels forever. It feels awful. W. E. B. Du Bois, *The Souls of Black Folk* (New York: Vintage, 1990), 7; W. E. B. Du Bois, "The Study of the Negro Problems," *Annals of the American Academy of Political and Social Science* 11 (January 1898): 1–23; Nahum Chandler, *X—The Problem of the Negro as a Problem for Thought* (New York: Fordham University Press, 2014); Paul Gilroy, *Against Race: Imagining Political Culture beyond the Color Line* (Cambridge, MA: Harvard University Press, 2000). She is a loose cannon, a problem. Remove her.

from—understands and reorders these geographies. I also focus on geography to dislodge crude identity politics, to cast the net beyond the individual and to emphasize that *where* we know from—rather than what we already know about our seemingly authentic selves—is a more generous and difficult political project that takes into account interhuman geographies. With this in mind, I suture a black sense of place to these mathematics and problem-solving practices in order to unthink the violence that often accompanies the production of space.

An algorithm "applies to any mathematical procedure consisting of an indefinite number of steps, each step applying to the one preceding it."[13] The steps are, in fact, massive calculations that are set up to accomplish a task; most algorithms stop on finding the answer. In addition, algorithms are intended to solve problems correctly and efficiently.[14] According to Khan Academy, the reason algorithms matter is that the massive calculations "do things people care about."[15] While algorithms are best known within the context of computer science, they are attached to longer practices of statistical data collection. The aforementioned "hot spots," "hot lists," and "risky people" were the result of computer algorithms, as are trending hashtags, credit application scores, job application scores, prison sentencing decisions, publication impact factors, Netflix and Amazon recommendations, and so on. Algorithms also assess voter information environments, extract personal information, accumulate data sets, transfer data to capitalist stakeholders, ergo, profoundly remaking our sense of place (task accomplished).[16] These computer-generated algorithms are

13. Tobias Dantzig, *Number: The Language of Science* (1930; rpt., New York: Plume, 2007), 33.

14. Khan Academy, "What Is an Algorithm and Why Should You Care?," accessed May 19, 2016, https://www.khanacademy.org/computing/computer-science/algorithms/intro -to-algorithms/v/what-are-algorithms.

15. Khan Academy, "What Is an Algorithm and Why Should You Care?"

16. Carole Cadwalladr, "The Great British Brexit Robbery: How Our Democracy was Hijacked," *Guardian*, May 7, 2017, https://www.theguardian.com/technology/2017/may/07/the -great-british-brexit-robbery-hijacked-democracy?CMP=share_btn_link. In addition to being linked to the military industrial complex and surveillance, Cadwalladr likens voter information extraction to a "massive land grab." She also refers to the data and generation of computer information as an "ecosystem" that can be mapped. Data mining: to quarry, to excavate, to remove. The spatial terms are dizzying given that computer data is not, in fact, a three-dimensional space that we can touch and/or inhabit. Instead, the data ecosystem is made up of computer codes. The ecosystem is produced by scripting languages like C++ or Frege or Python or Objective-J and it is upheld by software architecture. In many

automated-decision-making-software: they are computer codes that are given a problem, that seek and compile patterns and themes, and then spit out solutions.

An important feature underlying many algorithms is predictability: they are not only used to work out problems; they know the problem in advance and are tasked to achieve a specified result. So the accomplishment, the answer, the result, what we care about, comes before the equation. An important example of this is predictive algorithm models. In his study of policing and profiling, Harcourt explores predictive parole models alongside the overlapping fields of sociology, criminology, and statistics. Beginning in roughly the 1930s, statistical information on prisoners—such as immigrant status, employment history, personality type, and characteristic traits—was gathered to determine the likelihood of repeat offenses.[17] While his study is very extensive, what can be deciphered from his text is that what these early statistical systems knew in advance was tied to "characteristic traits" that ostensibly shape recidivism and other decisions about prison life. It is not news, of course, that "characteristic traits" are underpinned by differential racial histories and privileges. What we learn from predictive algorithms, then, is that the mathematic

_____

ways, the land does not exist and therefore cannot be grabbed or mined: the goal is, Jiawei Han and Micheline Kamber argue, "the extraction of patterns and knowledge from large amounts of data, not the extraction (mining) of data itself." Jiawei Han and Micheline Kamber, *Data Mining: Concepts and Techniques* (Burlington, MA: Morgan Kaufmann, 2001), 5. However, Cadwalladr's language is powerful precisely because it nods to a much longer history of racial and colonial violence and, at the same time, allows our mind to leap and think about how data produces real three-dimensional geographies. Data grabbing and data mining are certainly not the same as massive transnational land transactions and land grabs, spurred by violent "development" logics that necessarily displace and destroy the lives of the world's most vulnerable. But the data grabbing—think Brexit and US president Trump, for example—remakes place and perhaps might be an anticipatory shadow in less immediate histories that were underwritten by displacement and accumulation by dispossession. Here, the work of Sharlene Mollett is instructive: land grabbing is not novel or recent; land grabbing is long-standing and routinely operationalized to naturalize racial hierarchies and racist "whitening logics." Sharlene Mollett, "The Power to Plunder: Rethinking Land Grabbing in Latin America," *Antipode* 48, no. 2 (March 2016): 412–432. Land grabbing is a self-replicating system that provides the avaricious conditions for the data grab. They are not the same, but they are both tied to colonialism and capitalism and they are both entwined with the production of space. The task of data grabbing is to remake our sense of place, heartlessly. Thank you, Paul Gilroy.

17. Harcourt, *Against Prediction*, 57.

answer or result is, at least in part and sometimes in whole, tied to a larger colonial and plantocratic logic: a trait is, as we know, a genetically determined characteristic—like eye color. Traits are the variables that underlie a biocentric system of knowledge.[18]

In contemporary contexts, sometimes race is written into the predictive formula. A Violence Prediction Model Variable counts and assesses:

African American;
Hispanic;
School Per Capita Shooting History;
Times Shot Previously;
Serious Misconducts Per Day;
Math Score; Reading Score;
Percent of Days Suspended;
Percent of Days Absent;
and so on.[19]

And sometimes race is obscured by the predictive formula. A Risk Terrain Model counts and assesses:

Drug Arrests, Gang;
Territory;
At-Risk Housing;
Risky Facilities;
Shootings;
Gun Robberies;
and so on.[20]

Violence. Terrain. Predictive algorithms and actuarial patterns did and still do rely on genetic variables to help solve problems and get results and do things people care about. We should also note that the characteristic traits that underlie early algorithms get coded over and coded

18. Sylvia Wynter and Katherine McKittrick, "Unparalleled Catastrophe for Our Species? Or, to Give Humanness a Different Future: Conversations," in *Sylvia Wynter: On Being Human as Praxis*, ed. Katherine McKittrick (Durham, NC: Duke University Press, 2015), 26–30.

19. Chandler, Levitt, and List, "Predicting and Preventing Shootings among At-Risk Youth," 288–292.

20. Leslie W. Kennedy, Joel M. Caplan, and Eric Piza, "Risk Clusters, Hotspots, and Spatial Intelligence: Risk Terrain Modeling as an Algorithm for Police Resource Allocation Strategies," *Journal of Quantitative Criminology* 27, no. 3 (2011): 339–362.

over and coded over, so that the variables (the traits) within the original equation that was fashioned to do things we care about sometimes get weighed down and lost underneath mathematical cyphers (as seen in the "Risk Terrain Model"). The weight that conceals traits also hides the work of the coders and translators: those workers who fuel algorithms by collecting and collating the data yet remain unseen and unacknowledged. These workers, Neda Atanasoski and Kalindi Vora write, are the "surrogate technologies" whose labor facilitates the ease of coming to an algorithmic conclusion.[21] The work and process of coding conceals a long biocentric statistical history that continues to define "traits"—our genetic characteristics—as variables. A variable is a symbol that represents a quantity in a mathematical expression. What unfolds are measurable numbers—often abstracted from human input—calculating resolutions that we care about.

If we understand algorithms in this vein, we can begin to tease out how numbers and mathematical equations are tied to a biocentric system of knowledge. What becomes increasingly clear, then, is not simply that the results and answers are racist (e.g., your traits mathematically result in your incarceration), but that the work of administrating algorithms (e.g., what we *do* to solve the problems that we care about) requires biocentric methods and methodologies that can only produce dehumanizing mathematical results. In other words, black inhumanity, specifically the biocentric racist claim that black people are nonhuman and unevolved and a priori deceased, is a variable in the problem-solving equation before the question is asked, which means that the work of the algorithm—to do things people care about, to accomplish the task—already *knows* that Flennoy's life and well-being are extraneous to its methodology. What comes into clear view, then, is not simply the racist result but the administrative and methodological steps that require racism before they begin to work through and toward the problem.

A large number of articles and books speak to these themes—particularly in relation to predictive policing but also in relation to other algorithmic patterns: predictive algorithms are racist, predictive algorithms imitate a racist system, predictive algorithms are technologies of racial

21. Neda Atanasoski and Kalindi Vora, "Surrogate Humanity: Posthuman Networks and the (Racialized) Obsolescence of Labor," *Catalyst: Feminism, Theory, Technoscience* 1, no. 1 (2015): n.p., http://feministtechnoscience.org/ojs/index.php/catalyst/article/view/ata_vora.

profiling, predictive algorithms are antiblack, algorithms harm communities of color, algorithms threaten democracy.[22] I subscribe to the "Algorithm" page on Flipboard, which algorithmically gathers a range of recommended articles on big data and algorithms and presents them to me because I care about algorithms. Headlines include "Beauty Contest Regrets Using Robots for Judges after Only White People Win," "Facebook Algorithms Can't Replace Good Judgment," "It's Getting Tougher to Tell if You're on the Phone with a Machine or Human: Algorithm Can Accurately Mimic Human Voices, Including Breathing," "Could an Algorithm Replace the Pill?," and "How Algorithms Can Destroy Your Chance of Getting a Job."[23] The widely circulated *ProPublica* article "Machine Bias" draws attention to how the software and formulas used to determine future criminals are racially biased: regardless of their criminal history—a history that may include no criminal activity at all—black people are cast as more unlawful and culpable than white people.[24] We also know, as well, that there is widespread support for predictive models, which are described as beneficial, proactive, promising, strikingly successful, cost-

22. Ezekiel Edwards, "Predictive Policing Software Is More Accurate at Predicting Policing," *Huffington Post*, August 31, 2016, http://www.huffingtonpost.com/entry/predictive-policing-reform_us_57c6ffe0e4b0e60d31dc9120; R. Joshua Scannell, "Broken Windows, Broken Code," *Real Life*, August 29, 2016, http://reallifemag.com/broken-windows-broken-code/; Cathy O'Neil, *Weapons of Math Destruction: How Big Data Increases Inequality and Threatens Democracy* (New York: Crown, 2016). Ruha Benjamin, *Race After Technology: Abolitionist Tools for the New Jim Code* (Cambridge: Polity, 2019).

23. Amanda Fama, "Beauty Contest Regrets Using Robots for Judges after Only White People Win," *Elite Daily*, September 9, 2016, https://www.elitedaily.com/news/beauty-contest-robot-judges-regrets/1606213; Navneet Alang, "Facebook Algorithms Can't Replace Good Judgment," *Globe and Mail*, September 9, 2016, https://www.theglobeandmail.com/opinion/facebook-algorithms-cant-replace-good-judgment/article31805498/; Dave Gershgorn, "It's Getting Tougher to Tell if You're on the Phone with a Machine or Human," *Quartz*, September 9, 2016, https://qz.com/778056/google-deepminds-wavenet-algorithm-can-accurately-mimic-human-voices/; Cory Doctorow, "Blackballed by Machine Learning: How Algorithms Can Destroy Your Chance of Getting a Job," *BoingBoing*, September 8, 2016, https://boingboing.net/2016/09/08/blackballed-by-machine-learnin.html; Emma Lundin, "Could an Algorithm Replace the Pill?," *Guardian*, November 7, 2016, https://www.theguardian.com/lifeandstyle/2016/nov/07/natural-cycles-fertility-app-algorithm-replace-pill-contraception. Read with: Marcus Gilroy-Ware, *Filling the Void: Emotion, Capitalism, and Social Media* (London: Repeater Books, 2017).

24. Julia Angwin, Jeff Larson, Surya Mattu, and Lauren Kirchner, "Machine Bias," *ProPublica*, accessed June 20, 2016, https://www.propublica.org/article/machine-bias-risk-assessments-in-criminal-sentencing.

effective, incredibly accurate, and so on.[25] These incredibly accurate algorithms are also often posited as delinked from race, thus pushing up against the *ProPublica* thesis. The website for PredPol (a well-known company that produces predictive policing software) reads, "PredPol uses only three data points in making predictions: past type of crime, place of crime and time of crime. It uses no personal information about individuals or groups of individuals, eliminating any personal liberties and profiling concerns."[26]

Type. Place. Time. In some of the studies I read, there are often short definitions of what a predictive algorithm is, or what predictive policing algorithms are, but the racial shadows behind numbers are often unspoken-unwritten. The already existing biocentric logic does not necessarily inform the administration of the algorithm (how we *get to* what we care about is not relevant). Instead, what is highlighted, discussed, are the answers: finding bad illegal geographies and disciplining the bad criminal people that inhabit these places. This kind of analytical move refuses racism, capitalism, and white supremacy while presenting their logics and outcomes—dysselection—as objective truths. Samuel Greengard writes:

> Feed reams of data—particularly data focused on the time, distribution, and geography of past events—into a database and ferret out patterns that *would not be apparent to the human eye or brain*. With the resulting data, it is possible to adjust patrols and other resources to create a stronger deterrent, but also to predict *where* crimes are likely to take place and be in a better position to apprehend suspects.[27]

What I am trying to work through is, then, how the racist biocentric logics that inform the algorithmic queries and their answers are quietly yet securely tied to the mathematics of black lifelessness. What we have is a system wherein black people are dehumanized in advance, and this

25. Walt L. Perry, Brian McInnis, Carter C. Price, Susan C. Smith, and John S. Hollywood, *Predictive Policing: The Role of Crime Forecasting in Law Enforcement Operations* (Santa Monica, CA: Rand, 2013); Andrew Guthrie Ferguson, "Predictive Policing and Reasonable Suspicion," *Emory Law Journal* 259 (2012): 261–313; Samuel Greengard, "Policing the Future," *Communications of the ACM* 55, no. 3 (March 2012): 19–21.

26. Predpol, "About," accessed February 1, 2017, http://www.predpol.com/about/.

27. Greengard, "Policing the Future," 19 (emphasis added).

dehumanization is hardened and made objective by mathematical codes. The tensions between these analytical approaches—the biological and the mathematical—function to produce a series of "objective facts" precisely because they are grounded in a positivist system of knowledge that indexes simultaneously, racial, sexual, economic, geographic, and temporal differences. The algorithm expresses, almost perfectly, the brutality of racism precisely because it is an accounting system that produces what Sylvia Wynter calls "adaptive truth-for" terms that are specific to our present order of consciousness.[28] The numbers that come before, comprise, and complete the algorithm are devoid of black life yet filled up with acts of black dysselection. It is a process typical to what we already know: a biocentric system is mathematically confirmed; it unfolds and is, in theory, seemingly absent of racism because the methodology cannot comprehend black well-being in the first place; the system and methodologies cannot bear black livingness, and the math and coding behind the algorithm provide an alibi for racism because black life is not relevant to the "things people care about." What is also revealed is the tendency to bifurcate the science of the biological and science of mathematics: even though we know in our hearts algorithms imitate a racist system, within our present system of knowledge, the numbers do not and cannot lie.

Josh Scannell adds to this by exploring how algorithms are "real social processes" that "enshrine contested neo-plantation systems of rule as technocratic abstractions, infrastructural, and inevitable."[29] The information behind algorithms is cast as "spectral data bodies" that produce a "metrics of prehension" that is spatially enacted. Indeed, if the numbers cannot lie, the spatialization of these numbers, expressed across multiscalar geographies, ensures what Ruth Wilson Gilmore calls the "fatal couplings of power and difference signified by racism."[30] Geography matters because it functions to illuminate how algorithmic answers to our problems—what we care about—are embedded in place. Interestingly, the more we research these connections between geography and algorithms, the more

28. Sylvia Wynter, "Unsettling the Coloniality of Being/Power/Truth/Freedom towards the Human, after Man, Its Overrepresentation—an Argument," CR: The New Centennial Review 3, no. 3 (Fall 2003): 280.

29. R. Joshua Scannell, "What Can an Algorithm Do?," DIS Magazine (2016), accessed September 26, 2016, http://dismagazine.com/discussion/72975/josh-scannell-what-can-an-algorithm-do/.

30. Ruth Wilson Gilmore, "Fatal Couplings of Power and Difference: Notes on Racism and Geography," Professional Geographer 54, no. 1 (February 2002): 22.

we notice how the former, geography, is racially codified. Predictive algorithms are not only imitating a racist system, they are refusing an already
refused black humanity by marking black geographies predictably criminal. In many ways, then, the answer to our problems is revealed as the
multiscalar dispossession of the dispossessed. This geographic layer per-
fects the algorithmic alibi by using mathematical procedures to abstract
human activity from racist problem-solving practices and by deperson-
alizing black geographies. PredPol: "Using only three data points—past
type, place and time of crime and a unique algorithm based on criminal behavior patterns, PredPol's powerful software provides each law enforcement agency with customized crime predictions for the places and
times that crimes are most likely to occur. PredPol pinpoints small areas,
depicted in 500 feet by 500 feet boxes on maps—that are automatically
generated for each shift of each day."[31] Type of crime, place of crime, time
of crime. Type. Place. Time.

In addition to studies like "Machine Bias," there has been some valuable work on reclaiming and recoding algorithms, recognizing coders
who critique and refuse predictive models, highlighting nonpredictive
and eternal algorithms, thinking about the algorithm as similar to the
Code Noir or as a form of plantation neoliberalism or as enacting a Foucauldian panopticon.[32] There are algorithmic poetics and code-work that
index and map different sites of safety and violence.[33] There have also
been algorithmic mappings of Negritude, opacity, slave ship routes, city
sounds, deaths since Ferguson, and more. So even though the numbers do
not lie, many are working hard to counter-code or renarrate or simply tell
the certainties that underlie the brutal statistics, traits, and mathematics
of dysselection.

31. Predpol, "About."

32. Wendy Chun, "On 'Sourcery,' or Code as Fetish," *Configurations* 16, no. 3 (Fall 2008):
299–324; Christopher Taylor, "Plantation Neoliberalism," *New Inquiry*, July 8, 2014, www
.thenewinquiry.com/essays/plantation-neoliberalism/; Louis Henderson, "Black Code/
Code Noir: The Algorithm as Necropolitical Control," *Khiasma*, June 2016, http://www
.khiasma.net/magazine/black-codecode-noir/; Colin Koopman, "The Algorithm and
the Watchtower," *New Inquiry*, September 29, 2015, http://thenewinquiry.com/essays/the
-algorithm-and-the-watchtower/.

33. Micha Cárdenas, "Trans of Color Poetics: Stitching Bodies, Concepts, and Algorithms," *Scholar and Feminist Online* 3, no. 13–4, no. 1 (2016), http://sfonline.barnard.edu
/traversing-technologies/micha-cardenas-trans-of-color-poetics-stitching-bodies-concepts
-and-algorithms/0/.

What all of this has led me to—the codes and the recodes, the equations and problems, the predictions and spatial alibis, the software and the numbers, all covered in blood and death and things we care about that would not otherwise be apparent to the eye or the brain—is a lesson in methodology. I am interested in algorithms because of what they tell us about *how* we do the things we care about. Much of this story has centralized how many algorithms are future-making mathematic equations. They are anticipatory computations that tell us what we already know, but in the future. If we want different or better or more just futures and worlds, it is important to notice what kind of knowledge networks are already predicting our futures. As we know, as well, futurity and futures are deeply meaningful to black folks: we see this playing out in a number of ways, in reconceptualizations of time and space, in Afrofuturisms, in black science fictions and speculative fictions, in the unmet promises of modernity, in the freedom yet to come; in the syllabi and the calls for papers and the conferences and the books and articles and blogs; in the keywords and in the museums; in the recent and not-recent-at-all turn to string theory and theoretical physics and quantum mechanics (within the context of black studies, for example); in the unending and open-ended circulation of the spectacles, the litanies, the lists of those we, you, I have lost; in the lists we cannot bear to draw up; in the poems and the theories we write and the poems and theories we will not write; on the streets, and in parks, and around our tables, and in artworlds, and in our sighs and side-eyes, in our tiredness and dreams; in the demand to keep it up, keep it up.[34]

If algorithms are future-making mathematical equations, they matter to black studies and black people because they are predicated on the negation of black life: this negation demands we keep an eye on algorithmic fictions because we cannot live with, we do not want to live with, the future outcome they produce; this negation also highlights, boldly, that black life is rebelling against that system of negation precisely because it is unimaginable within the practice of (automated) decision-making. Predictive black life is the antithesis to those technologies of race that repli-

34. "Never stop the action / keep it up / keep it up": Grace Jones, "Jones the Rhythm," *Slave to the Rhythm*, Island Records, 1985. Also recall Jones's live performances of "Slave to the Rhythm," where she hula-hoops throughout the entire song, often for over eight minutes— no beat lost. See Grace Jones, "Slave to the Rhythm—Live AVO Session," YouTube video, 8:33, posted June 26, 2010, https://www.youtube.com/watch?v=yPHmJLRFv8c.

cate what we already know about racial violence. Predictive black life. If algorithms provide a generalized template that requires the absolute negation of black humanity, and black life is in excess of this self-replicating system, then the equations, the algorithms, the big data, *cannot adapt to black life*. This opens up a methodological opportunity for us, because the algorithms signal that what is outside this and other systems of big knowledge—black life, black well-being, black livingness—is a genre of humanness that is poised to decode, or is already decoding, this system and, at the same time, enunciating a worldview that functions within, across, and outside oppressive technologies and infrastructures. This is the demonic ground Wynter writes about in her piece on *The Tempest*: a different and alternative space-time—a black sense of place, *where* we know from—that can and does reorder our present system of knowledge because it is not, in fact, measurable on colonial terms. Part of what I am suggesting is a monumental demand—to reorder how we know, to produce a new science of black mnemonic livingness—but I think it is a meaningful demand. We might engender and honor black life as methodology—human being as praxis coupled with diasporic interdisciplinarity that cannot be measured or pinned down. The demand can, therefore, be grasped on a smaller scale by posing new and different academic questions that emerge from a black sense of place (where we know from).

What happens to our questions if we insist our methodologies are, in themselves, forms of black well-being? What happens if the nonmeasurability-noncomputability of black life is indicative of, necessary to, our analytics? What if we are not seeking outputs, answers, conclusions that end with only describing racism within our present system of knowledge? What if the answers that emerge from our colonial and plantocratic blueprints are not good enough? What if there is not a learning outcome? What if we taught and wrote not as problem solvers who count and assess variables (and creative texts can, at times, be theorized as variables) but as intellectuals who, with all our hearts, believe in opacity and giving on and with rather than finding, grasping, and having?[35] The answers that emerge from our colonial pasts are not good enough precisely because they are given in advance of the questions. If the depth and richness of our lives are absented from our analytics—if our questions recite what we already know—we risk working with and reproducing a system that

35. Glissant, *Poetics of Relation*, 144.

cannot adapt to black life. This positions the algorithm not as something we should abandon but, instead, as a warning sign that signals the limits and possibilities of how we do what we do. The features of the algorithm are disquieting and familiar because they loom over and under the disciplining methodologies that make the academy what it is: the question, the answer, the massive calculations that are set up to accomplish a task; the push to solve problems correctly and efficiently. I am not arguing that the algorithm is the same, methodologically, as discourse analysis or text-based analyses or participant observation or other methodological processes we employ to do what we do. I am, though, suggesting that our academic worlds celebrate problem solving, learning outcomes, accomplishments, reviews, and mandates—and, in the case of my university, master plans, strategic plans—and that these features often lurk behind our questions. If we shift our focus to embrace, more boldly and confidently, an analytic of black life and livingness, we centralize black humanity—not eschewing racism and racial violence but, rather, understanding that these practices have always engendered a different form of life that privileges our collective well-being.

....

When I was writing this story, I stopped several times because I didn't want to finish it. I felt tired and defeated. In fact, I hated my argument and I came to despise algorithms. I realized that the work of coding—the practical science of computer science—was impenetrable and unwelcoming to a person who has not been trained in the discipline. I hated what I wanted to know and why I wanted to know it. My curiosity diminished. I am not a computer scientist: everything I read that *was* intelligible—the articles and books that spelled out how algorithms are undemocratic and racist—affirmed racism. What I read did not take me anywhere new and, at the same time, gave me a future I did not want. I didn't know anything yet I knew something. The only transparency for me, a non–computer scientist, was premature and preventable death. I also resented the context through which I and we are writing and thinking—normalized racial violence, lists of the dead and dying, the same old thing: "rampant textuality" coupled with excessive unspeakable violence that leads us on a linear path to a future of unfreedom.[36]

36. The term "rampant textuality" is from Paul Gilroy, *The Black Atlantic: Modernity and Double Consciousness* (Cambridge, MA: Harvard University Press, 1993), 78.

I confess my anger and frustration because I adore and believe, with all my heart, that radical (rogue) interdisciplinarity (method-making) and patient relational thinking offer ways to rethink our present system of knowledge; the reason I originally turned to algorithms is because I wanted to write a story about how these mathematical equations organize our world and I wanted to put them into conversation with creative texts that would, perhaps, take us somewhere new. What I also confronted, during my research, is that sometimes the seduction of interdisciplinarity can take us so radically outside our own sense of place that we lose sight of why we do the work we do. Part of my confession, then, is that I don't really know—in a confident and academic sense—how algorithms are made. I am still learning. It's like my interest in physics: I learned a lot and continue to learn, even though I am not sure I have the energetic knowledge base to unsettle *both* physics and blackness. What I learned from my research on computer science, for the most part, was the outcome. I came to despise the work because my interdisciplinarity project was foiled by what I did not know and what I could not know, as a non–computer scientist. I tried to make my own algorithm. I failed. I then had the grand idea to algorithmically mash up what I wrote here with something a colleague sent me. I wanted to produce an endless list of scrolling words that come from two senses of place. I could not do it. I did not know how to write the code. Defeated, the most I could bear was to input the words from this story into one of those word-cloud generators. I felt sick to my stomach. Those word clouds were, at one time, promotional narratives—part of the master plan, the strategic plan—for my university. "Gender" in large block letters, "women" in smaller letters, "queer" in tiny letters, "international" in medium-sized letters, "black" nowhere. I became and am offended and sickened by the word cloud.

But all of this led me to something I already know but keep returning to in a kind of compulsive and repetitive way. To do radical interdisciplinary work, from a black sense of place, that changes the kinds of questions we ask is not just about reading outside our discipline, researching, and using slices and terms from people we do not normally read; it is about sharing ideas comprehensively and moving these ideas into new contexts and places. In a different story I asked that we read creative texts *as* theoretical texts; I asked, What happens if the groove or the song gives insight to the theoretical frame? For this story, I checked in with my partner, Zilli, who is a musician and coder. When I told him what I wanted to do—to learn how to code, to create an algorithm that shows that predictive policing algorithms are not the only ways of knowing or doing black geographies, to learn how algorithms might be made into something new or different—he told me that was the wrong path. More specifically, he asked me: Why are you beginning with outcomes? What do you want the algorithm to do? I could not formulate satisfactory answers. I could only produce a nonfunctional and brutally individualistic formula: I begin with Flennoy, as outcome, I want my algorithm to change this outcome, or allow me to forget it, or bring him back, or give me some ethical distance, or . . . me, I want the algorithm to help me. Zilli and I had many conversations about the back end of algorithms, about how the politics of algorithms—even endless ones—are actually demands for clear and clean answers; they always already know. We also talked about Markov chains and Alan Turing, about AI and *Minority Report*. What I learned about algorithms is that the questions I ask in my own research emerge from difficult and often unbearable encounters—these encounters are riddled with impatience and are endless repetitive burdens that are ongoing and never resolved. I learned that I wanted something I could not get from an algorithm because all it could provide—in my reading, not everyone's reading!—was a predetermined codified answer. I also learned that there is a sexiness to algorithms—imagine, I thought, if I could actually code a poetic-politics of blackness, an algorithm of resistance, and publish it as part of my book.[37]

My conversations with Zilli led me down an important path because I came to understand that *not* knowing what an algorithm is, in an academic sense, opened up bigger questions about how we come to know blackness, in an academic sense. I began to dwell on praxis and methodology and to think differently about the production of knowledge in relation to race. The encounter did not produce a sexy coder with sexy codes; it produced an unfinished mess and a still-worried and still-curious person who continues to be deeply suspicious of how we come to know, where we know from, and the ways in which many academic methodologies refuse black life and relational thinking. But the conversation with Zilli is what I want to underscore—for if we are to reorient our analytics and privilege black life as we practice radical interdisciplinarity, we must engage, deeply, in conversation and share ideas generously. This is to say that relationality, like a black sense of place, must be praxis—a praxis that does not assume or desire resolved outcomes. Paying close attention to,

37. Disaster.

120   *Failure (My Head Was*

drawing out, and forging relational knowledges will provide us, as people who are invested in undoing the normalized workings of racial violence, with analytical mechanisms that allow us to do anticolonial work in a variety of university settings that, as we know, were not built to support or recognize black communities and black work.

Part of our intellectual task, then, is to work out how different kinds and types of texts, voices, and geographies *relate to each other* and open up unexpected and surprising ways to talk about liberation, knowledge, history, race, gender, narrative, and blackness. The task, as I have repeatedly noted throughout these stories, is not to track and quantify marginalized peoples and seek reparation through centering their objectification, but, rather, to posit that many divergent and different and relational voices of unfreedom are analytical and intellectual sites that can tell us something new about our academic concerns and our anticolonial futures. This story, then, is a long plea to be uncomfortably satisfied with the unmeasurability of black life and to engender interhuman relationalities, with all our heart; it is a plea to practice radical interdisciplinarity without fraying its connection to black life; it is a plea to honor a black sense of place and where we know from, rather than mobilizing crude identity politics as the answer and the fix. This is a plea to keep it up and a plea to foster and share intellectual spaces—sometimes crammed into the corners of the academy, sometimes not—for and with each other in order to methodologically and analytically redefine what they think we are.

....

THE KICK DRUM IS THE FAULT

....

Listen to.[1]

Adia Victoria, "The City"
A'maal Nuux, "Words Revealed"
Amadou and Mariam featuring Manu Chao, "Sénégal Fast Food"
Anita Baker, "Caught Up in the Rapture"
Aretha Franklin, "Save Me"
Azealia Banks, "Anna Wintour"
Bad Brains, "I Against I"
Bad Bunny, "Soy Peor"
Ben Harper, "Ground on Down"
Betty Davis, "Game Is My Middle Name"
Betty Davis, "They Say I'm Different"
Big K.R.I.T., "R.E.M."
Bob Marley and the Wailers, "Guava Jelly"
Brandy, "Necessary"
Charlie Chaplin, "Premier (Plaza) Explosion"
Cheryl Lynn, "Got to Be Real"
The Coasters, "Down in Mexico"

The title of this story is from "Housequake," by Prince, on *Sign o' the Times*, Paisley Park/ Warner Brothers, 1987.

1. This story was written with: AbdouMaliq Simone, Adam Elliott-Cooper, Alexander Weheliye, Barrington Walker, Carmen Kynard, Cora Gilroy-Ware, Eric Lott, Errol Nazareth, Esther Harvey, Kara Keeling, Kiese Laymon, Maya Stitski, Renée Green, SA Smythe, Shana M. Griffin, Shana Redmond, Simone Browne, Steven Osuna, Tia-Simone Gardner, Yaniya Lee.

Damon Davis featuring Tonina, "Light Years"
Dionne Warwick, "Don't Make Me Over"
Donna Summer, "I Feel Love"
Ebony Bones, "W.A.R.R.I.O.R."
The English Beat, "Twist and Crawl"
Erykah Badu, "Didn't Cha Know"
Erykah Badu, "The Healer"
Fauness, "Street Song"
FKA Twigs, "Cellophane"
Frank Ocean, "Nikes"
Gil Scott-Heron "The Revolution Will Not Be Televised"
Idris Ackamoor and the Pyramids, "Sunset"
Janelle Monáe, "Americans"
Jimmy Cliff, "Many Rivers to Cross"
J.O.E. featuring Konshens, "Fit"
Kamasi Washington, "Fists of Fury"
Kano, "Endz"
Kendrick Lamar, "i"
Khia, "My Neck, My Back (Lick It)"
Kojey Radical featuring Mahalia, "Water (If They Only Knew)"
Labi Siffre, "Remember My Song"
Laura Mvula, "That's Alright"
Layla Hendryx, "Rain or Snow"
Leikeli47, "Money"
Lion Babe, "Treat Me Like Fire"
Mariah Carey, "The Distance"
Max Roach and Abbey Lincoln, "Triptych: Prayer, Protest, Peace"
Millie Jackson, "Phuck U Symphony" (Live)
Millie Jackson, "Put Something Down on It" (Live)
Missy Elliott, "The Rain (Supa Dupa Fly)"
Mobb Deep featuring Lil' Kim, "Quiet Storm" (Remix)
Moor Mother, "By the Light"
Nas, "NY State of Mind"
Native, "Late September in May"
Neneh Cherry featuring Michael Stipe, "Trout"
Nina Simone, "Ain't Got No/I Got Life"
Nina Simone, "Pirate Jenny"
Nitty Scott, "BBYGRL"
OutKast, "The Whole World"

Paul Robeson, "Didn't My Lord Deliver Daniel?"
Pharoah Sanders featuring Leon Thomas, "The Creator Has a Master Plan"
Prince, "I Wanna Be Your Lover"
Prince, "Pop Life"
Public Enemy, "Welcome to the Terrordome"
Rihanna, "Higher"
The Roots, "Dynamite!"
Sade, "King of Sorrow"
Seinabo Sey, "I Owe You Nothing"
Shanique Marie, "Breezy Day"
Silvio Rodriguez, "La Maza"
The Slickers, "Johnny Too Bad"
Sly and the Family Stone, "If You Want Me to Stay"
Solange Knowles, "Cranes in the Sky"
Tina Turner, "Private Dancer"
Trina, "Da Baddest Bitch"
TV on the Radio, "Family Tree"
Vanity 6, "Nasty Girl"
Whitney Houston, "You Give Good Love"
YellowStraps, "Blame"

Pivot Reverse Turn. Thunder Clap. Free Spin. Twist . . .

*T*his is a relational story nested in black studies, science studies of blackness and race, and black creative text. Divided into different sections, the story uses columns, repetition, narrative blocks, and academic form to center black ways of knowing.[1] The method, while imperfect, hopefully offers a lens that will observe and critique the injustices of racism without revering and repeating and describing racial violence. The purpose of this story is to worry rather than replicate violence, while knowing that worry requires some kind of engagement—often an overbearing and anxious engagement—with harm. This is a story that does not want description or descriptive tactics (this is us, violated and dead) to solely define who and what we are. This is a story that lives with violence but cannot accurately describe violence. This is a story where I live with violence without knowing how to fully comprehend, or detail, violence. This is a story where we live with violence and do not ask for more and more and more evidence or proof of that violence. This story worries. It has been told before. Differently.[2]

This story will address how the social production of biologically determinist racial scripts—which extend from a biocentric conception of the human—can be dislodged by bringing studies of blackness in/and

The subtitle of this story, "Bad Made Measure," is from M. NourbeSe Philip, *Zong!* (Toronto: Mercury Press, 2008), 5.

1. See John Keene, *Counternarratives: Stories and Novellas* (New York: New Directions, 2015); and Richa Nagar, *Muddying the Waters: Coauthoring Feminisms across Scholarship and Activism* (Urbana: University of Illinois Press, 2014).

2. A different version of this paper can be found here: Katherine McKittrick, "Diachronic Loops/Deadweight Tonnage/Bad Made Measure," *Cultural Geographies* 23, no. 1 (December 2015): 1–16.

science into conversation with *autopoietics,* black Atlantic livingness, weights and measures, and poetry. A biocentric knowledge system and conception of the human, as noted throughout many of these stories, refers to the lawlike order of knowledge that posits a Darwinian narrative of the human—that we are purely biological and bio-evolutionary beings—as universal.[3]

A biocentric knowledge system assumes that, as a species, we have evolved differentially according to our ethnic-racial differences. The result is a kind of Malthusian spatial-racial fallout. Race functions to naturalize this conception of the human. We must keep in mind that biocentricity is not the same as scientific racism or biological determinism. Scientific racism and biological determinism are ideologies that *animate* a pervasive biocentric belief system.[4]

A biocentric conception of the human posits that we are bio-evolutionary beings who *do not author* this racially coded bio-evolutionary script.[5] A biocentric frame does not take into account stories and storytelling as modes of livingness; nor does it recognize biocentricity and Darwinism as fictive narratives.[6]

A biocentric conception of the human positions black subjects as naturally unevolved and less than human.[7] A biocentric conception of the human is tied to and follows a singular linear-teleological temporality.[8]

3. Joyce E. King and Sylvia Wynter, "Race and Our Biocentric Belief System: An Interview with Sylvia Wynter," in *Black Education: A Transformative Research and Action Agenda,* ed. Joyce. E. King (Washington, DC: American Educational Research Association, 2005), 361–366. Here Wynter provides us with an original formulation that is distinctly different from biocentrism (as taken up in environmental ethics). See Patrick George Derr and Edward M. McNamara, *Case Studies in Environmental Ethics* (New York: Rowman and Littlefield, 2003).

4. "The Negroes are animals. They go about naked." Frantz Fanon, *Black Skin, White Masks,* translated by Charles Lam Markmann (1952; rpt., New York: Grove, 1967), 165.

5. "My body was given back to me sprawled out . . . " Fanon, *Black Skin, White Masks,* 113.

6. "Recently an acquaintance told me a story. A Martinique Negro landed at La Havre and went into a bar . . . " Fanon, *Black Skin, White Masks,* 21.

7. "The Negro symbolizes the biological." Fanon, *Black Skin, White Masks,* 167.

8. "With the Negro the cycle of the biological begins." Fanon, *Black Skin, White Masks,* 161.

This story is an imperfect and unfinished working through of how we think about, study, and theorize racial violence. The story explores how racial violence is structured through the enmeshment of positivism and biocentricity—the social scientific and empirical verification of racial-gendered-classed-queered corporeal-locational differences among humans. Racial violence illuminates the difficult work of showing (proving) that discrimination, hate, racism, and other forms of oppression are unjust because they emerge from false claims of racial inferiority that are supported by bewitching scientific biases (a biocentric conception of the human assumes that we, as a species, have evolved differentially according to race-ethnicity; race functions to naturalize this conception of the human). Our work exposes the falsities. The exposed falsities, our proof, engenders hopeful anxiety.

A large cluster of analytical work on race—and specifically blackness—draws attention to the unjust violence done to black people's bodies. The body is the primary site of analysis. This work seeks to refuse scientific racism. Some analyses of the violated black body are coupled with oppositional narratives wherein black *embodied knowledge* is valued as a site of resistance. Black embodied knowledge radically overturns the normalizing workings of white supremacy by enunciating, demanding, and asserting black agency and humanity. At the same time, however, because the body and embodied knowledge are so tightly bound together—the physiological body imbues epistemology and ontology and comportment—often the black body, alone, is thrown into sharp (analytical) relief, displacing or hiding black agentive-intellectual labor. As a category of analysis (*not* an experiential physiology) the black body often signifies the "why" and "where" and "how" and "when" and "what" of racial violence; as a concept and category of analysis, the black body is the site where scrutiny and critique of violence takes place. The black body is never worn out or worn down. The black body is a site of experimentation, medicalization, study, data collection. The black body is the target (the bullseye and the objective) of hate and racist violence. The black body gives. The black body is scanned, worked on, and worked over. The black body carries and comports our liberation.

While theories of corporeality complement and complicate how we think through blackness, I wonder if the black body, as an analytic, can be imagined outside violation. This raises a number of open-ended questions: What happens when the black body is positioned, in itself and on its own, as racial knowledge? What happens when the black body is, in itself and on its own, proof of white supremacy? How is the black body, in itself and by itself, tasked with illuminating inequities? Are stories of black resistance *only legible in relation to* the body that bears racist violence and symbolizes preventable black death? How is black knowledge put forward as only emerging from, and only evidence of, biologic knowledge? Does the preoccupation with the black body, rather than black embodied knowledge and black extrahuman ways of being, foreclose alternative forms of liberation? We must ask ourselves—and I ask myself this often—how black *bodies* rather than *black people* are informing how we (I) understand liberation and the production of knowledge and, as well, how scholarly work may unintentionally replicate a biocentric order by leaning heavily on corporeal representation. These questions and tensions are urgent because when the black body, the concept, is required to do limitless theoretical work it is analytically posited as a priori biologic (a harmed body that body-knowledge emanates from) and is therefore already marginal or excluded or outside to how we *know* (because this framework abandons and obfuscates our black agentive-intellectual labor and casts black humanity as unknowing!).

This story hopes to face harm without harming while also recognizing that challenging biocentric logics is a painful and incomplete process. This story seeks to honor black ways of knowing by observing and critiquing the injustices of racism without revering and repeating and describing racial violence (description is not liberation). This is a story of where, I hope, the black body is not a concept. This is a story that does not want description or descriptive tactics (this is us, violated and dead) to define who and what we are. This is a story that lives with violence but is not sure how to describe violence. This is a story where I live with descriptive violence. This is a story where we live with violence and do not ask that violence be plain and clear and commonsense. This is a story that feels but cannot say what we saw. This is a story of the black body and black bodies unabandoned (agentive-intellectual).

Part 1 is an overview of how race is taken up in some areas of science studies; this section also thinks about how the glue that affixes race to science uncovers an *autopoietic* system. Part 2 provides an analytic pathway to reorienting the discursive scientific data of race and blackness. In part 3 I introduce the slave ship *Zong* through three columned vignettes: history; weights and measures; and social theory. This is followed by a discussion of M. NourbeSe Philip's *Zong!* The vignettes and *Zong!*, together, allow me to read the slave ship as a historically present living-system that articulates an unexpected scientific promise. The overarching work of the vignettes, the poetry, and the story as a whole is to push against the tendency to read blackness in/and science through a singular analytical model (one that classifies black people as less than human, or, one that leans on biological determinism and its bewitching misrepresentations of the black body). I conclude with a brief discussion that addresses the difficulties of reading, teaching, and analyzing racial violence, particularly when we rely on data sets that seek to grapple with race by relying on the axiom that biological race is socially produced. In this story, I am not dismissing or disputing the social production of race. I am, instead, questioning how comfortably falling back on this reasoning—that race is a fiction—can, in some (not all) instances, be underpinned by quiet biocentric logics. While each section has textual boundaries, the parts and pieces of data and theory and narrative, when read in tandem, draw attention to an analytical praxis that highlights how reading across (reading with, writing relationally, sharing with each other) is one way to counter the scholarly objectification of black people and their pain while also drawing attention to the richness of their geographies, stories, theories, songs, lovingness, effort.[9]

SCIENCE STUDIES, THE SINGULARIZATION
OF BLACK BIOLOGICS, *AUTOPOIETICS*

Since about the 1970s, feminist science studies and feminist philosophies of science have provided a theoretical critique of scientific neutrality and epistemological purity. Feminist science studies have developed research queries that are committed to challenging biological determinism and the absented role of women in the sciences.[10] These studies have also contrib-

9. "There was, quite simply, no secret about the killings of Africans on the Atlantic slave ships." James Walvin, *The Zong: A Massacre, the Law, and the End of Slavery* (New Haven, CT: Yale University Press, 2011), 115.

10. Anne Fausto-Sterling, *Myths of Gender: Biological Theories about Women and Men* (New York: Basic, 1985); Donna Haraway, *Primate Visions: Gender, Race, and Nature in the World of Modern Science* (New York: Routledge, 1989); Donna Haraway, *Simians, Cyborgs, and Women: The Reinvention of Nature* (New York: Routledge, 1991); Sandra Harding, *Whose Science? Whose Knowledge? Thinking from Women's Lives* (Ithaca, NY: Cornell University Press, 1991); David Noble, *A World without Women: The Christian Clerical Culture of Western Science* (Oxford: Oxford University Press, 1992); Sharon Traweek, *Beamtimes and Lifetimes: The World of High Energy Physicists* (Cambridge, MA: Harvard University Press, 1992).

uted to some incredible methodological and epistemological shifts that complement broader feminist and antiracist projects, specifically, the development of a standpoint feminist perspective and situated knowledge—which developed in different ways across feminist theory but, in feminist science studies specifically, are well-known in the research of Donna Haraway and Sandra Harding.[11] These feminist perspectives show that (feminist) identity-place calls into question scientific neutrality and other masculinist and colonial knowledge systems. In short, the demystification of scientific objectivity and the insertion of gendered voices into discourses of scientific knowledge inform the field of feminist science studies. Some areas of feminist science studies and feminist science and technology studies address how race informs the gendered workings of scientific knowledge and also track how race and racial apartheid are constituted through scientific knowledge and colonialism: here, for me, the work of Lundy Braun, Banu Subramaniam, Evelynn Hammonds, Dorothy Roberts, Karla F. C. Holloway, Simone Browne, and Alondra Nelson stand out.[12] While each of these thinkers have different projects, they importantly centralize the themes of the body, biological determinism, technology, scientific racism, and representation in relation to racial difference and, in this, destabilize the notion that the raced and gendered body can elicit transparent data. These studies also draw attention to how the prac-

11. Sandra Harding, ed., *The "Racial" Economy of Science: Toward a Democratic Future* (Bloomington: Indiana University Press, 1993); Haraway, *Simians, Cyborgs, and Women*. Notable, although often not mentioned, are the ways in which Haraway's landmark concept of "situated knowledge" is, in large part, made possible through her reading of the life and creative work of Nigerian author Buchi Emecheta.

12. Lundy Braun, *Breathing Race into the Machine: The Surprising Career of the Spirometer from Plantation to Genetics* (Minneapolis: University of Minnesota Press, 2014); Evelynn Hammonds and Banu Subramaniam, "A Conversation on Feminist Science Studies," *Signs* 28, no. 3 (2003): 923–944; Dorothy Roberts, *Fatal Invention: How Science, Politics, and Big Business Re-create Race in the Twenty-First Century* (New York: New Press, 2011); Banu Subramaniam, "Moored Metamorphoses: A Retrospective Essay on Feminist Science Studies," *Signs* 34, no. 4 (2009): 951–980; Karla F. C. Holloway, *Private Bodies, Public Texts: Race, Gender and a Cultural Bioethics* (Durham, NC: Duke University Press, 2011); Alondra Nelson, "Bio Science: Genetic Genealogy Testing and the Pursuit of African Ancestry," *Social Studies of Science* 38, no. 5 (2008): 759–783; Alondra Nelson, *The Social Life of DNA: Race, Reparations, and Reconciliation after the Genome* (Boston: Beacon, 2016); Simone Browne, *Dark Matters: On the Surveillance of Blackness* (Durham, NC: Duke University Press, 2015).

tice of documenting and knowing otherness and epidermal differences puts demands on how we ethically respond to processes of racialization, particularly wherein the black body is scanned, worked on, and worked over. They also punctuate, in terrifying ways, how race is knotted to mechanical infrastructures (labs, actuators, control panels, levers, switches, cylinders, motherboards, bearings, needles, vials, pullies, scales) and, as well, how these infrastructures bend and flex to accommodate biocentric ways of knowing.

In feminist science studies and science studies of race, then, three overlapping fields of study emerge: research that addresses the ways in which the racial underpinnings of science have long informed analyses of social inequities, poverty, racial and sexual discrimination, citizenship, and belonging; research on themes such as genomes, blood quantum, miscegenation, the bell curve, intelligence testing, and reproductive technologies, all of which bring into focus racial formations; investigations that examine and critique the ways in which the body, phenotype, skulls, height, hair, and gender comportment are indicators of biological differences among humans. In these areas of study two important themes are worth highlighting: that race is socially produced yet differentially lived vis-à-vis structural inequalities; and that the application of science can and does adversely shape the lives of women, poor, and nonwhite communities. In other words, although science is a knowledge system that socially produces what it means to be biologically human, it is also the epistemological grounds through which racial and sexual essentialism is registered and lived. These research foci and themes, for the most part, tend to focus on the long-standing prominence of scientific "facts" developed between the eighteenth and nineteenth centuries, the dominance of the colonial and patriarchal Western knowledge systems and scientific racism, and the project of undoing these histories. These foci and themes are anchored, implicitly or explicitly, to the body and bodies and, among these corporeal clusters, the black body is the fulcrum of experimentation, medicalization, study, data collection.

While feminist science studies and cognate studies of race in/and science constitute vast areas of inquiry—research themes range from equity in engineering to environmental racism—the question of *where* we know science from remains relevant precisely because, as Subramaniam has brilliantly argued, the field has actually continued without comprehensively attending to colonialism and has rarely moved beyond a critique of the biological sciences.[13] With Subramaniam's insights in mind, what the above overview of science studies reveals, as I see it and in terms of blackness and biology, is an analytical system that is closed: colonial and racial narratives are attached to and extend from the body outward, stabilize white supremacist logics, classify black life as unworthy, and loop back to mark the black body as an unworthy script that validates white supremacist logics. In her critical engagement with a range of scientific studies and stories, Dorothy Roberts shows that while race and blackness have been differently narrated over time and space, and meaningful openings have been made in scientific research, the analytical system through which race circulates is one laden with the strong *belief* that humans are genetically and naturally divided into races.[14] Karla Holloway's research on cultural bioethics complements Roberts's thinking by delineating how medical-legal-scientific infrastructures assure that some bodies, marginalized and/or black bodies, are cast as public "fleshy indignities."[15] Holloway also importantly notes that these assurances unveil and mirror society's "habits and traditions."[16] Simone Browne thinks through how habits, traditions, beliefs, and belief systems are tied to technologies of race (branding, passports, cameras, social media platforms, slave decks and holds, fingerprints, screening zones, and so on); these technologies confirm essentialist understandings of race, discipline black people, and materialize race thinking (in place and on the body).[17] Together, Browne, Roberts, and Holloway smartly sketch out how blackness is bound up in, and in fact necessary to, a self-replicating white supremacist system. They also uncover the profound ways in which the scientific narratives are racial narratives, populated by marginalized communities and strongly informing a publicly narrated belief system (or habits or traditions) that rests on credible scientific "facts" (data). To put it slightly differently, this biocentric belief system is ubiquitously ordinary because it is a habitual and public validation of eighteenth- and nineteenth-century racial-biological human differences that move forward in time (seemingly, at times, without interruption). The kind of ideas put forth by Browne, Roberts, Holloway, and other theorists of blackness in/and science crack open the quotidian

13. Subramaniam, "Moored Metamorphoses," 951–980.
14. Roberts, *Fatal Invention*.
15. Holloway, *Private Bodies, Public Texts*, 18.
16. Holloway, *Private Bodies, Public Texts*, 66.
17. Browne, *Dark Matters*.

and naturalized fictive truths of scientific racism by exposing how race underpins, and indeed propels, the autopoiesis of biocentricity.

In *Autopoiesis and Cognition: The Realization of the Living* Humberto Maturana and Francisco Varela track the discursive and biological enactment of social life through autopoiesis. By examining cellular networks, the theorists explain how the system that houses the cellular network is a closed and recursive system. The cellular network understands itself as bounded; any cellular growth or cellular changes that occur do so only through the reconstitution of the system that houses and sustains the cells. The system is closed and self-referential, and the cellular network is committed to this system because it realizes itself through the process of recursion.[18] The argument that follows is that the organization of human life—which underpins the enactment of ourselves and each other and our attendant environments—is comparable to, but not twinning, the cellular networks as just described. Here the practice of being human is relational to and embedded in a living-system that replicates itself and, in this, replicates what it means to be human according to the *parameters of the existing social system*. Autopoiesis is the process through which we repeat the conditions of our present mode of existence in order to keep the living-system—our environmental and existential world, our humanness—living. The living-system is normalized and inconspicuous and comfortable (our attachment and allegiance to the system keeps it living). Here, too, the processes of repetition and replication fold into each other demonstrating the corelational workings of how we *know* our human life and, simultaneously, do not notice the process of recursion: the practice of being human, and the enactment of social life, replicates itself with the analytic, affective, and material talisman of *realization* inducing the replication of how things already are and therefore normalizing the system as imperceptibly quotidian. As humans, we organize ourselves according to self-referential social systems: these systems are many and interconnected (and they can be bound up in our scholarly practices).[19]

Science studies of blackness, as noted above, expose a bundled *autopoietic* system that perpetuates and singularizes the logic of biological determinism. This disciplined and singularized logic, resting on a habit-

18. Humberto Maturana and Francisco Varela, *Autopoiesis and Cognition: The Realization of the Living* (London: D. Reidel, 1972).

19. Nikolas Luhmann, *Social Systems*, trans. J. Bednarz Jr. and D. Baecker (Stanford, CA: Stanford University Press, 1995).

ual belief system, renders other (scientific/empirical/experiential) experiences opaque. This logic also replicates what it means to be human and black according to the perimeters of the *existing* social system. Even as we urge and applaud social construction, the logic of biological determinism (and therefore racism) is necessarily within view. More specifically, social production of race can, inadvertently, mimic the crude classification and typology of humans according to racial-sexual differentiation: naming these racial and racist rankings and groupings and taxonomies of humans is replicated over and over again—whether as truth claims or socially produced fictions that seek to undo the weighty singularity of biological determinism. As science studies of race have shown, race is socially produced, yet our belief system perpetuates biological differences by nesting these socially produced differences in infrastructures and discourses that are *already* embedded with the racial differences they seek to make plain. Or, because "it is assumed that races differ biologically, the differences between them *appear* to be biological."[20] What is uncovered is a knowledge system that sustains itself through the repetition of biologically determinist stories. What becomes apparent, analytically, is a *loop* that leans on scientific racism—a closed system of knowledge *about* race-sex and *about* the body—that only knows itself through biocentric recursion: the organization of human life is conceptualized along racial-biological lines; evolutionary differences are illuminated as false; the *description* of difference—say, the wrongness of black inferiority—is repetitively constituted as socially constructed by science; the wrongness of science repeats the racial-biological description (black inferiority, black inferiority, black inferiority); the biocentric system of knowledge remains powerful and empowered and loops around, again, to naturalize racial-sexual differentiation. The axiom "social construction of race" thus describes our existing (biocentric) system of knowledge as wrong and, while centering its wrongness, nonetheless reifies biocentricity.

It follows that the symbolic code of blackness—signified by the black body, alone, pried away from experience, cognition, agency—can only, in this figuration, be scientifically imagined as already oppressed by non-white flesh (because "the black" is already prefigured as outside the family of humans). All other scientific matters or possibilities are foreclosed by biological determinism because blackness must be positioned as purely biological and scientifically inferior in order for the critique, "social con-

20. Roberts, *Fatal Invention*, 119 (emphasis added).

struction," to make sense. The analytical and methodological purpose then—to name and dismantle race and racism—tends to move from the (firmly entrenched) racialized physiological figure outward. Black lives are reduced, in this process, to analytical data and are cast as figures that are biologically determined to become factual parts of a bigger habitual belief system invested in racial differentiation. This uncovers a teleological narrative where the body violated by racist scientific narratives is the anchor to a liberatory trajectory and thus can, in this closed system, only realize itself and keep living by—to paraphrase Frantz Fanon—moving from subhumanness toward a genre of humanness that despises blackness.[21]

With this in mind, it is notable that some analyses of black lives and black histories that solely focus on *naming* scientific racism fall back on a biocentric model. As such, some analytical approaches to race—across disciplines—inadvertently produce blackness as less-than-human in order to point to the problematic narratives that are attached to those who are socially produced as less-than-human. Biological determinism and the critique of biological determinism, together, flatten out and singularize the biologics of blackness. This forecloses the relational and complicated interdisciplinary workings of black studies. In this formulation, scientific racism continues to have the last word precisely because it is recursively enacted *as socially constructed*. Conceptually, the critique is useful—the work of demystifying race and racism is difficult and important and urgent. However, at times, this demystifying work necessarily involves marking blackness as a site of false racial defectiveness that reinforces, analytically, black-as-always-defective. An analytical conundrum is thus posed, one that echoes the concerns Fanon identified in 1952: How might we think about the social construction of race in terms that notice how the condition of being black is knotted to scientific racism but not wholly defined by it?[22]

21. Frantz Fanon, *The Wretched of the Earth*, trans. Constance Farrington (New York: Grove, 1963), 163. Fanon writes: "Bourgeois ideology, however, which is the proclamation of an essential equality between men, manages to appear logical in its own eyes by inviting the sub-men to become human, and to take as their prototype Western humanity as incarnated in the Western bourgoisie."

22. Fanon, *Black Skin, White Masks*.

If we turn to the writings of Sylvia Wynter we can observe how the repetitive naming and critique of biological determinism is nested in a monumental system of biocentricity. Wynter allows us to work through the ongoing predicament Fanon identified (the condition of being black is knotted to scientific racism but not wholly defined by it). This narrative block takes us back in time, momentarily returning to the above section, in order to prepare for the forthcoming columns and the discussion of *Zong!*

Wynter's writings demonstrate the ways in which moments of scientific thought ushered in broad cognitive ruptures, with the Copernican leap pointing to how new conceptions of the physical cosmos exemplified particular "discoveries" that led to a radical, albeit gradual, shift in how we collectively perceive the world and its inhabitants. She also demonstrates the ways in which scientific matters gradually came to be articulated as an objective system of knowledge that enumerates and classifies "difference." With this, the scientific expressions of modernity—newly rational Man, cartographies of colonialism and the plantation, the metrics of gendered and sexed bodies, the mathematics of nature, the sorting of biological data—disclose the ways in which the question of human life is mapped out by scientific imperatives that increasingly profit from positing that we, humans, are fundamentally biocentric and natural beings.[23] Here the critique of biological determinism recursively circulates, while the work of Wynter yields another set of questions through her extension of Maturana and Varela. She argues that the concept of autopoiesis not only identifies a recursive looping system but also demonstrates that particular radical perspectives can observe this system and name its normalcy, and thus provide the conditions to assert different living systems and/or breach the existing social system. The consensual circular organization of human life through which we scientifically live and die as a species must also draw attention to what she describes as "a new frame of meaning, not only of *natural* history, but also of a newly conceived *cultural* history specific to and unique to our species, because the history of those

23. Sylvia Wynter, "Unsettling the Coloniality of Being/Power/Truth/Freedom: Towards the Human, after Man, Its Overrepresentation—an Argument," CR: *The New Centennial Review* 3, no. 3 (Fall 2003): 257–337.

'forms of life' gives expression to [a] . . . hybridly organic and . . . *languaging* existence."[24]

Wynter draws attention to the ways in which alternative human formations inform our worldview. She writes, then, that there is "always something else besides the dominant cultural logic going on, and that something else is constituted another—but also transgressive—ground of understanding . . . not simply a sociodemographic location but the site both of a form of life and of possible critical intervention."[25] Importantly, the possible critical interventions are not the oppositional narratives or reclamations that prize what Wynter calls the overpresentation of Man-as-human.[26] Wynter's project, instead, demonstrates the ways in which the practice of opposing and/or reclaiming can, in fact, be made through and against, and thus *in* the image of Man-as-human (the organization of human life is conceptualized along racial-biological lines; evolutionary differences are tagged as false; the *description* of difference—say, the wrongness of black inferiority— is repetitively constituted as socially constructed by science; the wrongness of science repeats the racial-biological description [black inferiority, black inferiority, black inferiority]; the biocentric system of knowledge [expressed as Man-as-human] remains powerful and empowered and loops around, again, to naturalize racial-sexual differentiation).

The "something else" that is "going on" is a new worldview, or an interhuman lens, that moves beyond the bio-evolutionary story of Man and toward the inscriptions of being human that unsettle this racial logic. Part of Wynter's concern is that the dominant belief system about what it means to be human follows governing codes that divide and sort science and creativity: the human, in this formulation, is primarily *physiological* while *creativity is an extrahuman* activity. With the category of race in mind, we can observe how the bifurcation of science and creativity can reify racial differentiation: the bifurcation posits, in advance, that all humans are bio-evolutionary beings that develop and progress *toward* creative acts that are nonphysiological. Wynter argues however, that we must notice the ways in which we, as humans, are simultaneously biological *and* cultural and alterable beings—skin *and* masks, bios *and* mythoi. This positions humans as beings whose *physiological origins* are *relational* to representation and narrative.

24. Sylvia Wynter, "1492: A New World View," in *Race, Discourse, and the Origin of the Americas: A New World View,* ed. Vera Lawrence Hyatt and Rex Nettleford (Washington, DC: Smithsonian Institution Press, 1995), 7 (emphasis in the original).

25. David Scott, "The Re-enchantment of Humanism: An Interview with Sylvia Wynter," *Small Axe* 8 (September 2000): 164.

26. Wynter, "Unsettling the Coloniality of Being/Power/Truth/Freedom," 257–337.

The simultaneity of bios *and* mythoi-skins *and* masks, must be emphasized here, for she is not suggesting that we evolve, grow, develop *and then*, once "developed," we narrate our world; rather, she is arguing that we *come into being as languaging humans.* This is a significant point to keep in mind, because it notices that some social systems are constituted through consensual circular organization and rooted in epistemological trappings (e.g., science is objective and oppressive). These social systems can be, and are, breached by creative human aesthetics that generate a point of view *away from* this consensual circular social system. This framework also points to relational and connective knowledges rather than positioning, say, science first, social construction second, and resistance third/later. Following these insights, I suggest, then, that the racial and racist underpinnings of scientific knowledge and the application of this knowledge to black bodies has, at times, foreclosed interdisciplinary conversations and a "hybridly organic" and "*languaging* existence."[27] Yet a transgressive ground of understanding, a new form of life, and critical intervention are, I think, available if we shift our analytical frame away from the lone site of the suffering body and toward corelational texts, practices, and narratives that emphasize black life.

It is worth repeating that I am not disputing that race is socially constructed; it is worth repeating that this story is one of methodological and analytical worry.

This is a story where we live with violence and do not ask for more and more and more evidence or proof of that violence. This is a story of unabandonment. In reading the slave ship and the story of the *Zong* as assertions of black life and black poetic effort, I hope to dislodge, at least momentarily, the biocentric codes that offer this site up as the location of black death and instead bring into focus how this history doubles as a critique and undoing of biocentricity.

27. Wynter, "1492," 7.

I read the *Zong*, a slave ship, as a historically present conceptual device that opens up two overlapping analytical pathways: first, the histories embedded on and around the slave ship anticipate our ecocidal and genocidal present because they are part of an identifiable biocentric loop—the ship incites an analytical leaning toward racism and black death; second, the *Zong* allows us to think about racial matters anew and interrupt this loop because it holds in it the possibility to foster different knowledges and, simultaneously, be understood as a location through which many knowledges are constituted. To put it simply, the ship imparts *and* creates knowledges. It follows that the scientific underpinnings of modernity— biocentricity, positivism—are aligned with, not preceding, human practices. The *Zong* cannot be contained by a singular theoretical frame or story—instead, it demands and is an articulation of multiple historically present black lives. Below I present three columns—history, weights and measures, social theory—before a discussion of the long poetry cycle *Zong!*, by M. NourbeSe Philip.[28] I ask that the reader read both down and across these columns in order to notice how the slave ship is a device that points to the ways in which the brutal histories of racial violence—that is, a technology that houses and makes legible the indexical, the measurable, the disposable—ask not how we describe and get over the awfulness and brutality but, rather, how we live with our world, differently, right now and engender new critical interventions.

28. The references informing the three columns are James Walvin, *The Zong*, 11, 95–98, 101, 213; Paul Gilroy, *The Black Atlantic: Modernity and Double Consciousness* (Cambridge, MA: Harvard University Press, 1993), 16; Sonjah Stanley Niaah, *DanceHall: From Slave Ship to Ghetto* (Ottawa: University of Ottawa Press, 2010), 19; Treva B. Lindsey and Jessica Marie Johnson, "Searching for Climax: Black Erotic Lives in Slavery and Freedom," *Meridian* 12, no. 2 (2014): 169–195; Saidiya Hartman, "Venus in Two Acts," *Small Axe* 12, no. 2 (June 2008): 4, 1–14; Katherine McKittrick, "Mathematics Black Life," *Black Scholar* 44, no. 2 (Summer 2014), 16–28; Erin McMullen Fehskens, "Accounts Unpaid, Accounts Untold: M. NourbeSe Philip's *Zong!* and the Catalogue," *Callaloo* 35, no. 2 (Spring 2012), 407–424; Joshua Smyth, "How to Calculate Dead Weight," *Sciencing*, accessed March 25, 2018, https:// sciencing.com/calculate-dead-weight-7289046.html. See also Ian Baucom's *Specters of the Atlantic: Finance Capital, Slavery, and the Philosophy of History* (Durham, NC: Duke University Press, 2005), which tracks how slavery and capitalism, key sites of modernity, contextualize the historically present workings of credit, insurance, liability, recompense.

Some History

James Walvin wrote a legal history of the slave ship the *Zong*. Walvin's research tracks the deliberate killing of enslaved black people that occurred in 1781 so that the slavers could both survive and collect insurance on their massacred human cargo. Walvin writes:

"It was calculated that the ship now had enough water for only four days, but that it would take between ten and fourteen days to sail back to Jamaica. . . . On 29 November [1781] the crew were assembled and asked what they thought of the suggestion that, faced with the water crisis, 'Part of the slaves should be destroyed . . .' At 8 pm that evening fifty-four women and children were pushed overboard. . . . Two days later . . . a group of forty-two men were thrown overboard from the quarterdeck. A third batch of thirty-eight Africans were killed some time later: ten Africans, realizing what was about to happen, jumped to their deaths."

Weights and Measures

If the history Walvin uncovers (to the left) is one of public racial violence and the anticipation of different instances of postslave premature death, we would do well to think through how the seeming scientific underpinnings of modernity—acts that weigh and measure and differentiate—are insinuated into, and push up against, the knowledge systems that narrate the *Zong*.

We might dwell, even more, on the measurements that make this difficult diasporic life possible, in part because the practice of empirical containment provides the conditions for social theories (to the right) to interrupt and undo the biocentric logic of race. It is through conceptualizing weights and measures as relational to *and* distinguished from black life that the promise of the slave ship emerges.

Here the positivist underpinnings of modernity open

Some Social Theory

There are many social theories that attend to the slave ship, the Atlantic slave triangle, and the Middle Passage. I will outline a few that have most directly informed this story and lead to my discussion ahead and look back on Walvin's history and deadweight (left). The first is Paul Gilroy's discussion of the slave ship in *The Black Atlantic*, where he argues that the slave ship is a technology of modernity that connected various diasporic geographies and histories of terror; Gilroy's discussion of the ship underscores—or presupposes, to use his word—his critique of ethnic absolutism thus demonstrating how slave and postslave struggles evidence the complicated work of belonging. Gilroy's analysis draws attention to J. M. W. Turner's 1840 painting *The Slave Ship (Slavers Throwing Overboard the Dead and Dying — Typhoon Coming On)*, which was inspired by the *Zong* massacre (and

Some History, *cont.*

The history Walvin uncovers is disturbing: he evidences that the killings were premeditated and situates this racial violence within the context of the slave trade:

"Killing Africans was not unusual" and, moreover, was "not a matter of murder."

What emerges first, through this narrative of history, is the closed system circulating through and beyond the *Zong*. The history conveyed points to the acceptability of black death. The archival research done by Walvin, which I won't replicate here, demonstrates the ways in which the legal landscape simply oversees racial violence. Indeed, as one reads his text, the historian Walvin refers to the justified, admissible, commonsense killing of human cargo throughout the slave trade multiple times, thus remarking that the violence aboard the *Zong* was not unusual; as a result he lays bare for the reader the mundane

Weights and Measures, *cont.*

up, just fleetingly, to reorder or mark black life and breach the closed system that is so often understood as a location that houses objecthood and death.

Maritime knowledge systems are grounded by weights and measures. There are numerous scientific and mathematic calculations that underwrite ship design, safety measures, port fees, manning regulations, and so forth. But most interesting to me is the concept of deadweight tonnage—a postslavery term—for it is this measure of weight that brings together and collapses the entirety of the ship's weight. This is to say that unlike gross tonnage or net tonnage—which measure internal volume and cargo, respectively—the deadweight tonnage, or deadweight capacity measurement, takes into consideration all provisions, crew, fuel, cargo, and so forth.

Deadweight tonnage is everything and everyone as viewed and calculated

Some Social Theory, *cont.*

enlivens black premature death through descriptively coding the enslaved as not simply dead, but also "dying"). Gilroy theorizes the slave ship as purposeful and *living*.

Gilroy theorizes the slave ship as purposeful and *living* and thereby provides the conceptual platform for Sonjah Stanley Niaah's research, which discusses the restless resistances that emerge when black geographies are under siege.

Niaah works through how those aboard the slave ship and the Middle Passage reorder linear time through rhythm, with the Brathwaitian "limbo" signifying the simultaneity of displacement and reinvention. She dwells on livingness not to refuse violence and loss but to illuminate the ways in which black aesthetics—dance, song, diasporic literacies—engender alternative modes of freedom.

Alternative modes of freedom are expressed

Some History, *cont.*

workings of racist violence. In many ways, this history is a closed system—for the pages claim to uncover a "murderous secret" that is, as you continue to read, not a secret at all. Indeed, the text needs an engagement with explicit and mundane antiblack violence to move forward: racism and black death provide the conditions through which British-ness makes itself known and realizes itself, for the *Zong* would, Walvin argues, figure into antislavery campaigns and then lead to British rejection of their "lucrative habit." This is a biocentric history, so there is little to no room for an unusual or alternative tale or the promised secrets: the dimensions of racial difference stay in place while emancipatory tenets are soldered to exploitation that is shrouded in white benevolence.

At the same time, though, the historian provides a mathematical opening. Walvin initially puts forth confident numbers—those just listed above—which

Weights and Measures, *cont.*

through the lens of weights and measures.

What these weights and measures offer is a way to remathematize black life, for in deadweight the entirety of the ship is subjected to a measure-ment system that bundles everything and everyone together.

There is only a singu-lar deadweight tonnage measurement even though there are a range of people and objects that make this weight possible. The mea-surement erases human-ness just as it enacts it, for the deadweight signals the unfolding of modernity and collective human lives alongside, rather than be-fore or after, the biological determinant.

The deadweight measure tasks us to review the ship through relational and con-nective means—bundled data sets that are both closed and open, past and present—without losing those biocentric codes that differentiate the weight sources and noticing, of course, that the dead-

Some Social Theory, *cont.*

through a range of black sexual identifications and practices, as noted by Treva Lindsey and Jessica Marie Johnson. Alternative modes of freedom, a range of sexual identifications and practices, yoked to but not replicating a closed system.

These insights can be thought about alongside Saidiya Hartman's research that dwells on the ways in which the data of the ship renders the enslaved part of a register, a record, a ledger, a tally of debits.

(Labs, actuators, control panels, levers, switches, cylinders, motherboards, bearings, needles, vials, pullies, scales.)

Hartman's thinking demon-strates how the tabulation of antiblack violence and unfreedom are legible only as a loss.

No matter how hard we try to retell the story, the quantitative matters of the slave trade emerge as the official story. No matter how hard we try.

Any discussion of archival loss asks that we recognize

Some History, *cont.*

allow the reader to tabulate the number of Africans killed: 186. Despite Walvin's data, though, he also exclaims that these numbers are unreliable: "There is some confusion," he writes, "about the precise numbers killed." He follows this with a series of other numbers: 150, 142, 122, one-third of the Africans on board. Other histories of the *Zong* are also unclear about the number of Africans killed: 150, 133, 132, 123. The death tabulation is, as I read it, best understood as a range of numbers gathered from many texts and sources. The inability to count the dead allows us to doubt knowable data and a singular analytical frame, and therefore to open ourselves up to another set of questions and numbers that follow alongside and after the *Zong*. With this opening in place, one cannot help but think about these deliberate killings alongside a whole host of contemporary premature and preventable deaths that continue to realize the closed system—deaths that

Weights and Measures, *cont.*

weight will be relieved in crisis through the loss of black life.

Here the biocentric narrative is not situated as the *primary* analytic story; instead, biocentricity is correlational to transport and other scientific matters that, together, are brought into being by black and other human lives.

The weights and measures, the bundled (anachronistic) deadweight tonnage, provide the conditions for us to, analytically, shift our focus away from the always oppressed black body and toward a different set of questions that ask how the measurability of violence—and thus the body— lends a voice to black life.

The closed analytical system, wherein we theoretically describe the brutalities of slavery as the origin of black oppression, is breached on the recognition of the analytics of black life: 150, 142, 122, one-third of the Africans on board . . .

Some Social Theory, *cont.*

the archives as tracking the incomplete project of freedom. This incompleteness opens up the work of imagination—iterations of black life that cannot be contained by official history.

Keep trying.

These theorists (differently) provide a conceptual frame that can be stacked onto and situated alongside Walvin's history and the weights and measures (left). In these texts, one can read the ways in which the technology and science of the slave ship not only reduced black humans to cargo but also, in this process of objectification, provided the conditions through which blackness is rearticulated as rebelliously diasporic.

Likewise, there is a naming of violence and death as an insistence that black life—not just black survival—informs modernity. In short, the empirical purpose of the slave ship belies its ongoing living history.

Some History, *cont.*

are too many to list and too many to grieve (miners shot, killing black youths to bring silence to black music, executing the unarmed).

(No matter how hard we try to retell the story, the quantitative matters of the slave trade emerge as the official story.)

In many ways, the deliberate murdering of black slaves on the *Zong* eerily anticipates our contemporary struggles with racial violence. This is not to conflate time and space but, rather, to notice how the *Zong* moves forward in time and becomes implicated in a similar circular closed system: in naming these histories as evidence of the violent, ongoing, but differential workings of premature or preventable death, the history of the *Zong* points to how we *know* our human life through instances of black death; the practice of being human and the enactment of social life is sustaining itself through the replication of how things already are. With this history in

Weights and Measures, *cont.*

Things Needed*: ship; draft marks; calculator or computer: Note all provisions and cargoes being loaded onto the ship. Add together the weights of each piece of cargo, each passenger or crew member, and all provisions that have been loaded onboard. Calculate the weight of fuel: multiply the volume of fuel taken aboard by its density. Calculations are commonly performed in metric units. Fuel oil has a density of 890 kilograms per cubic meter, meaning that a ship that has loaded 1 cubic meter (or 100 liters) of fuel has added 890 kilograms to its weight. Add the fuel weight to the weight of cargo, passengers, and provisions to calculate total deadweight. Or: Find the ship's displacement marks. These are white ruler lines on the bottom of the bow and stern of the hull. Note which displacement line is sitting at the water level before loading the ship. Load the ship with all crew, cargo, fuel, and provisions. Note which*

Some Social Theory, *cont.*

The closed analytical system, wherein we theoretically describe the brutalities of slavery as the origin of black oppression, is breached on recognition of the analytics of black life.

Noticeably, across these theoretical texts, the mathematical data of the slave ship is continually interrupted by an assertion of life and therefore a new definition of livingness.

I read these texts, and the actors within—diasporic figures in limbo—as a disruption of racist violence.

These texts offer a genre of black life and a way of being black.

Here, then, racist violence —normalized premature death as well as the slow death that informs black life, black lives, and black histories—is animated by a relationality wherein a different kind of living figure emerges.

These texts do not move from racial violence *toward* a freedom that houses and replicates racial violence.

mind, the *Zong* stands as a
cosmogony of contemporary
racial violence, throwing
blackness overboard, again
and again, and thus real-
izing—in the present—a
living network of scientific
racism and despair where
black life has no beginning
and a discourse of eman-
cipatory benevolence—the
Zong as antislavery technology—expresses Fanon's
predicament.

displacement mark is now
at the waterline. Consult
the ship's displacement
tables, which have formu-
las to calculate how much
water has been displaced
based on the shape of the
ship's hull. The weight
of the displaced water is
equal to the weight loaded
onto the ship—that is, the
deadweight.

Instead, they differently
notice that the slave ship
and the horrors of slavery
engendered difficult forms
of diasporic livingness that
that cannot write itself-say-
itself-know-itself *within*
the logics of plantocratic-
colonial registers.

ZONG!

It is in concert with and within NourbeSe Philip's long poem *Zong!* that
history, weights and measures, and social theories of the slave ship and
the Atlantic emerge and intertwine. Reading the creative text with and
through the columned vignettes both reveals and disproves biocentric
logics, therefore also reaching and bending back to the narrative blocks
above. *Zong!* works within and thinks outside a closed system, and this
inside-outside uncovers an autopoietic system. Because I am focusing on
a text-based analysis and working with autopoiesis and network systems,
I have found diachronic loops a useful and complementary concept. In
their theories of loops and self-referencing, David Levary and his colleagues explore how words, definitions, and concepts are interrelated.
Their research examines lexical networks—which we can here, in a small
way, liken to the aforementioned social systems and cellular networks.
The study shows how distinct semantic ideas remain coherent even when
new words are introduced into the network. Levary and his colleagues
use etymological data to show that even as new words disrupt and reimagine the broader definitional and conceptual ideas, this is done within
a self-referencing system. Within this system are diachronic loops—clusters of words, definitions, and concepts that are introduced into the system at different times and thus hold in them the possibility to question

its coherency yet remain verifiable within the context of the broader lexicon.[29]

If we read NourbeSe Philip's *Zong!* as a diachronic loop, the logic of racism, the naming of the dead and dying, are understood alongside the cyclical structure of the poem and the attendant texts within and outside the work, including the columns above. Notably, the text in its entirety iterates racist violence within the context of slavery; but the text also produces a network of words that unfold to produce a knowledge system that momentarily moves outside itself. Specifically, the structure of the text, which Philip calls an "extended poetry cycle," is one where words and voices are dismembered and put back together, with the reader implicated in the recovery of the lost voices.[30] One must work hard to make sense of the words, locutions, and voices in order to envision the bigger conceptual picture that turns back on itself only to remark on the unspeakability of violences. Overall, the reader can approach the text from many perspectives and across overlapping and stacked histories in order to glean how it requires multiple narratives in order to represent black loss and pain.

Within the context of a history of calculated and measurable racial violence, *Zong!* offers a thread that cannot simply bear witness to and recall racist violence within the biocentric and empirical terms that made this violence possible. Instead, the text is an attempt to capture *and* unlearn the complexities of the events that took place on the *Zong* in 1781: to suggest that this poetry cycle is *only* reclamation (resuscitating the unliving) forecloses the ways in which the poet is, in my view, attempting to trouble practices of reclamation. Indeed, by inserting an additional recursive narrative that continually warns that the story is *untellable* (this is, she writes, a "story that can only be told by not telling") Philip signals that reclamation is impossible.[31] The poetry is scattered text—not linear or horizontal, but scattered; the words and ideas and names and places are carefully placed on each page in a nonlinear fashion. Philip's cross-referential framing of the *Zong* massacre is complex: to produce the scattering she

29. David Levary, Jean-Pierre Eckmann, Elisha Moses, and Tsvi Tlusty, "Loops and Self-Reference in the Construction of Dictionaries," *Physical Review X* 2, no. 3 (2012), https://journals.aps.org/prx/abstract/10.1103/PhysRevX.2.031018.

30. Marika Preziuso, "M. NourbeSe Philip—*Zong!*," accessed December 22, 2013, http://latineos.com/articulos/literatura/item/46-m-NourbeSe-philip-zong.html?lang=es.

31. Philip, *Zong!*, 191

deploys and enjoins the law, the data of the slave ship, unusual and norma-tive calendars, songs, prayers, biblical and philosophical citations, histori-cal narratives, archives, verses, multiple languages, phrases, ledgers, fugal and counterpointed repetition, inventories, in order to exhibit the poetry cycle.[32] The poem includes a glossary, a journal entry, a legal document, songs, a ship's manifest, and a coauthor—Boateng—who is the voice of the ancestors.

NourbeSe Philip's poem and poetry cycle cannot, in my view, with-stand an analysis that dwells on simply naming and reclaiming black death. Indeed, I would argue that the poetry cycle is not preoccupied with the past and resuscitating the dead but instead provides a future—and part of this future involves reading black cultural production as invested in history-making that names the data of violence in order to creatively interrupt it and intentionally point to, and undo, the empirical and ana-lytical violence that cannot sustain its own brutalities in the present. With the creative in mind, the logistics of the history of slavery might be read through the kind of lens NourbeSe Philip puts forth in *Zong!*: in these poetics we not only find loss, history, and the anticipation of the ongoing racial violences that engender and define us; we also notice in the text a place where the data of the massacre, the calculated empirical and theo-retical and public and scientific accumulation of black death, can no lon-ger tell itself, in the present, within the terms that made it possible.

Of particular significance, then, is the livingness of the slave ship—precisely because robust racial logics institute the *Zong* as predicated on the dead and dying. The livingness of the ship forges the columns—intimacies, rebellions, weights and measures, secrets that are not secret at all—with Philip's textual history. Here the voices within (sometimes faded and in italics, sometimes in plain text, sometimes songs, sometimes data) can be read alongside and with the empiricism of weights and mea-sures that contain and extend black life beyond the ship itself. Most obvi-ously, the excerpt "uncommon weight / great weight / uncommon weight / great weight / new weight" brushes up against "perils of necessity / mor-tality / slave / them was slaves not evidence."[33] As one reads through, dif-ferent histories take place—more words, more concepts, more diachronic loops that cut across and refuse a narrative of deadness and lend them-selves to the livingness of the ship itself. The text gives us clues to what a

32. Preziuso, "M. NourbeSe Philip—*Zong!*"
33. Philip, *Zong!*, 54–56.

different form of life might look like (say) by centralizing an articulation of freedom by the unfree and noticing that the logic of race, as we know it (biocentrically), cannot tell this story ethically.

I read Philip's work—the story that can only be told by not telling— not as one that is preoccupied with return but, rather, as a poem that historicizes racial violence to demonstrate how transatlantic slavery prefigures our contemporary planetary troubles and a closed biocentric system that thrives on racial terror. In this formulation, I put forth that black cultural production that attends to slavery not only involves the work of re-memory and return but also contains within it an anticipatory urgency that looks forward, to the present, and surveys the unsurprising and mundane work of contemporary racial violences. Because Philip denotes the text as a poetry cycle—a series of events that are repeated and bend back into themselves—there is a circuitous logic that frames the story she is telling yet continually gestures to how this violence is enacted in post-slave contexts. I am signaling that this creative text, if read through the lens of black life and livingness, reveals a diachronic loop that undoes a biocentric logic by naming it and, simultaneously, demanding the reader contend with the ability for this logic to sustain itself.

Some black creative works, then, allow us to see into the future. I would argue, in fact, that the creative text that returns to the past *intends* to give blackness a future (rather than reading blackness as socially produced and/or naturally biologically violable).[34] With this, the creative return to slavery and the slave ship might be read not as a way to delineate the causes and the effects of racial violence but, instead, as a text that puts forth a different set of preoccupations that are interested how this past has shaped what we have come to know as freedom, in the present. This kind of framing asks: What are the ideological histories that construct freedom through persistent violence, and how might the creative reenactment of racist violence offer commentary that honors this persistence by interrupting it?

34. See, for example, Octavia Butler, *Kindred* (New York: Doubleday, 1979).

This is, in part, then, about teaching and learning from the analytics of violence and race—for the story of the *Zong* asks that we be cautious about singular (linear-enclosed) narratives while also noticing the ways in which the logic of race is anchored to a monumental biocentric narrative that is invested in replicating scientific racism (even in critique). The intellectual work of honoring complex racial narratives that name struggles against death can be, paradoxically, undermined by the analytical framing that dwells on and concretizes racial violence. The conceptual difficulty lies in the ways in which *descriptions* of racial violence actually contribute to the ongoing fragmentation of human relationships. While biocentric narratives have certainly been contested—social construction, sociocultural practices, nonlinear space-time experiences and experiments, and performativity are just some ways our biocentric world has been challenged—the language and process of explicating racial violence often tends to fall back on an axiomatic frame of survival (wherein the suffering body and the dying have always been the marginalized human other who stands in opposition to the white Western liberated human norm, precisely because *black death precedes and is necessary to this conceptual frame*). This is a frame that delineates how the analytical stakes of studying race and racism often only provide us with a descriptive story that corresponds with our existing system of knowledge, one that has *already* posited blackness and a black sense of place as dead and dying.

Here we would do well to notice how the inhabitants of spaces of absolute otherness can be, quite easily, discursively colonized by our intellectual investigations.[35] There is a tendency to focus on a certain mode of appropriation and codification within mainstream academic questions that profit from simultaneously devaluing and damning racial-sexual intellectual narratives as we empirically collect wretched bodies. Within this framework we can apparently fix and repair the racial other by producing knowledge about the racial other that renders them less than human (and so often biologic skin, only and all body, is the dehumanizing proof). No one moves. It is worth thinking about how the cyclical and

35. See Chandra Talpade Mohanty, "Under Western Eyes: Feminist Scholarship and Colonial Discourses," *boundary 2* 12, no. 3–13, no. 1 (1984): 333–358.

death-dealing analytical *descriptions* of the condemned remain conceptually intact, at least in part, because thinking otherwise demands attending to whole new systems of knowledge—and therefore honoring radical relational reading practices, stories, and knowledges—wherein the brutalities of racial violence are not descriptively rehearsed but always demanding and participating in practical activities of resistance and encounter, disobedient inquiries, wonder, and anticolonial thinking.

The rhythm, the beat, was to become the central underlying principle.

—Sylvia Wynter, *Black Metamorphosis*

*I*n her essay on jazz, Dionne Brand writes that black music "leaves you open, and up in the air and that this is the space that some of us need, an opening to another life tangled up in this one but opening."[1] Writings on black music abound, tracking a range of social, political, economic, affective, and geographic patterns and contexts, as well as the biographical narratives that inform music, music-making, and musicians. These writings also draw attention to the tensions between the materiality of black music (the racial economies and racial histories that underpin the production and distribution of black creative works), lyrical content (if the tune indeed has lyrics), and the waveforms that underpin and sonically frame song (beats, rhythms, acoustics, notational moods, frequencies). Black musical aesthetics not only emerge within and against long-standing antiblack practices; they are heard and listened to across and in excess of the positivist workings of racism. Waveforms—beats, rhythms, acoustics, notational moods, and frequencies that intersect with racial economies and histories and available lyrical content—cannot be exacted, yet they speak to exacting racial technologies. With this, black music, what we hold on to and what we hear, moves between and across and

The title of this story, "I Got Life," is from a song by Nina Simone and is on her album *Nuff Said* (New York: RCA Studios, 1968). This story, with minor differences, was previously published as "Rebellion/Invention/Groove," *Small Axe* 49 (March 2016): 79–91.

1. Dionne Brand, "Jazz," in *Bread out of Stone* (New York: Random House/Vintage, 1994), 161.

outside ungraspable waveforms, the anticolonial politics underpinning black cultural production, and the racial economy of white supremacy that denies black personhood. In this story, I think about these tensions—between waveforms, anticolonial politics, the memory of slavery, and long-standing practices of racial violence—as they emerge in Sylvia Wynter's *Black Metamorphosis*.

Before turning to an analysis of *Black Metamorphosis*, it is important to briefly situate this monograph in relation to Wynter's thinking on art, cultural production, and music. Wynter's dramatic plays and her novel *The Hills of Hebron*, as well as her analyses of films, poetry, drama, music, and fiction, demonstrate a steady critical engagement with creative worlds. Wynter works out how creative narratives (including but not limited to the works of Ellison, Shakespeare, Cervantes, Morrison, Glissant, Césaire, and Marley) simultaneously narrate and disrupt normative assertions of humanism.[2] Her research draws attention to the overlapping epistemologies fostered during and after imperialism, colonialism, and transatlantic slavery, and uncovers the ways in which black worldviews are relational to overarching systems of European and Western knowledge. Indeed, overarching systems are powerfully anchored to uneven practices of accumulation and dispossession that thrive on replicating themselves through rewarding human activities that validate inequities. Wynter's insights on creative works are therefore not simply a call to integrate "race" or "black art" into the global histories of the West; rather, she argues that the perspectival economic imperialism of the planet, and attendant racial processes such as plantation slavery, produced the conditions through which the colonized would radically and creatively redefine—re*word*, to be specific—the representative terms of

2. See, for example, Sylvia Wynter, *The Hills of Hebron: A Jamaican Novel* (New York: Simon and Schuster, 1962); Sylvia Wynter, "The Eye of the Other," in *Blacks in Hispanic Literature: Critical Essays*, ed. Miriam DeCosta (New York: Kennikat, 1977), 8–19; Sylvia Wynter, "Rethinking Aesthetics," in *Ex-iles: Essays on Caribbean Cinema*, ed. Mbye Cham (Trenton, NJ: Africa World Press, 1992), 238–279; Sylvia Wynter, "On Disenchanting Discourse: 'Minority' Literary Criticism and Beyond," in *The Nature and Context of Minority Discourse*, ed. Abdul R. JanMohamed and David Lloyd (New York: Oxford University Press, 1990), 432–469; Sylvia Wynter, "One Love—Rhetoric or Reality?—Aspects of Afro-Jamaicanism," *Caribbean Studies* 12, no. 3 (October 1972): 90–97; Sylvia Wynter, "Ethno or Socio Poetics," *Alcheringa/Ethnopoetics* 2, no. 2 (1976): 78–94; Sylvia Wynter, "Jonkonnu in Jamaica: Towards the Interpretation of Folk Dance as a Cultural Process," *Jamaica Journal* 4, no. 2 (1970): 34–48; Sylvia Wynter, "Maskarade," in *West Indian Plays for Schools*, by Easton Lee, Sylvia Wynter, and Enid Chevannes, vol. 2 (Kingston, Jamaica: Jamaica Publishing House, 1979), 26–55.

the human.[3] It is suggested, therefore, that such inequitable systems of knowledge can be, and are, breached by creative human aesthetics. In *Black Metamorphosis* Wynter thinks through the ways in which the Middle Passage and plantation systems produced the conditions for a range of black rebellions that were initiated by figures that reinvented and affirmed black humanity and black life and engendered New World cultural inventions.[4] These inventions were, largely, musical inventions that, in their waveform and lyrical enunciations, expressed in new forms what it means to be human.[5]

In what follows I trace Wynter's exploration of the plantation economy, racism, and the negation of black humanity. In *Black Metamorphosis* Wynter unveils how the plantation slavery system and its postslave expressions produced black nonpersons and nonbeings (through brutal acts of racist violence designed to actualize psychic and embodied alienation) just as this system generated black plantation activities that rebelled against the tenets of white supremacy. This first section is titled "Rebellion." I then explore how black plantation activities engendered music and creative spaces that wrote, rewrote, and continue to write and rewrite black life, from the perspective of the ex-slave archipelagos, as the "imposition of style in chaotic circumstance."[6] Steadily, throughout *Black Metamor-*

3. Demetrius Eudell, "Afterword: Toward Aimé Césaire's 'Humanism Made to the Measure of the World': Reading *The Hills of Hebron* in the Context of Sylvia Wynter's Later Work," in Sylvia Wynter, *The Hills of Hebron* (1962; rpt., Kingston, Jamaica: Ian Randle, 2010), 311–340; Carole Boyce Davies, "From Masquerade to Maskarade: Caribbean Cultural Resistance and the Rehumanizing Project," in *Sylvia Wynter: On Being Human as Praxis*, ed. Katherine McKittrick (Durham, NC: Duke University Press, 2015), 203–225.

4. I use the term "New World" following Sylvia Wynter, "1492: A New World View," in *Race, Discourse, and the Origin of the Americas: A New World View*, ed. Vera Lawrence Hyatt and Rex Nettleford (Washington, DC: Smithsonian Institution Press, 1995), 5–57.

5. To clarify my terms: *reinvention* is the process through which enslaved and postslavery black communities in the New World came to *live and construct* black humanity within the context of racial violence: a range of rebellious acts that affirmed black humanity and black life were and are imperative to reinvention. *Invention* is meant to signal those cultural practices and texts—marronages, mutinies, funerals, carnivals, dramas, visual arts, fictions, poems, fights, dances, music-making and -listening, revolts—that emerged *alongside* reinvented black lives. I want to point out, too, the relational workings of reinvention and invention: the reinvention of black life *and* attendant cultural inventions were engendered by the Middle Passage and plantation systems dynamically and simultaneously. One cannot reinvent the human without rebellious inventions, and rebellious inventions require reinvented lives.

6. Sylvia Wynter, *Black Metamorphosis: New Natives in a New World* (unpublished ms., n.d.), 196.

phosis, Wynter draws attention to how the creation of culture, the making and praxis of music—within the context of hateful and violent racist axioms—is underwritten by "the revolutionary demand for happiness" that, at the same time, demonstrates that creative acts mark the affirmation of black life.[7] This second section is titled "Invention." Finally, in the section titled "Groove," I read Wynter's discussion of musical beats to think about black waveforms as rebellious enthusiasms. I argue that waveforms—the beats, rhythms, acoustics, notational moods, frequencies that undergird black music—affirm, through cognitive schemas, modes of being human that refuse racism just as they restructure our existing system of knowledge. I focus on the waveforms, rather than solely lyrical content, to draw attention to how an ungraspable resonance—sound—allows us to think about how loving and sharing and hearing and listening and grooving to black music is a rebellious political act that is entwined with neurological pleasure and the melodic pronouncement of black life.

REBELLION

Sylvia Wynter explores many layered and knotted plantation narratives in *Black Metamorphosis*. The monograph begins with a discussion of enslaved Africans who, following Middle Passage terrors, were forced to occupy and work violent plantation economies. The Middle Passage and plantation systems transformed—or more specifically converted—the enslaved into units of labor. The enslaved perceptively and conceptually became homogeneous units of labor, planted in the New World not to inhabit (people, settle) the land but to mechanically produce monocrops and fuel the economic system.[8] Above all, the plantation system sought profit. It follows that the enslaved units of labor, as owned property, were embedded in a system that benefited from, and calcified, their nonpersonhood and nonbeing; and it is precisely because they were planted in the New World not as "buyers and sellers" but as commodities, things "bought and sold," that black enslaved peoples in the New World were at once alienated from and implicated in the racial economy as nonbeings/nonconsumers/mechanized labor.[9] To put it differently, the plantation context required the impossibility of black humanity. At the same time, trans-

7. Wynter, *Black Metamorphosis*, 198.
8. Wynter, *Black Metamorphosis*, 1–3.
9. Wynter, *Black Metamorphosis*, 232.

atlantic slavery—the Middle Passage and plantation systems—totally cut the enslaved off from their former cultures and histories while normalizing a collective "mode of knowing" that sustained white supremacy and geographically codified racial differences.[10] Indeed, the economic mechanization and negation of blackness was entwined with the geographic removal from the continent of Africa, geographic estrangement upon arrival in New World, and plantation geographies designed to simultaneously immobilize and mechanize black labor units. Imposed placelessness was accompanied by the negation of black humanity and the "alienated reality" experienced by enslaved people.[11] These same processes, we can conclude, *humanized* white colonial geographies as productive sites of settlement, belonging, and capital accumulation. Belonging and settlement and accumulation were thus entangled with dispossessed black labor units and entrenched, extrahumanly and not, the "nothing" of the enslaved and the "being" of the settler.[12]

Later in the manuscript Wynter rethinks her initial black-labor-unit model to argue that the plantation economy must, in fact, be understood alongside the widespread assault on *all aspects* of black life. Calling into question and reworking Karl Marx's "factory" hypothesis, and reading a series of black intellectual texts, Wynter identifies that practices of "nigger-breaking" *initiated* the enslaved black population *and* the colonizing white population, through acts of violence, *as asymmetrically raced black nonbeings and raced white beings,* and through the colonization of consciousness:

> Nigger-breaking reveals itself as an initiation rite in which the task of social inscription was at least as important as the task of economic extraction. . . . The plantation and the nigger-breaking model of exploitation reveals that the social order of production, in order to function, needs to establish fixed coefficients of social exchange, and that the strategy of the economic is a central means of establishing these fixed coefficients of exchange.[13]

In *Black Metamorphosis* Wynter shows that the unsettling workings of racism and violence grew out of and were sustained by a plantation sys-

10. Wynter, *Black Metamorphosis*, 387.
11. Wynter, *Black Metamorphosis*, 7.
12. Wynter, *Black Metamorphosis*, 146.
13. Wynter, *Black Metamorphosis*, 590–591.

tem that, geographically, economically, socially, and psychically, produced the punished and punishable laboring black body (*not* the laboring black *person*) as necessary to socialization through/as racism, across racial identifications. What Wynter traces, then, are not only the historical plantocratic processes through which blackness becomes an absolute a negative sign "in the mathematics of inequality," but also how the interpellation of the self-as-free, in knotted slave-plantation-and-postslave-plantation contexts, is produced within a normative bourgeois *order of consciousness*—propped up by a global political economy of race—*that is antiblack racism.*[14]

Slavery was, Wynter writes, "the first large-scale intensive attempt at the *mechanization* of human existence."[15] The mechanization of the black labor-unit-status was anchored to a range of racist practices (premature and preventable deaths, lashings, segregations, bindings, lynchings, cuttings, brandings, dismemberments, malnourishments, rapes, impoverishments, incarcerations, thrashings designed to break black into absolute negation) that expertly located black nonpersonhood and nonbeing within the fabric of, and therefore necessary to, collective social consciousness. In many ways, what can also be observed is what I consider one of Wynter's more provocative insights: how practices of racism and narratives of racism not only permeate how we collectively understand one another but also inform negative *physiological and neurobiological* responses to blackness.[16] What Wynter offers in her unraveling of the plantation in *Black Metamorphosis* is how psychic and affective negative feelings about blackness—feelings that are so often experienced as though they are truthful *bio-instinctual* responses—are implicit to a symbolic belief system of which antiblackness is constitutive.[17] Antiblackness informs neurobiological and physiological drives, desires, emotions—and negative feelings—because it underwrites a collective and normalized, racially coded, biocentric belief system wherein narratives of natural selection, and the dysselection of blackness, are cast as, and *reflexively* experienced as, common sense. Social consciousness, then, *across racial identi-*

14. Wynter, *Black Metamorphosis*, 214, 593.

15. Wynter, *Black Metamorphosis*, 107 (emphasis added).

16. It is worth thinking about this alongside Wynter's "Towards the Sociogenic Principle: Fanon, Identity, the Puzzle of Conscious Experience," in *National Identities and Sociopolitical Changes in Latin America*, ed. Mercedes F. Durán-Cogan and Antonio Gómez-Moriana (New York: Routledge, 2001), 30–66.

17. Wynter, *Black Metamorphosis*, 569.

fications, includes physiologically and neurobiologically *feeling and sensing and knowing antiblackness as a normal way of life. Feeling normal is feeling, as if bio-instinctually, black-as-worthless.* It is worth repeating that Wynter also identifies racist violence, emerging from plantation logics, as initiation; rites of passage mark entrance into, and therefore replicate and normalize, a European-centered bourgeois social order.[18] Importantly, then, the process of *coming into* and *being accepted into* the world relies on conceptions of, or more brutally and dismally *acts of,* racist violence that reinforce the *physiological and neurobiological* refusal of black humanity.

Black Metamorphosis does not, however, descriptively rehearse the refusal of black humanity. Every line of the text is sutured to black life. As one reads the monograph, the brutal and racist imperative to totally negate enslaved and postslave peoples is undone by Wynter's documentation of a range of black rebellions: marronages, mutinies, funerals, carnivals, dramas, visual arts, fictions, poems, fights, dances, music-making and -listening, revolts, "periodic uprisings and . . . the ongoing creation of culture."[19] Every line of this text is sutured to black life *as* the rebellious *impulse* to indict and overturn the dominant values that engender and profit from the imposition of black nonbeing and nonpersonhood.[20] The total negation of blackness described above (the widespread oppression that normalized white supremacy, the calcified racist plantation logics, the psychic and neurological and physiological negative responses to blackness, the racist violence) is always written as analytically *relational* to a series of rebellions that affirm black life. Wynter's reading of oppression and resistance is therefore not dichotomous but, rather, a "question mark . . . a dynamic dialectic of terror and hope."[21]

Significantly, the racial order of things that followed Middle Passage terror also produced the conditions to reinvent and reorder black life.

18. Wynter, *Black Metamorphosis,* 423.

19. Wynter, *Black Metamorphosis,* 83.

20. I am paraphrasing and bringing together two moments in *Black Metamorphosis.* When discussing rebellions and religious ceremonies performed by the enslaved on the plantation—acts that undermined the dominant colonial ways of knowing—Wynter writes, "One central impulse was clear, the impulse to enslave the system which negated them" (82). Later in the monograph (on p. 232) she describes the pathologization of black communities (through official documentation and data collection on black victimhood, e.g., the Moynihan Report) as conducted and written by figures that "internalized market values" and saw the "failure of blacks as an incapacity rather than as an indictment of the dominant values to which they subscribe."

21. Wynter, *Black Metamorphosis,* 225.

The negation of black humanity *within* the plantation context provided new and different ways to pronounce black life. It is important to note here that the affirmation of black life includes, but is not restricted to, the repurposing of multiethnic African traces and phantasies—not as vestiges of nostalgic idealization, but as adaptive social innovations.[22] The affirmation of black life, then, requires thinking across a range of racial identifications and practices (African and non-African, black and non-black) within a system that axiomatically situates black life *outside* plantocratic conceptions of humanity and, in this, reinvents black selfhood-community-life anew.

Notable here is Wynter's concept of indigenization.[23] Throughout the manuscript she tracks the different ways displacement, negation, and racist violence fostered radical practices of black humanization—marronages, mutinies, funerals, carnivals, dramas, visual arts, fictions, poems, fights, dances, the blues, jazz, revolts, "periodic uprisings and . . . the ongoing creation of culture."[24] These practices delineate a "sustained and prolonged attempt to reinvent the black as human."[25] What she begins to open up, then, is the perceptive and groundbreaking claim that *making black culture* (marronages, mutinies, funerals, carnivals, dramas, visual arts, fictions, poems, fights, dances, music-making and -listening, revolts) *reinvents* (black) humanity and life. The affirmation of black humanness is enunciated through an "alienated reality" that is rooted in plantocratic histories, practices, and geographies. This alienated-reality status does

22. Wynter, *Black Metamorphosis*, 243–244, 506. It important to underscore that the specificity of African-ness, the varying intimacies of multifarious African indigenous lives, are not exactly replicated by the enslaved—retention in the New World is trace, and trace is repurposed in the context of the New World plantation logic.

23. In *Black Metamorphosis* Wynter's concept of indigenization is not, it should be noted, a discussion of teleological-temporal New World arrivals and here-first-spatial-birth-claims; indigenization is a verb. It is, then, a thinking through of the ways in which Middle Passage and plantation systems produced a range of differential modes of knowing and uneven perceptions of humanness (of which the enslaved black was excluded altogether as labor-unit). This analytical approach allows us to address and discuss: the heavy weight of normative ideologies and values and the brutally oppressive technologies of slavery and colonialism that, all together, produce modern relational histories and narratives and dynamic acts of rebellion—rebellion is indigenization—against the codes of unfreedom that violently marginalize global damnés. See her discussion of the "underlife" throughout the manuscript, too.

24. Wynter, *Black Metamorphosis*, 83.

25. Wynter, *Black Metamorphosis*, 248.

not provide a New World cosmogony that situates the black enslaved as settlers and/or property holders and/or autochthonous; the alienated-reality status instead draws attention to black diaspora activities as geopolitical responses that unsettle racism and objectification. This means the affirmation of black humanness is both relational to and in contradistinction to the dominant order of consciousness, because rebellions—which are activities! not identities! not places!—honor black life as an ongoing struggle against what is represented as and believed to be preordained dysselected objecthood and placelessness. It is the process of creating blackness anew within the context of white supremacy that shifts our focus away from perceiving a range of New World inhabitants as differently occupying resolved knowable and distinct noun-places (settler/property holder/autochthonous/labor-unit) and toward the politics of being human as praxis.

Let me explain this a little further: Sylvia Wynter writes that (mythic and real) autochthonous cultures of Africans from various locations and those indigenous to the New World were violently disrupted—*in their own lands*—by *both* transatlantic slavery and colonialism.[26] The forced movement of Africans *into* the New World meant that this disruption was extended to and reworked on the Middle Passage and the plantation. The loss of land to colonizing forces (experienced by those indigenous to Africa and those indigenous to the New World) was followed by a "change in continent" and the "total conditioning power of the plantation" for black enslaved people.[27] The change in continent required—unlike those indigenous to the New World, who were violently initiated into "Indian-ness" through genocidal practices and reserve systems in their own lands—black rebirth and cultural recreation in an entirely new geographic context. The reinvention of the human that took place in black communities, Wynter writes, was folded into the collective rebellions against plantation and colonial capitalist structures and their attendant modes of knowing.[28]

As noted above, the geographic stakes of enslavement and colonialism unveil ungeographic black labor units (planted in, not intended to *people*, space) and settler geographies that are humanized through production, accumulation, and profit generation. Indeed, in this model the normative

26. Wynter, *Black Metamorphosis*, 13–14.
27. Wynter, *Black Metamorphosis*, 17.
28. Wynter, *Black Metamorphosis*, 83.

human is produced, and revered, as a *geographic* actor whose belonging is buttressed by consumerism and ownership. The racial economy that designated the enslaved as nonbeings/nonconsumers/mechanized labor requires that the radical affirmation of black life be sought and claimed outside colonial—land settling and land claiming and land exploiting and genocidal—paradigms. It follows that the reinvention of black life must be engendered outside the logics of accumulation, land ownership, and profit generation, regardless of racial identification, while also paying close attention to rebellious acts that indict and counter-poeticize a system of knowledge that venerates practices of racial violence as initiatory acts of humanization. This means, too, noticing that the process of black objectification implicit to the Middle Passage and plantation systems also required that the enslaved be indispensable to wider global interhuman exchanges and initiations and inventions—including, of course, African traces and black rebellions and subversive cultural texts. Indigenization, then, is not bound up in spatial claims (which are always, within our present system of knowledge, decidedly ethnically absolutist claims). Nor is indigenization held in strict and steady opposition to, say, oppressive homogeneous colonizing powers. Indigenization is rebellion. Indigenizations are *ongoing* rebellions that demand we think outside our normalized order of consciousness (an order that sites and cites the consumer-driven-accumulating-property-owning-always-wealthy-noun-place human as a finished, settled, thrived-for figure seemingly unmitigated by the messy consequences of interhuman exchanges that were [and are] engendered by our collective plantation histories and futures) and uncover the potentiality of rehumanized liberation and joy.

INVENTION

Black Metamorphosis traces the ways in which the Middle Passage and plantation systems produced the conditions to reinvent new forms of human life. Rebellions, uprisings, and cultural production, Wynter writes, disclose black intellectual strategies that "operated by a different principle of thought from that of the rational mind related to that of the plantation."[29] She continues: "Revolts were, at one and the same time, a form of praxis and an abstract theoretical activity. Neither could be separated from the other. Theory existed only in praxis; praxis was inseparable

29. Wynter, *Black Metamorphosis*, 109.

from theory."[30] Part of Wynter's underlying claim in this text is that black rebellion—marronages, mutinies, funerals, carnivals, dramas, visual arts, fictions, poems, fights, dances, music-making and -listening, revolts, "periodic uprisings and . . . the ongoing creation of culture"—is an intellectual breach. It is worth repeating that what is being breached (a dominant order of consciousness and its attendant initiation system that rests on entwining biocentric and economically racist practices) is heavy: it is a naturalized and normalized teleological *belief* system that preordains a racial economy of racism and normalizes the objectification of black people; it is narrated as a commonsense cosmogony and "destiny."[31] Rebelling against this heaviness calls into question the preordained, profitable, and reflexively felt (as if bio-instinctually) workings of racism.

Rebellious activities honor black life through expressing a model of liberation that is a "subversion of the axiomatic culture [and] the axiomatic psyche."[32] Reading across a range of creative and intellectual texts, Wynter's discussion of black music and popular culture illuminates the interrelated praxes of inventing culture and reinventing black life *through* alienated realities. Her analyses of reggae, the blues, and jazz, for example, think through music as, among other things: a layered site of mythical, symbolic, and experiential histories; a secularizing ritual; tempos and beats that recode normative time; repurposed and shared (among a range of black and nonblack artists) texts and rhythms; intertextual; citing suffering, survival, love, happiness, revolution; a kinship-making activity. With this, "[black music] was created in this exterior [alienated reality] social space, out of an outlier consciousness that was born from the sustained experience of social marginality. Because of this even as the record industry makes black music the 'raw material' of its profit production, and diffuses it globally, the bourgeoisie order itself creates the condition of possibility of its own subversion."[33] The creation of culture, black inventions, animate liberation as praxes of rebellious subversions. Related, inventing black music out of our plantation pasts demonstrates that the figure that was never intended to *be*—because *being* is iconized as property-owning-settled-geographically-belonging-nonblack—in fact, empirically and experientially questions the ontological terms of humanness and therefore

30. Wynter, *Black Metamorphosis*, 139.
31. Wynter, *Black Metamorphosis*, 444.
32. Wynter, *Black Metamorphosis*, 387.
33. Wynter, *Black Metamorphosis*, 896.

becomes through subversive rebellion and as subversive rebel. The black figure that emerged from an alienated-reality status *as* black-human-life therefore reorients us to radical praxes of liberation that do not replicate a colonial order of knowledge. The reinvention of black life and community, and inventive rebellious practices, regardless of scale, clearly demonstrate a revolt against an entire belief system, including a sanctioned order of consciousness, that negates black humanity; these reinventions and inventions transform an impossibility—black humanity—into an imaginable and valuable and expressive form of black life.

In the early portions of the manuscript Wynter delineates how black rebellions, uprisings, and cultural production, together, were resistances and critical responses to the labor-unit-status imposed on the enslaved.[34] Black cultural production and inventions were, of course, seen as *noncultural* within the dominant order of knowledge—for the enslaved were, first and foremost, labor units bereft of humanity and therefore without cultural-intellectual acuity.[35] Black culture was (is) therefore logically stigmatized because it resides outside normative, respectable, cultural codes. Wynter also outlines how black cultural practices were threats ("property that had rebelled, thereby affirming its status as human, [was] burnt (i.e. tortured) as a terror," and overseers thwarted dances that "serve[d] to keep alive that military spirit").[36] In mapping out how those deemed nonpersons were punished for producing noncultural inventions that critiqued and reimagined the dominant system, *Black Metamorphosis* opens up a way to think about how the reinventions of black life were tied to "mechanisms of rebellion . . . sited in culture" that "profoundly undermine[d] the bourgeoisie utilitarianism and the instrumental rationality of the dominant order."[37] In several instances Wynter therefore shows how the plantocratic values that negated and objectified blackness were subverted and restructured by black cultural practices such as work songs, stories, dramas, dances, poems. She writes that the "subversive quality of black popular music has been primarily its assault on this [colonial] sense of time, its freeing of time from a market process, its insistence on time as a life process."[38] She continues, later, to write that the "paradox

34. Wynter, *Black Metamorphosis*, 117.
35. Wynter, *Black Metamorphosis*, 467.
36. Wynter, *Black Metamorphosis*, 79, 82, 129.
37. Wynter, *Black Metamorphosis*, 411–412, 545–546.
38. Wynter, *Black Metamorphosis*, 198–199, 202.

of black culture is that, stigmatized as the negation of the norm, it was left alone to develop alternative possibilities; to provide the ground, the basis, for subversion of the dominant values of the hegemonic culture."[39] In *Black Metamorphosis*, the invention of black music is a revolutionary act that keeps heretical (nonmarket) time, negates black nonbeing by honoring and recoding black life, repurposes and interrupts linear temporalities, and is expressed in the midst of a violent and stigmatizing knowledge system. These musical practices, generated out of time and place, were also collaborative inventions because they were anchored to associative and collectively shared sounds, lyrics, myths, rituals, songs, and experiences. Musical subversion is, importantly, tied to the development and legitimation of new modes of social kinship relations, reciprocal exchanges that do not replicate colonial heterosexual family figurations or individualist models but, rather, establish networks that collectively rebel.[40] Music, then, is not only an invention that subverts and undoes commonsense workings of racism; music, music-making, and music-listening, together, demonstrate the subversive politics of shared stories, communal activities, and collaborative possibilities wherein "one *must participate* in knowing."[41]

Wynter's work on music shows that the affirmation of black life and practices of rebellion are intimately tied to cultural production. Making, sharing, and listening to black music are rebellious activities that evidence "a long tradition of social resistance" and provide "a theoretical framework for social revolution."[42] What is at stake, then, are not texts and expressions and sounds that are disconnected from and oppositional to the dominant order but, instead, *activities* that are entangled with— *because they are plantocratic*—a range of racial identifications that provide clues about how we might think outside, and change, our present order of knowledge. Musical inventions subvert—overthrow, ruin, undermine— the existing system by exposing its inequities and limits, while also engendering black joy and collaborative acts.

39. Wynter, *Black Metamorphosis*, 478.
40. Wynter, *Black Metamorphosis*, 844–845.
41. Wynter, *Black Metamorphosis*, 546 (emphasis added).
42. Wynter, *Black Metamorphosis*, 849.

Musical inventions are anchored to associative sounds, lyrics, myths, rituals, songs, and experiences.[43] In addition, musical inventions not only cushion "the shock of dispossession"; they also "oppose it, by reminding, at deep psychic levels, of a potential return to humanity."[44] I conclude this story with a discussion of sound and grooving to argue that waveforms are reparative rebellious inventions. I draw out some of the beats and grooves and feelings that Wynter writes into *Black Metamorphosis* to suggest that these are waveforms that undo the aforementioned negative physiological and neurobiological responses to black life. My discussion of sound, then, seeks to demonstrate that one of Wynter's rebellious analytical moves in this manuscript is to provide an opening to think about how sounds, and grooving to music and beats, necessarily complement the aforementioned reinventions, inventions, subversions, collaborations. Indeed, part of my claim here is that listening to and grooving to black music provides the conditions to intellectually engage and love black ethically. Music waveforms allow us to glean that reinventing black life anew is bound up in cognitive schemas that envision, and feel, black sound outside normative structures of desire. This is to say that in order to be newly human, one does not only rebelliously *site* and *make* black culture in a world that despises blackness, one also *engages* cultural inventions and sounds and ideas and texts, deeply and enthusiastically, in order to affirm humanity: one grooves *out* of the logics of racism and *into* black life.

As I noted above, in *Black Metamorphosis* Wynter traces how reinvented black life forms and creative inventions emerged out of a range of violent racist acts. Throughout the text there are many instances where she identifies the profoundly human consequences of racist violence and what she describes as "death in life" and the "long and sustained agony of black experience."[45] She writes of, for example, intolerable psychic pressures, anxieties, alienations, unsettling modes of cognition, colonized desires, among other neurobiological, physiological, and affective responses to oppression.[46] These responses to racism clearly delineate how the overarching extrahuman system of knowledge imposes itself on, and shapes,

---

43. Wynter, *Black Metamorphosis*, 185–187, 191–197.
44. Wynter, *Black Metamorphosis*, 114.
45. Wynter, *Black Metamorphosis*, 212, 627.
46. For example, Wynter, *Black Metamorphosis*, 243–244, 248, 387, 403.

black and nonblack consciousness, with those cast as nonpersons neuro-biologically, physiologically, and affectively occupying a world that makes humanness known through refusing black life. I draw attention to these neurobiological, physiological, and affective moments in *Black Metamorphosis* because it is, in part, within the realm of consciousness that Wynter explores black rebellion. The brutality of racism is relational to, she notes, the *impulse* to resist, the *impulse* to produce oppositional narratives, the mind *feeling* theory, a profound *enthusiasm* for black culture, and longings *felt* in the flesh.[47] Again, these are not bio-instinctual impulses, feelings, and enthusiasms—although they may be experienced as such; they are, rather, indicators of a normalized, racially coded, biocentric belief system that shapes how we collectively *feel* and *know* and *affectively negotiate* the world. These specific impulses, feelings, and enthusiasms delineate the limits of the overarching system in that black *life*—neurobiological, physiological, and affective life—is enunciated as rebellious life *at the level of consciousness* and, *simultaneously*, through the reinventions and inventions noted above. This claim, then, totally undoes the mode of knowing that extracts livingness from blackness and black life by drawing attention to correlational (reinventions-as-inventions-as-rebellions-as-consciousness-as-being-as-praxis) human activities rather than unchanging biocentric *categories* of being that cosmogonically anticipate black dysselection.[48] This alternative order of consciousness emerges from knotted and messy and awful plantocratic pasts that, I argue, are relational creative acts that unfold as reparative possibilities rooted in black intellectual activities.

The impulse and enthusiasm to subvert indicates the powerful possibilities that music, music-making, and other creative acts engender. Wynter suggests that because systems of oppression and racism were and are so brutal, deep, and heavy, black cultural activities are embedded with, and thus invite, "emotional charge."[49] She also writes: "Music is strictly structured and thinks itself through the senses."[50] These insights, together, begin to

47. For example, Wynter, *Black Metamorphosis*, 82, 109, 412, 545–546, 817.
48. See also Wynter's discussion of bios-mythoi and human being as praxis: Sylvia Wynter and Katherine McKittrick, "Unparalleled Catastrophe for Our Species? Or, to Give Humanness a Different Future: Conversations," in *Sylvia Wynter: On Being Human as Praxis*, ed. Katherine McKittrick (Durham, NC: Duke University Press, 2015), 1–89.
49. Wynter, *Black Metamorphosis*, 412.
50. Wynter, *Black Metamorphosis*, 245.

frame up how the relational acts of making and engaging black music—grooving—are collaborative rebellion. In her discussion of religious and secular music and dance, for example, she documents how tempos, steps, groans, shuffles, abrupt turns, laughter, hip-sways, beats, songs, foot-stamping, arm movements, and other beats and grooves are expressions of conscious art, renewed realities, and life forces for the dispossessed.[51] While the music, sound, and dance archived in *Black Metamorphosis* point to a number of entwining practices and sources (African and non-African, black and nonblack), what I want to emphasize are the ways that Wynter couples rebellion, critique, invention, and reinvention with rhythms and grooves. She writes, for example, that rhythm is "the aesthetic/ethic principle of the gestalt" and thus central to the reconstitution of black life.[52] Indeed, the beats and grooves within the monograph shed light on an "alternate way of thought, one where the mind and senses coexist, where the mind 'feels' and the senses become theoreticians."[53] It follows, then, that the aforementioned alternative mode of consciousness—the impulse to innovatively subvert—is, in part, constituted through "a radicalization of desire."[54]

Wynter writes of beats and grooves and waveforms as productive sites of resistance that are relational to revolution and the affirmation of black life. She writes that drums are "the enabling mechanism of consciousness reversal" and that listening to beats, grooves, and music fosters collective "cosmic unity" between the self and the social body: people "listening or dancing participate in the experience of the music [and are] linked to the physiological experience of the beat."[55] Indeed, in sharing and grooving to music, histories are renarrated, kinships are reimagined, and a different mode of representation is performed, heard, repeated, enjoyed: this is a very different kind of initiation into humanness than a normative model that requires racism and racial violence. With this, Wynter writes, "enthusiasm and exaltation are the uncolonized flow of desire that expresses liberation from societal codings."[56] Enthusiasm radically challenges and overturns the dominant order: the feeling of exaltation, emerging as a form of knowledge that is necessarily collaborative praxis, cites and sites

51. Wynter, *Black Metamorphosis*, 191–197.
52. Wynter, *Black Metamorphosis*, 245.
53. Wynter, *Black Metamorphosis*, 109.
54. Wynter, *Black Metamorphosis*, 817.
55. Wynter, *Black Metamorphosis*, 878–879.
56. Wynter, *Black Metamorphosis*, 549.

black joy and love. For it is in the waveforms of music—beats, rhythms, acoustics, notational moods, and frequencies that intersect with racial economies and histories—that rebelliousness is enunciated as an energetic (neurological, physiological) *affection for* black culture *as* life. In this, *Black Metamorphosis* asks for an engagement with music that couples rebelliousness and subversion with the act of making, hearing, listening to, and moving to, song. The aesthetic waveforms offer a way to call attention to the ways in which the praxis of black life—as well as the behaviors and brain activities that find pleasure in song—is articulated through music, music-making, music-listening, orchestration, beats, bass, notations, lyrics, rhymes, soul, groove. This opens up a meaningful way to think about how the politics of sound, and grooving to song, are assertions of black life that indict and subvert racism and, at the same time, notice the inventive aspects of our collective and difficult plantocratic histories, traces, and memories: "The ethic is the aesthetic."[57]

57. Wynter, *Black Metamorphosis*, 900.

I have told this story elsewhere. Differently.[1] This story has three sections that work toward reimagining the spatial politics of the black diaspora. These sections can be read separately, together, or in any order. I begin with method and the framing and organization of the story. The first section, "The List," is an excerpt of a human geography encyclopedia entry on diaspora.[2] The entry has been revised, amended, and modified; it also contains many ellipses, pauses . . . indicating breaks, breaths, erasures that are not found in the original encyclopedia entry. The list, with any luck, will hint at how cataloguing a material, conceptual, and imaginative site—diaspora—does little to undo, and indeed reconstitutes, our present geographic order. "The List" serves as a guide, or an opening, to the second section, "Ungeographic," which outlines the limits of mapping diaspora through prevailing geographic concepts. In that section I discuss how listing functions to affirm mapping—a cartographic practice that is laden with oppressive geographic techniques: in short, to map the diaspora by enfolding it into a human geography encyclopedic entry and listing its fundamental characteristics forecloses the radical spatial politics diaspora offers. In the final section of this story, "Tormented Chronologies," I work with the writings of Édouard Glis-

The title of this story, "(I Entered the Lists)," is from Frantz Fanon, *Black Skin, White Masks* (New York: Grove, 1952), 114.

    1. A very different version of this story was written as "I Entered the Lists . . . Diaspora Catalogues: The List, the Unbearable Territory, and Tormented Chronologies—Three Narratives and a *Weltanschauung*," *XCP: Cross Cultural Poetics* 17 (2007): 7–29. Thank you, Alexander Weheliye, for sharing that this imperfect story of lists, now and then, matters.

    2. Katherine McKittrick, "Diaspora," in *International Encyclopedia of Human Geography*, ed. Rob Kitchin and Nigel Thrift (London: Elsevier, 2009), 156–161.

sant to consider how we might undo the colonizing desire that underpins place-making (ownership as authenticated by list and map and list and map as coveted objects). To do this, I think through Glissant's concept of "tormented chronology."

ONE METHOD

I entered the lists

—FRANTZ FANON

I begin with a somewhat crude remixing and mashing-up of the language that animates human geography and diaspora studies.[3] I remix and mash up an encyclopedia entry I wrote in 2009. The scholarly remix and mash-up used in the section "The List" is one method that hopes to illuminate the limits of what is on the page; point to what we can do *with* the page itself; wander off the page. The method draws on Mark V. Campbell's study of the remix. In theorizing turntabling and DJing, he asks that we think about how an original text—a sample, a tune, a beat, a song—is reinvented to produce new modes of relationality. Campbell observes how black cultural production is intellectual work that consists of layering, interrupting, fusing, and grooving to narratives that might otherwise be disconnected. He also theorizes remix as a way to call into question racial authenticities by centering how members of the black diaspora lyrically, sonically, and rhythmically write race outside normative biocentric categories. Black music—scratch, boom—is a generative expression of diasporic unbelonging. "Mash-up" refers to the process of layering songs on top of one another. In mash-ups we see and hear and feel long bars, riffs, and scores that are sonically pressed together. These overlaid tracks offer a familiarity (we recognize something, we recognize a piece of that song we love) that is re-expressed in a slightly different context (through doubling or tripling musical scores on top of one another, through pressing that song we love into the bass line of the song we remember). The mash-up produces a new and different song while also pointing to for-

3. Mark V. Campbell, "Everything's Connected: A Relationality Remix, a Praxis," *C. L. R. James Journal* 20, no. 1 (Fall 2014): 97–114. See also Alexander Weheliye, *Phonographies: Grooves in Sonic Afro-Modernity* (Durham, NC: Duke University Press, 2005); Paul Gilroy, *The Black Atlantic: Modernity and Double Consciousness* (Cambridge, MA: Harvard University Press, 1993).

mer "umashed" or "unmixed" texts and sounds. *Donuts* by J Dilla is exemplary.[4] The remix and the mash-up are useful, as method and model, because these creative activities reveal the lived and expressive poetics of the black diaspora (the sound, the grooves, the collaborative narratives, the reinvention of text and sway, as well as those moments of love and other sonic mnemonics). We might imagine the black diaspora, and expressions of black life, to be constituted through and by the remix mash-up and the mash-up remix. Thus, the crude remix and mash-up in part 1 might inform how the reader attends to parts 2 and 3 (in these sections I tease out how normative modes of belonging, which are determined by the geographies of market-time-nation-time-blood-and-land, are mashed up and undone by diasporic logics). This, ideally, interrupts and reimagines and creates new stories by

- inventing with found objects;
- breaking free of old associations;
- engendering new contexts from old histories;
- flipping the script;
- learning to speak in new forms;
- noticing how the sound of thought becomes legible;
- producing work at the edge of new meanings;
- taking an idea and folding it in on itself.[5]

Remixing and mashing-up reconfigure text on the page, within the story, and in extant of the story. Imperfectly, this story is an experiment in unmapping the diaspora and recognizing black methodologies as reworking and re-creating what they think we are—and where we are, spatially—through the study, praxis, and reinvention of black life. The story believes that the black diaspora is not a settled place, but a way of being. Black geography is, perhaps, a method of living outside geographic norms.

4. J Dilla, *Donuts*, Stone's Throw, 2006. Thank you, Elliot Jun. See also Aram Sinnreich, *Mashed Up: Music, Technology, and the Rise of Configurable Culture* (Amherst: University of Massachusetts Press, 2010).

5. The list is from Paul D. Miller aka DJ Spooky that Subliminal Kid, *Rhythm Science* (Cambridge, MA: MIT Press, 2004), 25.

I entered the lists

—FRANTZ FANON

Glossary: for readers *from elsewhere*, who don't deal very well with unknown words or who want to understand everything. But, perhaps, to establish for ourselves, ourselves as well, the long list of words within us whose sense escapes or, taking this farther, to fix the syntax of this language we are babbling. The readers of *here* are the future.[6]

GLOSSARY OF TERMS

Creolization: . . . the coming together of diverse cultural traits or languages . . . a new or different (rather than subordinate/dominant) cultural practice that encompasses the social and political relations of two or more ethnic groups . . . unlike hybridity (see below) . . . renewed socio-spatial consequences . . .

Displacement: the geographic process of being removed, exiled, or marginalized . . . displacement can occur due to racism, sexism, homophobia, or other acts of discrimination and violence that subordinate particular communities, even though these communities may not have the means to escape . . . discrimination . . .

Homeland: a territory to which one belongs, was born in, or is tied to ancestrally . . . also understood as a "country of origin," . . . in the past or the present . . .

Migration, Migratory Subjects: any movement of humans from one location to another . . . the experiential tenets of migration that . . . forced expulsions, colonial displacements, or economically induced movements . . .

Nation: . . . demarcates the geographic location of a particular ethnic group . . . a government manages and protects . . .

6. Édouard Glissant, *Poetics of Relation*, trans. Betsy Wing (1990; rpt., Ann Arbor: University of Michigan Press, 1997), xxi.

... "diaspora" is inherently geographical ... exile, displacement, and resettlement ... migratory processes and experiences as well as imagined communities ... anti-Semitism, war, transatlantic slavery, colonial violence, homophobia, or poverty ... diaspora challenges and contributes to the ways in which modernity, nation, identity, and place are understood and experienced ...

Diaspora: ... the scattering of people across spaces, borders, and nations ... ethnic and racial traumas as well as geographic losses have underwritten the scattering of people ... particular groupings of people have been violently forced to leave their homeland because they are racially, ethnically, and/or religiously different from those in power ... forced expulsion might be coupled with ethnic cleansing ... Jewish exiles, for example, have been regarded as forced scatterings instigated by anti-Semitism, genocide, and war ... in addition to physical violence that targets and expels a particular ethnic group ... lack of a stable nation-space and geopolitical independence, and transnational dispersals ... the desire to establish and secure a location that can replace former geographic losses ... World War II, Shoah ... Israel in 1948 ... neighboring states ... attendant and diasporic Middle Eastern communities ... new spaces of settlement in North America, Africa, Australia, South America, and Asia ... memorials have been constructed in various sites internationally ... African peoples ... violently exiled ... expulsion and bondage ... sold and transplanted into the Americas and Europe, and geographically disconnected from their former African homelands ... sociocultural ruptures ... expunged ... entangled with centuries of violence wherein the question of homeland and geographic loss shapes how belonging and nationhood are experienced within the new region of relocation ... human removal, death, and displacement ... Palestine.

settling after such exile carries with it ... history of removal, death and displacement ... relocation in the Americas is, at times, understood through their diasporic relationship to the Middle Passage, the continent of Africa and/or transatlantic slavery ... debates over this ... some memories too unbearable to return to, some generations rethinking the past ... the Armenian community ... displacement and exile ... centuries of ethnic and religious subordination ...

massacres of 1915–1916 . . . mass genocide and displacement . . . discrimination, war, poverty, colonialism, ethnic cleansing and violence have removed and moved Irish, Asian, South Asian, Caribbean, Eastern European, and Middle Eastern groups from their countries of birth . . . war, ethnic cleansing, colonialism, and various genocides

paved the way for . . . gay, lesbian, transgendered, and bisexual communities . . . queer diasporas . . . spaces of resettlement . . . homophobia and heterosexual gender conventions . . .

. . . returns . . . the process of returning, whether imaginary, real, filmic, fictional . . . what returns are possible . . . through travel, remembrance, imagination, remittances, yearnings, stories, or songs? are past cultural practices retained on relocation, and do these cultural practices carry in them the history of violence, dispersal, and memories of home? . . . Afrocentrism, Negritude, and Pan-Africanism produce links . . . funds are sent "home" to assist family and friends or to secure future departures . . . films that take up departures or violence, novels that remember slavery, poetry that explores forced human migrations, internet sites that map Holocaust memorials and record the lives of survivors, songs that sample the music of Bob Marley and are then played on local radio stations, globally, live performances of Ghidda in the UK or Canada . . . diasporic returns . . . real, imaginary, political, economic, and creative . . . if diaspora fundamentally centers on the movement of people, are not all traveling cultures diasporic . . . if departure is voluntary, or individual rather than collective, is this diasporic process . . . do all diasporic subjects return? . . . all diasporas are historically contingent on the specificities of time and space . . .

- Exile of a substantial population based on ethnicity, race, religion, or difference that is often coupled with violence and/or genocide
- Loss of or displacement from homeland
- The mutual construction of identity and place as they are experienced by migratory diasporic communities

RETURNS

"routes and roots" . . . diasporic cultures are not traveling and migrating with ease . . . a particular event or events—poverty, violence, war—initiated flight and this movement is difficult (psychically, physiologically) because it is wrapped up in loss . . . exiled communities formulate their collective identities not as victims but, rather, as subjects who negotiate, transgress, and fracture the boundaries of and between nation, territory, and culture . . .

territorialization (the jurisdiction and regulation of land and its citizens by a particular government) . . .

alternative understandings of modernity, nation, identity, and place . . . do not assume a clear or stable "beginning" and "end" . . . site and cite human violence, but do not explicitly locate a region of liberation or freedom at the end of diasporic travels . . . are concerned with nation, are critical of borders, nationalism, and the limits of nation-state citizenship . . . imagine homelands and returns, but do not assume that "home" is either returnable or innocent . . .

modernity . . . transnational flows beginning in the fifteenth century (colonial expansion, exploration, transatlantic slavery, indenture) . . . crystallized in the seventeenth century during . . . multiscalar social hierarchies began to shape economic, political, cultural, and social systems inside and outside imperial nations . . . the shift away from feudal political systems, the development of the modern nation-state, and new international economic profits . . . systems of knowledge became increasingly based on categorization in the name of rationality, progress, and democratic liberalism . . . a corporeal hierarchy based on sexuality, race, ethnicity, phenotype, and gender wherein the white man symbolically came to represent and embody democracy and rationality . . .

close studies of plants, insects, animals, women, the poor, the insane, and positivist mappings of European, indigenous, and colonial physical and human geographies . . . "discover" and ultimately transform "primitive" or "nonrational" cultures or "enlightened" justifications for racial-sexual subordination . . . trains, gas chambers, work camps, plantations, ghettos, ethnic enclaves, reservations . . . [7]

7. "The homeless, the jobless, the semi-jobless, the criminalized drug offending prison population, the damnés, the global archipelago, constituted by the Third- and Fourth-World peoples of the so called 'underdeveloped' areas of the world." Sylvia Wynter, "Unsettling the Coloniality of Being/Power/Truth/Freedom: Towards the Human, After Man, Its Over-representation—an Argument," CR: The New Centennial Review 3, no. 3 (Fall 2003): 261.

. . . the disappearance of indigenous communities . . . bondage, genocide, violence, and colonialism are . . .

progress, enlightened reason, democracy . . . negotiate and enlightened modernity if, in its various implementations, it negates their worldview and figures, even prefigures, them as irrational, uncivilized, and worthy of expulsion and bondage? . . . is often equated with democratic citizenship, technological progress, and new ways of organizing the world . . . validated the expulsion of particular groups from their country of origin . . . nation is central to theorizing diasporas . . . forced dispersal carries with it the idea of "displacement from" somewhere and "displacement to" somewhere . . . how diasporic communities understand themselves in relation to the nation . . . racial identities within a prescribed country or region (Vietnamese only live in Vietnam . . .)

. . . the nation, as a political bounded entity that safely houses and supports its citizens, is constantly being breached . . . some citizens are not, in fact, welcome or at ease within the boundaries of their country of birth . . . as a refugee, economic migrant, or exiled subject . . . fraught with ambivalence . . . acts of discrimination . . .

. . . not outside of modernity . . . the experiences of removal, travel, and return are indicative of how roots and routes (indeed diaspora spaces) intersect with, and therefore are indicative of, modern geographies . . . these processes of displacement, outer-national ties, and settlement demonstrate the workings of modernity and the modern nation not as bounded or unchanging but as a territory inflected with difference . . . this formulation attempts to recuperate or restore a broken past . . . anticolonial struggles . . . how masses of people might, together, relate to this history vis-à-vis their common identities and contemporaneous political struggles against oppression . . . identities were and are soldered as a counter-narrative to Eurocentric modernity and the nation-state . . . absolutely other or wholly different from the bourgeois hegemonic class . . . diaspora identities change from moment to moment and place to place . . . original geographic loss . . . can only be understood as fluid and changing: there is no satisfactory relationship with historic regions of displacement . . .

... as they continue to experience discrimination within the nation of relocation (racial profiling, segregations, incarcerations, poverty) ...
neither outside modernity or the nation ... combine and creolize
multiple points of identification ... a process of entanglement ...

... diaspora as a fundamentally geographic process, as it is underwritten by exiles, displacements, and regional specificities ... use the
term "diaspora" as a descriptor for movement ... not exploring
questions of identity, modernity, violent exile, collective histories,
and ambivalent nation-making ... diaspora is simply synonymous
with migration and immigration ... those geographers interested
in ... trauma, displacement, and identity shape and are shaping the
production of space ... advance a unique conceptualization of what
is often called diaspora spaces ... diaspora and diaspora studies is
focused on the highly metaphoric ... diaspora is primarily theorized through the production of identity, rather than a materiality
of displacement ... many geographers have noted that questions
of hybridity, imagined communities, and returns are ... collective
histories lack geographic specificity and political economy ... frus-
trated with the unrepresentability of the psychic themes in diaspora
studies ... three-dimensionality and geographic specificity—are
coupled with emotional and psychic processes ... the materiality of
modernity ...

positivist mappings ... difficult spatial conditions through which diasporic exile is a part ... this critique of the unrepresentability of
diaspora experiences is hasty ... questions of memory, psychic attachment, past exiles, and collective histories always carry in them
the materiality of displacement ... the language of diaspora, one
must always imagine the three-dimensionality of expulsion, in order to fully grasp that diaspora is a human phenomenon ...

APA REFERENCES / THEORISTS USED ABOVE: Anderson, B. R. O. G. (1983).
Imagined communities: Reflections on the origin and spread of nationalism.
London: Verso Editions / NLB ... Anthias, F. (1998). Evaluating "dias-
pora": Beyond ethnicity? *Sociology, 32*(3), 557–580 ... Blunt, A. (2003).
Geographies of diaspora and mixed descent: Anglo-Indians in India and
Britain. *International Journal of Population Geography, 9,* 281–294 ... Brah,
A. (1996). *Cartographies of diaspora: Contesting identities.* New York: Rout-
ledge ... Brand, D. (2001). *A map to the door of no return: Notes on belong-*

ing. Toronto: Doubleday . . . Carter, S. (2005). The geopolitics of diaspora. *Area, 37*(1), 54–63 . . . Clifford, J. (1994). Diasporas. *Cultural Anthropology, 9*, 302–338 . . . Cohen, R. (1997). *Global diasporas: An introduction.* Seattle: University of Washington Press . . . Davies, C. B. (1994). *Black women, writing, and identity: Migrations of the subject.* London: Routledge . . . Gilroy, P. (1993). *The black Atlantic: Modernity and double consciousness.* Cambridge, MA: Harvard University Press . . . Gopinath, G. (2005). *Impossible desires: Queer diasporas and South Asian public cultures, perverse modernities.* Durham, NC: Duke University Press . . . Habib, J. (2004). *Israel, diaspora, and the routes of national belonging.* Toronto: University of Toronto Press . . . Hall, S. (1990). Cultural identity and diaspora. In J. Rutherford (Ed.), *Identity: Community, culture, difference* (pp. 222–237). London: Lawrence and Wishart . . . Lowe, L. (1996). *Immigrant acts: On Asian American cultural politics.* Durham, NC: Duke University Press . . . Patton, C., & Sánchez-Eppler, B. (2000). *Queer diasporas.* Durham, NC: Duke University Press . . . Shilav, Y. (1993). Ethnicity and geography in Jewish perspectives. *GeoJournal, 30*(3), 273–277 . . . Yeoh, B. S. A., & Willis, K. (1999). "Heart" and "wing," nation and diaspora: Gendered discourses in Singapore's regionalisation process. *Gender, Place and Culture, 6*(4), 355–372.

KEYWORDS: colonialism, diaspora, displacement, exile, holocaust (Shoah), home, homeland, identity, migration, modernity, nation, transatlantic slavery

UNGEOGRAPHIC

I entered the lists

—FRANTZ FANON

In 2007 or 2008 I was invited to write a "diaspora" entry for the *International Encyclopedia of Human Geography.* I envisioned that this task would be relatively straightforward: I had planned to provide a genealogy of sorts, tracing displacements experienced by Jewish, African, Armenian communities, outlining exiles instigated by war, violence, and then taking up contemporary debates on queer diasporas and migration and globalization. I had planned to outline, furthermore, some of the central questions selected diaspora theorists raised: how expulsion is attached to memory and modernity; how traveling cultures are not always diasporic; how nostalgia and/or the nation underwrite many diasporas. While writing up these themes, ideas, and histories, I was asked to pay close attention to the "aims and scope" provided by the *International Encyclopedia of*

Human Geography editors: my entry must be detailed, authoritative, and comprehensive; my entry must be inclusive and global in scope; my entry must be written in English, four thousand words long, and an invaluable source of information on diaspora. My entry must be multidisciplinary yet focused on the key debates in human geography. I was also asked to provide a list of defined key terms and a limited bibliography that would serve as a next step for the interested reader. This bibliography and my dictionary entry, ideally, would *not* rely on a singular "seminal work" (see APA References above); an ideal entry would, then, draw on my broad knowledge of the available literature on the subject without paraphrasing any central theorists of diaspora.

Since about the mid-1990s, and in human geography alone, there has been an expanding and expansive production of dictionaries, encyclopedias, and reference primers written in English.[8] Excluding world and regional atlases and popular travel guides like the *Lonely Planet* series, there are dictionaries on feminist geographies, historical geographies, modern geographies, and premodern geographies. There are the "classic" human geography dictionaries produced by publishers such as Oxford, Penguin, and Blackwell; there are interdisciplinary texts, like the *Encyclopaedia of Housing*.[9] Sage Publications has produced primers on human geography, geographic methods, key geographic thinkers, and geographic

8. Outside the discipline of human geography, primers, lists, and encyclopedias abound—too many to compile here, subjects range from bird guides, plant guides, car guides, and other object, animal, people guides, to the texts like Michael Gray's *Bob Dylan Encyclopedia* (New York: Continuum, 2006), which is over seven hundred pages long. The interested list-reader might also look to the Routledge "Key Guides," which includes texts such as Diané Collinson, Kathryn Plant, and Robert Wilkinson, *Fifty Eastern Thinkers* (London: Routledge, 2001); Yvone Tasker, *Fifty Contemporary Filmmakers* (London: Routledge, 2002); Diané Collinson, *Fifty Major Philosophers* (London: Routledge, 1988); G. R. Evans, *Fifty Key Medieval Thinkers* (London: Routledge, 2006); Martin Griffiths, *Fifty Key Thinkers in International Relations* (London: Routledge, 1999); John Lechte, *Fifty Key Contemporary Thinkers: From Structuralism to Post-modernity* (London: Routledge, 1994); Martha Bremser and Lorna Sanders, *Fifty Contemporary Choreographers* (New York: Routledge, 2011). These primers, lists, might be thought about alongside the too-brief discussion of syllabi in the story "Footnotes (Books and Papers Scattered about the Floor)."

9. For example, Alisdair Rogers, Noel Castree, and Rob Kitchin, *A Dictionary of Human Geography* (Oxford: Oxford University Press, 2013); Derek Gregory, Ron Johnston, Geraldine Pratt, Michael J. Watts, and Sarah Whatmore, eds., *The Dictionary of Human Geography*, 5th ed. (Oxford: Wiley, 2009). Yes, there is *A Dictionary of Geography* and *The Dictionary of Geography* . . . Andrew T. Carswell, *The Encyclopedia of Housing* (London: Sage, 2012); W. G. Moore, *The Penguin Dictionary of Geography* (New York: Penguin, 1978).

concepts.[10] These sources of geographic knowledge do not pay close attention to geographies of race and racism or what we might call alternative geographies: the Middle Passage, W. E. B. Du Bois's urban studies, Toni Morrison's site of memory are not to be found. Sometimes key thinkers of race are included (Gayatri Spivak, bell hooks, Edward Said). Of course, opening up the possibility of nonwhite geographic knowledge is not the point of the texts—they are designed to outline and therefore fashion a particular geographic story.

The production of knowledge within the discipline of geography is closely related to the discipline's history of positivism and exclusion. While many human geographers, anxiously and not, name legacies of whiteness, colonialism, and heterosexism that inhabit their areas of study, the production of the discipline—*as disciplined*—thrives. When the production of specialized handbooks, lists, and encyclopedias are incorporated into academic and nonacademic spheres, they follow similar guidelines to the *International Encyclopedia of Human Geography*. This emphasizes the ways in which the production of knowledge is intimately bound to the production of space. Indeed, the work of cataloguing and naming diaspora is a mapping exercise; it is a renewed enlightenment exercise of classifying, finding, discovering, and documenting. With this in mind, there are written and unwritten codes within the discipline of human geography that understand knowledge to be fundamentally spatial; the spatialization of ideas—material, metaphoric—can easily replicate colonial efforts.[11] That is, the knowledge that is documented and collected and listed is tied to a legacy of colonialism, extraction, and cataloguing.

Given our present and prevailing geographic system—wherein we are rewarded for owning things and places and ideas—spatializing the black diaspora (and by extension the subdiscipline of black geographies) in normative ways risks partaking in a politics of territorialization. More specifically, the exercise of authenticating an authoritative and compre-

10. See Phil Hubbard, Rob Kitchin, and Gill Valentine, eds., *Key Thinkers on Space and Place* (London: Sage, 2004); Stuart Aitken and Gill Valentine, eds., *Approaches to Human Geography* (London: Sage, 2006); Nicholas Clifford and Gill Valentine, eds., *Key Methods in Geography* (London: Sage, 2003); Sarah Holloway, Stephen Rice, and Gill Valentine, eds., *Key Concepts in Geography* (London: Sage, 2003). In fact, the "reference" series from Sage is unending. See http://sk.sagepub.com/reference.

11. Neil Smith and Cindi Katz, "Grounding Metaphor: Towards a Spatialized Politics," in *Place and the Politics of Identity*, ed. Michael Keith and Steve Pile (New York: Routledge, 1993), 67–83.

hensive understanding of diaspora enacts the jurisdiction and regulation of diaspora-lands and its diaspora-citizens even though diaspora, ideally, works to undo this jurisdiction and regulation. All of the entries in the *International Encyclopedia of Human Geography*—from whiteness and postcolonialism to Global Information Systems and the entry on David Harvey—are intended to literally map out, and therefore stake a claim to, some kind of space. Diaspora, then, is to be mapped and disciplined and institutionalized, unfolding as a "conceptualization of geography that is reassuringly secure and familiar."[12] The rigor of cataloguing, classifying, and mapping knowledge on the terms outlined by the *International Encyclopaedia of Human Geography* corresponds with familiar (normative, prevailing) geographic patterns that frame our spatial world as it already is (transparent, colonizing, knowable). My entry was and is a project of disavowal. That is, our present geographic system demands an authoritative diasporic map, with classificatory regions easily corresponding with their inhabitants, thus obscuring the potential geographic trouble diaspora—and blackness—can actually do.

What are the politics of mapping the black diaspora, and how is this mapping done? In 2015 a map titled "The Atlantic Slave Trade in Two Minutes" circulated online. The viewer is invited to watch dots on an animated map moving quickly between different sites on the continent of Africa toward the Americas and parts of Europe. Numbers are provided: 20,000+ voyages are tracked, slave-trading countries are counted, the enslaved are enumerated (315 years; 20,528 voyages; millions of lives).[13] The map is interactive, and "if you pause the map and click on a dot, you'll learn about the ship's flag—was it British? Portuguese? French?—its origin point, its destination, and its history in the slave trade."[14] I am not sure why we need to observe the Atlantic slave trade in two minutes. I do not find it easy to interact with this map. Watch it. Watch it disappear black life. The supplemental materials (there is a piece on Olaudah Equiano, there are links to studies on Equiano, there are links to other slave histories)

12. Philip Crang, Claire Dwyer, and Peter Jackson, "Transnationalism and the Spaces of Commodity Culture," *Progress in Human Geography* 27, no. 4 (2003): 446.

13. Andrew Kahn and Jamelle Bouie, "The Atlantic Slave Trade in Two Minutes," *Slate*, June 25, 2015, http://www.slate.com/articles/life/the_history_of_american_slavery /2015/06/animated_interactive_of_the_history_of_the_atlantic_slave_trade.html. See also http://www.slate.com/articles/life/the_history_of_american_slavery.html, accessed April 23, 2018.

14. Kahn and Bouie, "The Atlantic Slave Trade in Two Minutes."

do not undo the feeling of dread that accompanies witnessing centuries of racial violence in two minutes. You watch and you know the timing—so fast, so dehumanizing—is awful and unspeakable.[15]

The interactive map is, in theory, diasporic (it shows that transatlantic slavery, beginning in the fifteenth century, forcefully moved black peoples—in slave ships represented as dots—from the continent of Africa to a range of non-African geographies). It shows dispersal, displacement, exile. It shows 315 years, 20,528 voyages, millions of lives, in two minutes. It is nauseating. This is one way to map the black diaspora. But there are other ways, too: mapping the creative works of authors, musicians, and poets, analyzing postslave travels or the work of scholars like NourbeSe Philip or Jennifer Morgan or Gayl Jones or . . . The two-minute map is not enough. The map needs . . . [16]

While I was writing the encyclopedia entry, I was preoccupied with two other geographic concerns: the expulsion of black and poor peoples from New Orleans, and a paper by Carole Boyce Davies and Babacar M'Bow titled "Towards African Diaspora Citizenship: Politicizing an Existing Global Geography."[17] The black diaspora—the process of dis-

15. Pair with the interactive map of lynchings in the United States: *The Map of White Supremacy Mob Violence*. This reflects the difficult research conducted by Monroe Nathan Work. I am uncertain how to interact. I look. Ida B. Wells. She was the first. I stop.

Home: the horror of these gruesome killings was surging.

Instructions: zoom in using slider; click on the points that appear; drag the timeline that appears.

This is a learning tool. I hate the map.

Monroe Work Today, accessed December 21, 2018, http://www.monroeworktoday.org/index.html?u=2.

16. We need Treva C. Ellison and Romi (Ron) Morrison, "Decoding Possibilities: An Alluvial Map of Black Feminist Praxis," paper presented at *Black Geographies: A Symposium*, University of California, Berkeley, October 12, 2017.

17. Karen Bakker, "Katrina: The Public Transcript of Disaster," *Environment and Planning D: Society and Space* 23, no. 6 (2005): 795–801; Neil Smith, "There's No Such Thing as a Natural Disaster," *Understanding Katrina: Perspectives from the Social Sciences*, June 11, 2006, https://items.ssrc.org/understanding-katrina/theres-no-such-thing-as-a-natural-disaster/; Bruce Braun and James McCarthy, "Hurricane Katrina and Abandoned Being," *Environment and Planning D: Society and Space* 23, no. 6 (December 2005): 802–809; Carole Boyce Davies and Babacar M'Bow, "Towards an African Diaspora Citizenship: Politicizing an Existing Global Geography," in *Black Geographies and the Politics of Place*, ed. Katherine McKittrick and Clyde Woods (Toronto: Between the Lines Press, 2007), 14–45; Katherine McKittrick and Clyde Woods, "No One Knows the Mysteries at the Bottom of the Ocean," in *Black Geographies and the Politics of Place*, ed. Katherine McKittrick and Clyde Woods (Toronto: Between the Lines Press, 2007), 1–13.

placement and unbelonging—is a human phenomenon that has high-lighted, called into question, and refused the positivist contours of human geography and thus worked toward creating alternative spaces for political struggle. It is unlisted. It offers a perspective that is not always understood by the geographic language of insides and outsides, margins and centers, borders and nations. Black diaspora and diasporic communities engender poetic spaces that redraw and remap the landscape. Part of this redrawing and remapping offers a black sense of place: the sustained production of multiple and overlapping (past and present) liberation praxes that are not legible on cartographic maps but, instead, notice black ways of being. Diaspora geography is not the act of making maps; rather, it is the act of sharing ideas about where liberation is and might be. In this way, diaspora (black geography) is not a legible geography or geographic process, per se, but the practice of recognizing black life and livingness. Here colonial-imperial-capitalist geographic processes—violent removal from one's homeland, Middle Passage terror, slave labor—unfold into a geographic praxis that is outside the colonial-imperial-capitalist logics (ungeographic).

Black diaspora narrates livingness underneath and across existing maps, while recognizing how these maps are constituting diaspora itself; the material and imaginative geographies of the black diaspora are boundary-less (beyond a boundary), global, unfinished, dispersed, migratory, underwater, routed-rooted, underground, and inflected by the local.[18] Rather than participating in reterritorialization, engaging the black diaspora and its attendant communities involves recognizing, without officially demarcating, spaces that are not normally celebrated—or even noticed—in our present geographic order. These texts, experiences, resistances, places, and narratives are wide-ranging, sometimes (not always) legible in their materiality and their opaque black epistemological work—the Middle Passage, the plantation, the slave ship, the prison, the regions of the "underdeveloped" and "global South," the underground, the elsewhere, the nowhere, the out there, the invisible. Depending on our vantage point, black diaspora spaces, and what we do within them, are right in front of us while also hidden from view. Black diaspora spaces are nowhere and everywhere, practical and rebellious.

18. C. L. R. James, *Beyond a Boundary* (1963; rpt., Durham, NC: Duke University Press, 1993).

I am in search of an expansive methodology . . .[19]

The one hundred years and 133 troubling cases of Black criminals covered in these pages . . .[20]

You better go back in and ask her to draw you a map . . .[21]

TORMENTED CHRONOLOGIES

I entered the lists

—FRANTZ FANON

The violent dislocation that accompanied the slave trade, Édouard Glissant notes, reconfigures black diasporic time. Black consciousness, too, is dislocated and reconfigured. The question of History—linear, totalitarian, clear—cannot account for black time.[22] Glissant writes that History (colonial) narratively erases black history (nonhistory), but he also thinks through how the violent dislocation produced a sense of time that "came together in the context of shock, contraction, painful negation, and explosive forces."[23] He is keenly aware of, but not preoccupied by, discursive erasure because the Middle Passage and forced plantation labor (time characterized by ruptures) produced totally different temporal conditions for Caribbean populations. This is a meaningful analytical move, one that recognizes that erasure from history is oppressive yet, at the same time, draws attention to how the material conditions of displacement— the punishing expulsion of black peoples—lead to "a painful notion of time and its full projection into the future."[24] This painful notion of time, expulsion, and loss can be theorized in tandem with diaspora space (ungeographic), thus totally calling into question the Eurocentric inventories and geometrics that dominate how we know where and who we are.

19. Jennifer L. Morgan, *Laboring Women: Reproduction and Gender in New World Slavery* (Philadelphia: University of Pennsylvania Press, 2004), 201.

20. Barrington Walker, *Race on Trial: Black Defendants in Ontario's Criminal Courts, 1858–1958* (Toronto: University of Toronto Press, 2010), 23.

21. Alice Walker, "Looking for Zora," in *In Search of Our Mothers' Gardens: Womanist Prose* (New York: Harcourt and Brace and Company, 1983), 103.

22. Édouard Glissant, *Caribbean Discourse: Selected Essays*, trans. J. Michael Dash (Charlottesville: University Press of Virginia), 61–65.

23. Glissant, *Caribbean Discourse*, 62.

24. Glissant, *Caribbean Discourse*, 64.

Glissant, extending a thread from Edward Kamau Brathwaite, theorizes this—(ungeographic)—as subterranean convergence: "all those Africans weighed down with the ball and chain and thrown overboard whenever a slave ship was pursued by enemy vessels and felt too weak to put up a fight. *They sowed in the depths the seeds of an invisible presence . . .* floating free, not fixed in one position in some primordial spot, but extending in all directions in our world through its network of branches."[25]

Glissant asks that we reconstitute the "tormented chronology" of the History described above (imposed erasure, broken memory, rupture) by holding on to multiple and converging versions of (ungeographic) time and space.[26] He reimagines the work of history by creatively restructuring time and space. This "new methodology" repoliticizes lists and list-making by offering different modes of periodization and temporalities and identifications.

> If therefore one abandons the absurd catalogue of official history . . . and one tries to see what really happened . . .[27]

> . . . the directions he will provide will have nothing to do with the precise and objective nature of the location that is at stake . . . you will also find that he will not attempt to impose on you any set notion of time. He will offer a version *parallel* to your own.[28]

> We, thereby, live, we have the good fortune of living, this shared process of cultural mutation, this convergence frees us from uniformity.[29]

Our tormented chronologies (lists, registers, entries, catalogues, cartographies that function to erase and objectify) must therefore be understood through "*all* the perspectives of the human sciences."[30] And here we should not be distracted by Glissant's use of "sciences" and fear a return to another objective, measurable listing of things and places, for his conception of science here is importantly human, and includes, among other intellectual spaces and processes, literatures, poetics, nonhistories, the everyday world, latent memories, explosive emotions, nature, cultural

25. Glissant, *Caribbean Discourse*, 66–67 (emphasis in the original).
26. Glissant, *Caribbean Discourse*, 65.
27. Glissant, *Caribbean Discourse*, 88–89.
28. Glissant, *Caribbean Discourse*, 93 (emphasis in the original).
29. Glissant, *Caribbean Discourse*, 67.
30. Glissant, *Caribbean Discourse*, 65 (emphasis added).

production, creativity, and beyond. The tormented chronology, read with and alongside black humanity (black ungeographic time space), turns the lists upside down, tears them up, adds and discards, not with the ongoing fear of disavowal but, rather, through the pain and pleasure of what is made possible, and new, as our listings converge, confront one another, and overlap. While lists function to catalogue and affirm geopolitical boundaries (territories of Man and his human others), Glissant reads them as changeable and always changing precisely because they emerge from the material conditions of displacement that engender submarine roots and the alterability of time and space.

....

History has its dimension of the unexplorable, at the edge of which we wander, our eyes wide open.[31]

> . . . they burned the pages/they signed the papers/she signed the paper/I better get some sleep . . . it is possible to reduce our chronology to a basic skeleton of "facts," in any combination . . . Saturday July 19, 2025: Time drags! . . . my name is . . . one eleven . . . five haunted years.[32]

31. Glissant, *Caribbean Discourse*, 66.
32. Gayl Jones. Nina Simone. Édouard Glissant. Toni Morrison. Octavia Butler. J Dilla.

*D*ear Science,

When I last wrote, I told you about how I am trying to work out—without descriptively writing out—the intellectual-physiological effort that emerges alongside black rebellion. You didn't write back. Alone, without your response, I had to confront something I keep grasping for but cannot seem to explicate well: black rebellion, the work of liberation, regardless of scale, is livingness; black livingness is unmeasurable; our despair and heartbreak and friendships and ways of loving and moving, are tethered to a dehumanizing system of knowledge, a monumental story, that is measured (unfaltering) and precise (quantifiable). I wonder if the effort to live this world should be told at all. Maybe you can help me with the wording.

I finished the book I told you about and it was sent to Reader. They urged the praxis of story. They reminded me that we are not outside science, we are of science, and that the book holds in it mnemonics that repeat and restore not dehumanization but unfurled and hidden ideas about collaboration and liberation. This is where you, Science, took me. To be black is to live through scientific racism and, at the same time, reinvent the terms and stakes of knowledge. The reinvention becomes an invention-appreciation of our relational lives, I suppose, which is especially urgent given that we continue to collectively struggle against racial violence, premature death, and ecocide. To be black is to recognize and enervate the fictive perimeters of you, Science, and notice that the enclosures of biological determinism and the potentials of opacity, together, provide the conditions to concoct a different story altogether. There is more to you than I know. The concoction—secret, fiction, detailed, unclear, momentary, forever—accounts for how we live through the wreckage of the plantation and displace its racist logics and accompanying geographic weights and measures. What the plantation did to us, globally! Still. Reader wrote of implications, future pathways, provisional pursuits, recombinant possibilities, incomputables, quarks and curved space. I offer mnemonic black livingness: fluctuating codes and stories of black life, new and long-standing, that honor and study, imperfectly, our collaborative efforts to seek liberation. This is mindful work that is not interested in seizing, expropriating, place. Mnemonic black livingness is liberation unrealized (black geography, verb, is the process of seeking liberation).

I remember writing to you about physics and computer science and mathematics. I remember the failure and disappointment. I did not understand the syntax, the source codes, or the energy properties. I was left with numbers that could only produce what I could not bear and cannot forget. Like the Greenhill auction block. Like the girl. I asked for help. People shared and collaborated generously. We are curious. I want to sustain wonder.

Until soon,

Katherine xo

NOTES AND REMINDERS

Ahmed, Sara. *Living a Feminist Life*. Durham, NC: Duke University Press, 2017.

Ahmed, Sara. "White Men." *Feministkilljoys* (blog), November 4, 2014. https:// feministkilljoys.com/2014/11/04/white-men.

Alang, Navneet. "Facebook Algorithms Can't Replace Good Judgement." *Globe and Mail*, September 9, 2016. https://www.theglobeandmail.com/opinion /facebook-algorithms-cant-replace-good-judgment/article31805498/.

Alderson, Jonathan. *Challenging the Myths of Autism: Unlock New Possibilities and Hope*. Toronto: HarperCollins, 2011.

Analogue University. "Control, Resistance, and the 'Data University': Towards a Third Wave Critique." AntipodeFoundation.org, March 31, 2017. https:// antipodefoundation.org/2017/03/31/control-resistance-and-the-data -university/.

Angwin, Julia, Jeff Larson, Lauren Kirchner, and Surya Mattu. "Machine Bias." *ProPublica*, accessed June 20, 2016. https://www.propublica.org/article /machine-bias-risk-assessments-in-criminal-sentencing.

Atanasoski, Neda, and Kalindi Vora. "Surrogate Humanity: Posthuman Networks and the (Racialized) Obsolescence of Labor." *Catalyst: Feminism, Theory, Technoscience* 1, no. 1 (2015): n.p.

Bailey, Marlon M. *Butch Queens Up in Pumps: Gender, Performance, and Ballroom Culture in Detroit*. Ann Arbor: University of Michigan Press, 2013.

Bakker, Karen. "Katrina: The Public Transcript of Disaster." *Environment and Planning D: Society and Space* 23, no. 6 (2005): 796–802.

Banks, Taunya Lovell. "Still Drowning in Segregation: Limits of Law in Post–Civil Rights America." *Law and Inequality* 32, no. 2 (Summer 2014): 215–255.

Bannerji, Himani. "Returning the Gaze: An Introduction." In *Returning the Gaze: Essays on Racism, Feminism, and Politics*, edited by Himani Banerjee, ix–xxix. Toronto: Sister Vision, 1994.

Baucom, Ian. *Specters of the Atlantic: Finance Capital, Slavery, and the Philosophy of History*. Durham, NC: Duke University Press, 2005.

Benjamin, Ruha. *Race After Technology: Abolitionist Tools for the New Jim Code*. Cambridge: Polity, 2019.

Benjamin, Walter. "Unpacking My Library." In *Walter Benjamin: Illuminations,* edited by Hannah Arendt, translated by Harry Zohn, 59–67. New York: Schocken Books, 1968.

Bennett, Matthew. "Drexciya Interview: The Anonymous Protagonists of Detroit Electro." *Clash Music,* May 12, 2012. http://clashmusic.com/features /drexciya-interview.

Berlant, Lauren Gail. *The Female Complaint: The Unfinished Business of Sentimentality in American Culture.* Durham, NC: Duke University Press, 2008.

Biko, Steve. "The Definition of Black Consciousness." In *I Write What I Like: Selected Writings.* 1978. Reprint, Chicago: University of Chicago Press, 2002.

Birchmeier, Jason. "James Marcel Stinson | Biography and History." *AllMusic,* accessed January 8, 2017. https://www.allmusic.com/artist/james-marcel -stinson-mn0001315741/biography.

Bloom, Harold. *The Western Canon: The Books and School of the Ages.* New York: Harcourt Brace, 1994.

Boggs, Abigail, and Nick Mitchell. "Critical University Studies and the Crisis Consensus." *Feminist Studies* 44, no. 2 (2018): 432–463.

Brand, Dionne. *Bread out of Stone: Recollections, Sex, Recognitions, Race, Dreaming, Politics.* Toronto: Coach House Press, 1995.

Brand, Dionne. *Inventory.* Toronto: McClelland & Stewart, 2006.

Brand, Dionne. "Jazz." In *Bread out of Stone: Recollections, Sex, Recognitions, Race, Dreaming, Politics.* Toronto: Coach House Press, 1995.

Brand, Dionne. *Land to Light On.* Toronto: McClelland & Stewart, 1997.

Brand, Dionne. *A Map to the Door of No Return: Notes to Belonging.* Toronto: Vintage, 2002.

Brand, Dionne. *Ossuaries.* Toronto: McClelland & Stewart, 2010.

Braun, Bruce, and James McCarthy. "Hurricane Katrina and Abandoned Being." *Environment and Planning D: Society and Space* 23, no. 6 (December 2005): 795–809.

Braun, Lundy. *Breathing Race into the Machine: The Surprising Career of the Spirometer From Plantation to Genetics.* Minneapolis: University of Minnesota Press, 2014.

Bremser, Martha, and Lorna Sanders. *Fifty Contemporary Choreographers.* New York: Routledge, 2011.

Brown, Jacqueline Nassy. *Dropping Anchor, Setting Sail: Geographies of Race in Black Liverpool.* Princeton, NJ: Princeton University Press, 2009.

Brown, Jacqueline Nassy. "Stuart Hall's Geographic Refusals: A Response to Katherine McKittrick." Paper presented at Stuart Hall: Geographies of Resistance, CUNY GC, New York, March 26, 2015.

Brown, Wendy. *Undoing the Demos: Neoliberalism's Stealth Revolution.* New York: Zone Books, 2015.

Browne, Simone. *Dark Matters: On the Surveillance of Blackness.* Durham, NC: Duke University Press, 2015.

Butler, Judith. "After Loss: What Then?" In *Loss: The Politics of Mourning,* edited by David L. Eng and David Kazanjian. Los Angeles: University of California Press, 2003.

Butler, Judith. *Excitable Speech: A Politics of the Performative*. New York: Routledge, 1997.

Butler, Octavia. *Kindred*. New York: Doubleday, 1979.

Butler, Octavia. *Parable of the Sower*. New York: Time Warner, 1993.

Butler, Octavia. *Patternmaster*. New York: Avon, 1976.

Cadwalladr, Carole. "The Great British Brexit Robbery: How Our Democracy Was Hijacked." *Guardian*, May 7, 2017. https://www.theguardian.com /technology/2017/may/07/the-great-british-brexit-robbery-hijacked -democracy.

Campbell, Mark V. "Connect the T.Dots—Remix Multiculturalism: After Caribbean-Canadian, Social Possibilities for Living Difference." In *Ebony Roots, Northern Soil: Perspectives on Blackness in Canada*, edited by Charmaine Nelson, 254–276. Cambridge: Cambridge Scholars Publishing, 2010.

Campbell, Mark V. "Everything's Connected: A Relationality Remix, a Praxis." *C. L. R. James Journal* 20, no. 1 (2014): 97–114.

Campbell, Mark V. "Sonic Intimacies: On Djing Better Futures." *Decolonization: Indigeneity, Education and Society*, March 25, 2015. https://decolonization .wordpress.com/2015/03/25/sonic-intimacies-on- djing-better-futures/.

Carby, Hazel V. *Imperial Intimacies: A Tale of Two Islands*. London: Verso, 2019.

Carby, Hazel V. *Race Men*. Cambridge, MA: Harvard University Press, 1998.

Cárdenas, Micha. "Trans of Color Poetics: Stitching Bodies, Concepts, and Algorithms." *Scholar and Feminist Online* 3.13–4.1 (2016). doi:http://sfonline .barnard.edu/traversing-technologies/micha-cardenas-trans-of-color -poetics-stitching-bodies-concepts-and-algorithms/.

Carrington, André M. *Speculative Blackness: The Future of Race in Science Fiction*. Minneapolis: University of Minnesota Press, 2016.

Carswell, Andrew T. *The Encyclopedia of Housing*. London: Sage, 2012.

Carter, Perry, David L. Butler, and Derek H. Alderman. "The House That Story Built: The Place of Slavery in Plantation Museum Narratives." *Professional Geographer* 66, no. 4 (2014): 547–557.

Castree, Noel, Rob Kitchin, and Alisdair Rogers. *Dictionary of Human Geography*. Oxford: Oxford University Press, 2013.

Césaire, Aimé. "Demeure I." In *Solar Throat Slashed*, edited and translated by A. James Arnold and Clayton Eshleman, 36. Middletown, CT: Wesleyan University Press, 2011.

Césaire, Aimé. *Discourse on Colonialism*. Translated by Joan Pinkham. 1955. Reprint, New York: Monthly Review Press, 2000.

Césaire, Aimé. "Poetry and Knowledge." In *Lyric and Dramatic Poetry*, translated by Clayton Eshleman and Annette Smith, xlii–lvi. Charlottesville: University Press of Virginia, 1990.

Chandler, Dana, Steven D. Levitt, and John A. List. "Predicting and Preventing Shootings among At-Risk Youth." *American Economic Review* 101, no. 3 (2011): 288–292.

Chandler, Nahum. *X—The Problem of the Negro as a Problem for Thought.* New York: Fordham University Press, 2014.

Christian, Barbara. "The Race for Theory." *Feminist Studies* 14, no. 1 (Spring 1998): 67–79.

Chuh, Kandice. *Imagine Otherwise: On Asian Americanist Critique.* Durham, NC: Duke University Press, 2003.

Chun, Wendy. "On 'Sourcery,' or Code as Fetish." *Configurations* 16, no. 3 (Fall 2008): 299–324.

Clark, VèVè. "Developing Diaspora Literacy: Allusion in Maryse Condé's *Hérémakhonon.*" In *Out of the Kumbla: Caribbean Women and Literature,* edited by Carole Boyce Davies and Elaine Savory Fido, 303–319. Trenton, NJ: Africa World Press, 1990.

Clark, William. *Academic Charisma and the Origins of the Research University.* Chicago: University of Chicago Press, 2006.

Cliff, Jimmy. "Many Rivers to Cross." On *The Harder They Come.* Island Records, 1972, CD.

Clifford, Nicholas, and Gill Valentine, eds. *Key Methods in Geography.* London: Sage, 2003.

Cole, Teju. "Double Negative." In *Known and Strange Things,* 69–73. New York: Random House, 2016.

Collins, Patricia Hill. *Black Feminist Thought: Knowledge, Consciousness, and the Politics of Empowerment.* 1990. Reprint, New York: Routledge, 2000.

Collinson, Diané. *Fifty Major Philosophers.* London: Routledge, 1988.

Collinson, Diané, Kathryn Plant, and Robert Wilkinson. *Fifty Eastern Thinkers.* London: Routledge, 2001.

Cornew, Lauren, Karen R. Dobkins, Natacha Akshoomoff, Joseph P. McCleery, and Leslie J. Carver. "Atypical Social Referencing in Infant Siblings of Children with Autism Spectrum Disorders." *Journal of Autism and Developmental Disorders* 42, no. 12 (2012): 2611–2621.

Crang, Philip, Claire Dwyer, and Peter Jackson. "Transnationalism and the Spaces of Commodity Culture." *Progress in Human Geography* 27, no. 4 (2003): 438–456.

Crenshaw, Kimberlé. "Mapping the Margins: Intersectionality, Identity Politics, and Violence against Women of Color." *Stanford Law Review* 43, no. 6 (1991): 1241–1299.

Daigle, Michelle. "The Spectacle of Reconciliation: On (the) Unsettling Responsibilities to Indigenous Peoples in the Academy." *Environment and Planning D: Society and Space* (January 2019): 1–19.

Dantzig, Tobias. *Number: The Language of Science.* 1930. Reprint, New York: Plume, 2007.

Davies, Carole Boyce. "From Masquerade to Maskarade: Caribbean Cultural Resistance and the Rehumanizing Project." In *Sylvia Wynter: On Being Hu-*

man as Praxis, edited by Katherine McKittrick, 203–225. Durham, NC: Duke University Press, 2015.

Davies, Carole Boyce. *Left of Karl Marx: The Political Life of Black Communist Claudia Jones*. Durham, NC: Duke University Press, 2007.

Davies, Carole Boyce, and Babacar M'Bow. "Towards African Diaspora Citizenship: Politicizing an Existing Global Geography." In *Black Geographies and the Politics of Place*, edited by Katherine McKittrick and Clyde Woods, 14–45. Toronto: Between the Lines Press, 2007.

Davis, Angela. *Women, Race, and Class*. New York: Vintage, 1982.

Davis, Betty. "They Say I'm Different." On *They Say I'm Different*. Seattle: Light in the Attic Records, 1974, CD.

Derr, Patrick George, and Edward M. McNamara. *Case Studies in Environmental Ethics*. New York: Rowman and Littlefield, 2003.

Doctorow, Cory. "Blackballed by Machine Learning: How Algorithms Can Destroy Your Chances of Getting a Job." *BoingBoing*, September 8, 2016. https://boingboing.net/2016/09/08/blackballed-by-machine-learnin.html.

Drexciya. *Harnessed the Storm*. Tresor Records, 2002, CD.

Drexciya. "Wavejumper." On *The Quest*. Submerge, 1997, CD.

Du Bois, W. E. B. *Black Reconstruction in America, 1860–1880*. New York: Atheneum, 1935, 1992.

Du Bois, W. E. B. *The Souls of Black Folk*. 1903. Reprint, New York: Vintage, 1990.

Du Bois, W. E. B. "The Study of the Negro Problems." *Annals of the American Academy of Political and Social Science* 11 (February 1898): 1–23.

Edwards, Ezekiel. "Predictive Policing Software Is More Accurate at Predicting Policing." *Huffington Post*, August 31, 2016. http://www.huffingtonpost.com/entry/predictive-policing-reform_us_57c6ffe0e4b0e60d31dc9120:.

Elliott, Missy. "Work It (Official Video)." YouTube video, 4:25, posted October 26, 2009. https://www.youtube.com/watch?v=cjIvu7e6Wq8.

Ellison, Treva, C., and Romi (Ron) Morrison. "Decoding Possibilities: An Alluvial Map of Black Feminist Praxis." Paper presented at Black Geographies: A Symposium, University of California, Berkeley, October 12, 2017.

ESG. "Moody." On *A South Bronx Story*. Universal Sound, 2000, CD.

Eshun, Kodwo. "Further Considerations of Afrofuturism." *CR: The New Centennial Review* 3, no. 2 (2003): 287–302.

Eudell, Demetrius. "Afterword: Toward Aimé Césaire's 'Humanism Made to the Measure of the World': Reading *The Hills of Hebron* in the Context of Sylvia Wynter's Later Work." In Sylvia Wynter, *The Hills of Hebron*, 311–340. 1962. Reprint, Kingston, Jamaica: Ian Randle, 2010.

Evans, G. R. *Fifty Key Medieval Thinkers*. London: Routledge, 2006.

Fama, Amanda. "Beauty Contest Regrets Using Robots for Judges after Only White People Win." *Elite Daily*, September 9, 2016.

Fanon, Frantz. *Black Skin, White Masks*. Translated by Charles Lam Markmann. 1952. Reprint, New York: Grove, 1967.

Fanon, Frantz. *Black Skin, White Masks*. Translated by Richard Philcox. 1952. Reprint, New York: Grove, 2008.

Fanon, Frantz. *Peau noire, masques blancs*. Paris: Éditions Du Seuil, 1952.

Fanon, Frantz. *The Wretched of the Earth*. Translated by Constance Farrington. New York: Grove, 1963.

Fausto-Sterling, Anne. *Myths of Gender: Biological Theories about Women and Men*. New York: Basic Books, 1985.

Fehskens, Erin McMullen. "Accounts Unpaid, Accounts Untold: M. NourbeSe Philip's *Zong!* and the Catalogue." *Callaloo* 35, no. 2 (2012): 407–424.

Ferguson, Andrew Guthrie. "Predictive Policing and Reasonable Suspicion." *Emory Law Journal* 259 (2012): 261–313.

Ferguson, Roderick A. *The Reorder of Things: The University and Its Pedagogies of Minority Difference*. Minneapolis: University of Minnesota Press, 2012.

Fitzgerald, Ella. "My Happiness." CD. Brunswick, 1958.

Flack, Roberta. "The First Time Ever I Saw Your Face." On *First Take*. Atlantic, 1972, CD.

Forde, Kate. "Ellen Gallagher." *Frieze*, no. 124 (June–August 2009): 189.

Forman, Murray. "'Represent': Race, Space, and Place in Rap Music." In *That's the Joint! The Hip-Hop Studies Reader*, 2nd ed., edited by Murray Foreman and Mark Anthony Neal, 247–269. New York: Routledge, 2011.

Gaerig, Andrew. "Drexciya: Journey of the Deep Sea Dweller II." *Pitchfork*, May 31, 2012. http://pitchfork.com/reviews/albums/16678-journey-of-the -deep-sea-dweller-ii/.

Gallagher, Ellen. *Coral Cities*. London: Tate Publishing, 2007.

Gaskins, Nettrice R. "Deep Sea Dwellers: Drexciya and the Sonic Third Space." *Shima* 10, no. 2 (2016): 68–80.

Georgis, Dina. *Better Story: Queer Affects from the Middle East*. Albany: SUNY Press, 2013.

Gershgorn, Dave. "It's Getting Tougher to Tell If You're on the Phone with a Machine or Human." *Quartz*, September 9, 2016. https://qz.com/778056 /google-deepminds-wavenet-algorithm-can-accurately-mimic-human -voices/.

Gilmore, Ruth Wilson. "Abolition Geography and the Problem of Innocence." In *Futures of Black Radicalism*, edited by Alex Lubin and Gaye Theresa Johnson, 225–240. New York: Verso, 2017.

Gilmore, Ruth Wilson. "Fatal Couplings of Power and Difference: Notes on Racism and Geography." *Professional Geographer* 54, no. 1 (2002): 15–24.

Gilmore, Ruth Wilson. *Golden Gulag: Prisons, Surplus, Crisis, and Opposition in Globalizing California*. Berkeley: University of California Press, 2007.

Gilmore, Ruth Wilson. "Introduction." In *Development Arrested: The Blues and Plantation Power in the Mississippi Delta*, by Clyde Woods, xi–xiv. 2nd ed. London: Verso, 2007.

Gilroy, Paul. *Against Race: Imagining Political Culture beyond the Color Line*. Cambridge, MA: Harvard University Press, 2000.

Gilroy, Paul. *Between Camps: Nations, Cultures and the Allure of Race*. London: Allen Lane, 2000.

Gilroy, Paul. *The Black Atlantic: Modernity and Double Consciousness*. Cambridge, MA: Harvard University Press, 1993.

Gilroy-Ware, Marcus. *Filling the Void: Emotion, Capitalism, and Social Media*. London: Repeater Books, 2017.

Glissant, Édouard. *Caribbean Discourse: Selected Essays*. Translated by J. Michael Dash. Charlottesville: University Press of Virginia, 1999.

Glissant, Édouard. *Poetics of Relation*. Translated by Betsy Wing. 1990. Reprint, Ann Arbor: University of Michigan Press, 1997.

Gordon, Avery. *Ghostly Matters: Haunting and the Sociological Imagination*. Minneapolis: University of Minnesota Press, 1997.

Gordon, Avery. *The Hawthorn Archive: Letters from the Utopian Margins*. New York: Fordham University Press, 2018.

Grafton, Anthony. *The Footnote: A Curious History*. Cambridge, MA: Harvard University Press, 1999.

Gray, Michael. *The Bob Dylan Encyclopedia*. London: Continuum, 2006.

Greengard, Samuel. "Policing the Future." *Communications of the ACM* 55, no. 3 (March 01, 2012): 19–21. doi:10.1145/2093548.2093555.

Gregory, Derek. *Geographical Imaginations*. Oxford: Blackwell, 1994.

Gregory, Derek, Ron Johnston, Geraldine Pratt, Michael J. Watts, and Sarah Whatmore, eds. *The Dictionary of Human Geography*. Oxford: Wiley, 2009.

Griffiths, Martin. *Fifty Key Thinkers in International Relations*. London: Routledge, 1999.

Hall, Stuart. "Cultural Identity and Diaspora." In *Contemporary Postcolonial Theory: A Reader*, edited by Padmini Mongia, 110–121. London: Arnold, 1996.

Hall, Stuart. "Signification, Representation, Ideology: Althusser and the Post-Structuralist Debates." *Critical Studies in Mass Communication* 2, no. 2 (1985): 91–114.

Hammonds, Evelynn, and Banu Subramaniam. "A Conversation on Feminist Science Studies." *Signs: Journal of Women in Culture and Society* 28, no. 3 (Spring 2003): 923–944.

Han, Jiawei, and Micheline Kamber. *Data Mining: Concepts and Techniques*. Burlington, MA: Morgan Kaufmann, 2001.

Haqq, Abdullah. "The Book of Drexciya, Volume One." Accessed January 29, 2019. https://www.indiegogo.com/projects/the-book-of-drexciya-volume-one#/.

Haraway, Donna. *Primate Visions: Gender, Race, and Nature in the World of Modern Science*. New York: Routledge, 1989.

Haraway, Donna. *Simians, Cyborgs, and Women: The Reinvention of Nature*. New York: Routledge, 1991.

Harcourt, Bernard. *Against Prediction: Profiling, Policing, and Punishment in an Actuarial Age*. Chicago: University of Chicago Press, 2007.

Harding, Sandra, ed. *The "Racial" Economy of Science: Toward a Democratic Future*. Bloomington: Indiana University Press, 1993.

Harding, Sandra G. *Whose Science? Whose Knowledge? Thinking from Women's Lives*. Ithaca, NY: Cornell University Press, 1991.

Harris, Cheryl I. "Whiteness as Property." *Harvard Law Review* 106, no. 8 (1993): 1707–1791.

Hartman, Saidiya V. *Scenes of Subjection: Terror, Slavery, and Self-Making in Nineteenth-Century America*. New York: Oxford University Press, 1997.

Hartman, Saidiya. "Venus in Two Acts." *Small Axe* 12, no. 2 (June 2008): 1–14.

Harvey, David. *Key Concepts in Geography*. London: Edward Arnold, 1973.

Henderson, Louis. "Black Code/Code Noir." *Khiasma*, June 2016. http://www .khiasma.net/magazine/black-codecode-noir/.

Herrnstein, Richard J., and Charles A. Murray. *The Bell Curve: Intelligence and Class Structure in American Life*. New York: Free Press, 1994.

Holiday, Billie. "Strange Fruit." Commodore, 1939, CD.

Holloway, Karla F. C. *Private Bodies, Public Texts: Race, Gender and a Cultural Bioethics*. Durham, NC: Duke University Press, 2011.

Holloway, Sarah, Stephen Rice, and Gill Valentine, eds. *Key Concepts in Geography*. London: Sage, 2003.

Howard, Edward. "Liner Notes for Donny Hathaway." *Extension of a Man*. New York: Atco, 1973.

Hubbard, Phil, Rob Kitchin, and Gill Valentine, eds. *Key Thinkers on Space and Place*. London: Sage, 2004.

Hull, Gloria T., Patricia Bell-Scott, and Barbara Smith. *All the Women Are White, All the Blacks Are Men, but Some of Us Are Brave*. New York: Feminist Press at the City University of New York, 1982.

Hurston, Zora Neale. *Dust Tracks on a Road: An Autobiography*. 1942. Reprint, New York: HarperCollins, 1991.

Hurston, Zora Neale. *Mules and Men*. 1935. Reprint, New York: HarperCollins, 1990.

Hurston, Zora Neale. *Their Eyes Were Watching God*. 1937. Reprint, New York: HarperCollins, 1990.

Iton, Richard. *In Search of the Black Fantastic: Politics and Popular Culture in the Post–Civil Rights Era*. Oxford: Oxford University Press, 2008.

Iton, Richard. *Solidarity Blues: Race, Culture, and the American Left*. Chapel Hill: University of North Carolina Press, 2000.

Iton, Richard. "Still Life." *Small Axe* 17, no. 1 (2013): 22–39.

J Dilla. *Donuts*. Stone's Throw, 2006, CD.

J Dilla. "One Eleven." On *Donuts*. Stone's Throw, 2006, CD.

James, C. L. R. *American Civilization*. Oxford: Blackwell, 1992.

James, C. L. R. *Beyond a Boundary*. 1963. Reprint, Durham, NC: Duke University Press, 1993.

James, Joy. *Shadowboxing: Representations of Black Feminist Politics*. New York: Palgrave, 1999.

James, Robin. "Affective Resonance: On the Uses and Abuses of Music in and for Philosophy." *PhaenEx* 7, no. 2 (2012): 59–95.

James, Robin. *Resilience and Melancholy: Pop Music, Feminism, Neoliberalism.* Winchester and Washington: Zero Books, 2015.

Jones, Gayl. *Corregidora.* Boston: Beacon, 1975.

Jones, Gayl. *Eva's Man.* Boston: Beacon, 1976.

Jones, Grace. "Jones to the Rhythm." On *Slave to the Rhythm.* New York: Island Records, 1985, CD.

Jones, Grace. "Slave to the Rhythm—Live AVO Session." YouTube video, 8:33, posted June 26, 2010. https://www.youtube.com/watch?v=yPHmJLRFv8c.

Jordan, June. "Inaugural Rose." In *Directed by Desire: The Collected Poems of June Jordan*, edited by Jan Heller Levi and Sara Miles, 297. Port Townsend, WA: Copper Canyon Press, 2007.

Jordan, June. "My Sadness Sits around Me." In *The Black Poets*, edited by Dudley Randall, 248. New York: Bantam, 1971.

Jordan, June. "The Test of Atlanta." In *Directed by Desire: The Collected Poems of June Jordan*, edited by Jan Heller Levi and Sara Miles, 390–391. Port Townsend, WA: Copper Canyon Press, 2007.

Kahn, Andrew, and Jamelle Bouie. "The Atlantic Slave Trade in Two Minutes." *Slate*, June 25, 2015. http://www.slate.com/articles/life/the_history_of_american_slavery/2015/06/animated_interactive_of_the_history_of_the_atlantic_slave_trade.html.

Katz, Cindi. "Towards Minor Theory." *Environment and Planning D: Society and Space* 14, no. 4 (1996): 487–499.

Kay, Jackie. "Chapter Five: The Tweed Hat Dream." In *The Adoption Papers*, 19. Newcastle upon Tyne, UK: Bloodaxe Books, 1991.

Keeling, Kara. *The Witch's Flight: The Cinematic, The Black Femme, and the Image of Common Sense.* Durham, NC: Duke University Press, 2007.

Keene, John. *Annotations.* New York: New Directions, 1995.

Keene, John. *Counternarratives: Stories and Novellas.* New York: New Directions, 2015.

Kelley, Robin D. G. *Freedom Dreams: The Black Radical Imagination.* Boston: Beacon, 2002.

Kelley, Robin D. G. *Yo' Mama's Disfunktional! Fighting the Culture Wars in Urban America.* Boston: Beacon, 1997.

Kennedy, Leslie W., Joel M. Caplan, and Eric Piza. "Risk Clusters, Hotspots, and Spatial Intelligence: Risk Terrain Modeling as an Algorithm for Police Resource Allocation Strategies." *Journal of Quantitative Criminology* 27, no. 3 (2010): 339–362.

Khan Academy Computing. "What Is an Algorithm and Why Should You Care?" Khan Academy, accessed May 19, 2016. https://www.khanacademy.org/computing/computer-science/algorithms/intro-to-algorithms/v/what-are-algorithms.

King, Joyce E., and Sylvia Wynter. "'Race and Our Biocentric Belief System:

An Interview with Sylvia Wynter." In *Black Education: A Transformative Research and Action Agenda for the New Century,* edited by Joyce E. King, 361–366. Washington: American Educational Research Association, 2005.

Koopman, Colin. "The Algorithm and the Watchtower." *New Inquiry,* September 29, 2015. https://thenewinquiry.com/the-algorithm-and-the-watchtower/.

Kynard, Carmen. *Vernacular Insurrections: Race, Black Protest, and the New Century in Composition-Literacies Studies.* Albany: SUNY Press, 2013.

Lacharité, Yaniya Lee. "When and Where We Enter: Situating the Absented Presence of Black Canadian Art." MA thesis, Queen's University, March 2019.

Larsen, Nella. *Quicksand.* New York: Penguin, 1928.

Lechte, John. *Fifty Key Contemporary Thinkers: From Structuralism to Postmodernity.* London: Routledge, 1994.

Levary, David, Jean-Pierre Eckmann, Elisha Moses, and Tsvi Tlusty. "Loops and Self-Reference in the Construction of Dictionaries." *Physical Review X* 2, no. 3 (2012). https://journals.aps.org/prx/abstract/10.1103/PhysRevX.2.031018.

Levenstein, Rachel, Sue Sporte, and Elaine Allensworth. "Findings from an Investigation into the Culture of Calm Initiative." University of Chicago Consortium on School Research, accessed May 27, 2016. https://consortium.uchicago.edu/publications/findings-investigation-culture-calm-initiative.

Levitin, Daniel J. *This Is Your Brain on Music: The Science of a Human Obsession.* New York: Plume, 2007.

Lil' Kim. "Big Momma Thang." On *Hard Core.* Lil' Kim. Big Beat Records, 1997, CD.

Lindsay, Antoin. "Delving into the Drexciyan Deep: The Essential James Stinson." Thump. September 3, 2015. https://thump.vice.com/en_ca/article/8q7nnb/delving-into-the-drexciyan-deep-the-essential-james-stinson.

Lindsey, Treva, and Jessica Marie Johnson. "Searching for Climax: Black Erotic Lives in Slavery and Freedom." *Meridian* 12, no. 2 (2014): 169–195.

Lorde, Audre. "Letter to Mary Daly." In *Sister Outsider: Essays and Speeches,* 68. 1984. Reprint, Berkeley, CA: Crossing Press, 2007.

Lorde, Audre. *Sister Outsider: Essays and Speeches.* Berkeley, CA: Crossing Press, 1984.

Lorde, Audre. "Uses of the Erotic as Power." In *Sister Outsider: Essays and Speeches,* by Audre Lorde, 53–59. Berkeley, CA: Crossing Press, 1984.

Lowe, Lisa. *The Intimacies of Four Continents.* Durham, NC: Duke University Press, 2015.

Luhmann, Niklas. *Social Systems.* Translated by J. Bednarz Jr. and D. Baekker. Stanford, CA: Stanford University Press, 1995.

Lundin, Emma. "Could an Algorithm Replace the Pill?" *Guardian,* November 7, 2016.

Macharia, Keguro. "On Being Area-Studied." *GLQ: A Journal of Lesbian and Gay Studies* 22, no. 2 (2016): 183–189.

Manning, Erin. *The Minor Gesture.* Durham, NC: Duke University Press, 2016.

Martínez, Ernesto Javier. "On Butler on Morrison on Language." *Signs: Journal of Women in Culture and Society* 35, no. 4 (2010): 821–842.

Maturana, Humberto R., and Francisco J. Varela. *Autopoiesis and Cognition: The Realization of the Living*. London: D. Reidel, 1972.

McKay, Sally. "On the Brain." *Canadian Art* 35, no. 4 (Winter 2018): 62–63.

McKittrick, Katherine. "bell hooks." In *Key Thinkers on Space and Place*, edited by Phil Hubbard, Rob Kitchin, and Gil Valentine, 189–194. London: Sage, 2004.

McKittrick, Katherine. *Demonic Grounds: Black Women and the Cartographies of Struggle*. Minneapolis: University of Minnesota Press, 2006.

McKittrick, Katherine. "Diachronic Loops/Deadweight Tonnage/Bad Made Measure." *Cultural Geographies*, December 2015, 1–16.

McKittrick, Katherine. "Diaspora." In *International Encyclopedia of Human Geography*, edited by Rob Kitchin and Nigel Thrift, 156–161. London: Elsevier, 2009.

McKittrick, Katherine. "Fantastic/Still/Life: On Richard Iton (A Working Paper)." *Contemporary Political Theory*, February 2015, 24–32.

McKittrick, Katherine. "I Entered the Lists . . . Diaspora Catalogues: The List, the Unbearable Territory, and Tormented Chronologies—Three Narratives and a Weltanschauung." *XCP: Cross Cultural Poetics* 17 (2007): 7–29.

McKittrick, Katherine. "Mathematics Black Life." *Black Scholar* 44, no. 2 (Summer 2014): 16–28.

McKittrick, Katherine. "On Plantations, Prisons, and a Black Sense of Place." *Journal of Social and Cultural Geography* 12, no. 8 (2011): 947–963.

McKittrick, Katherine. "Plantation Futures." *Small Axe* 17, no. 3 (November 2013): 1–15.

McKittrick, Katherine, and Alexander Weheliye. "808s and Heartbreak." *Propter Nos* 2, no. 1 (Fall 2017): 13–43.

McKittrick, Katherine, and Clyde Woods. "No One Knows the Mysteries at the Bottom of the Ocean." In *Black Geographies and the Politics of Place*, edited by Clyde Woods and Katherine McKittrick, 1–13. Toronto: Between the Lines Press, 2007.

McKittrick, Katherine, and Sylvia Wynter. "Unparalleled Catastrophe for Our Species? Or, to Give Humanness a Different Future: Conversations." In *Sylvia Wynter: On Being Human as Praxis*, 9–89. Durham, NC: Duke University Press, 2015.

Mercer, Kobena. "Decolonization and Disappointment: Reading Fanon's Sexual Politics." In *The Fact of Blackness: Frantz Fanon and Visual Representation*, edited by Alan Read, 114–130. Seattle: Bay Press, 1996.

Miller, Paul D., aka DJ Spooky That Subliminal Kid. *Rhythm Science*. Cambridge, MA: MIT Press, 2004.

Mohanty, Chandra Talpade. "Under Western Eyes: Feminist Scholarship and Colonial Discourses." *boundary 2* 12, no. 3, and 13, no. 1 (1984): 333–358.

Mollett, Sharlene. "The Power to Plunder: Rethinking Land Grabbing in Latin America." *Antipode* 48, no. 2 (2015): 412–432.

Monroe Work Today. Accessed December 21, 2018. http://www.monroework today.org/index.html?u=2.

Moore, W. G. *The Penguin Dictionary of Geography*. New York: Penguin, 1978.

Morgan, Jennifer L. *Laboring Women: Reproduction and Gender in New World Slavery*. Philadelphia: University of Pennsylvania Press, 2004.

Morrison, Toni. *Beloved*. New York: Plume, 1987.

Morrison, Toni. "Disturbing Nurses and the Kindness of Sharks." In *Playing in the Dark: Whiteness and the Literary Imagination*, 62–91. New York: Random House, 1990.

Morrison, Toni. *Jazz*. New York: Alfred A. Knopf, 1992.

Moten, Fred. *In the Break: The Aesthetics of the Black Radical Tradition*. Minneapolis: University of Minnesota Press, 2003.

Mott, Carrie, and Daniel Cockayne. "Citation Matters: Mobilizing the Politics of Citation Toward a Practice of 'Conscientious Engagement.'" *Gender, Place and Culture* 24, no. 7 (2017): 954–973.

Nabokov, Vladimir. *Pale Fire*. New York: Vintage, 1989.

Nagar, Richa. *Muddying the Waters: Coauthoring Feminisms across Scholarship and Activism*. Urbana: University of Illinois Press, 2014.

Nelson, Alondra. "Bio Science: Genetic Genealogy Testing and the Pursuit of African Ancestry.'" *Social Studies of Science* 38, no. 5 (2008): 759–783.

Nelson, Alondra. *The Social Life of DNA: Race, Reparations, and Reconciliation after the Genome*. Boston: Beacon, 2016.

Niaah, Sonjah Stanley. *DanceHall: From Slave Ship to Ghetto*. Ottawa: University of Ottawa Press, 2010.

Noble, David. *A World without Women: The Christian Clerical Culture of Western Science*. Oxford: Oxford University Press, 1992.

O'Neil, Cathy. *Weapons of Math Destruction: How Big Data Increases Inequality and Threatens Democracy*. New York: Crown, 2016.

Patel, Aniruddh D. *Music, Language, and the Brain*. Oxford: Oxford University Press, 2010.

Perry, Walt L., Brian McInnis, Carter C. Price, Susan C. Smith, and John S. Hollywood. *Predictive Policing: The Role of Crime Forecasting in Law Enforcement Operations*. Santa Monica, CA: Rand, 2013.

Philip, M. NourbeSe. "Lessons for the Voice (1)." In *She Tries Her Tongue, Her Silence Softly Breaks*, by M. NourbeSe Philip, 72. Charlottetown, Canada: Ragweed Press, 1989.

Philip, M. NourbeSe. *A Genealogy of Resistance: And Other Essays*. Toronto: Mercury Press, 1997.

Philip, M. NourbeSe. *She Tries Her Tongue, Her Silence Softly Breaks*. Charlottetown, Canada: Ragweed Press, 1989.

Philip, M. NourbeSe. *Zong!* Toronto: Mercury Press, 2008.

Piccinini, Gualtiero. "Alan Turing and the Mathematical Objection." *Minds and Machines* 13 (2003): 23–48.

PredPol. "About Us." Accessed February 1, 2017. http://www.predpol.com/about/.

Preziuso, Marika. "M. NourbeSe Philip—Zong!" Latineos.com, accessed December 22, 2013. http://latineos.com/articulos/literatura/item/46-m-NourbeSe-philip-zong.html?lang=es.

Prince. "F.U.N.K." NPG Digital, 2007. Digital.

Prince. "Housequake." On *Sign o' the Times*. Paisley Park/Warner Brothers, 1987, CD.

Prince. "Love." On *3121*. NPG/Universal, 2007, CD.

Queen's University. "Queen's Learning Outcomes Assessment." Queen's University, Canada, accessed March 20, 2018. http://www.queensu.ca/qloa/home.

Ranganathan, Malini. "Thinking with Flint: Racial Liberalism and the Roots of an American Water Tragedy." *Capitalism Nature Socialism* 27, no. 3 (2016): 17–33.

Reel, Monte. "Chronicle of a Death Foretold: Predicting Murder on Chicago's South Side." *Harper's Magazine*, March 2014, 43–51.

Rennicks, Stephen. "The Primer." *Wire*, 321 (November 2010): 32.

Roberts, Dorothy. *Fatal Invention: How Science, Politics, and Big Business Recreate Race in the Twenty-First Century*. New York: New Press, 2011.

Rose, Nikolas. "At Risk of Madness." In *Embracing Risk: The Changing Culture of Insurance and Responsibility*, edited by Tom Baker and Jonathan Simon, 209–237. Chicago: University of Chicago Press, 2002.

Sacks, Oliver. *Musicophilia: Tales of Music and the Brain*. New York: Knopf, 2012.

Said, Edward W. *Culture and Imperialism*. New York: Vintage, 1993.

Samuels, A. J. "Master Organism: A. J. Samuels Interviews Gerald Donald." *Telekom Electronic Beats*, June 2015. http://www.electronicbeats.net/gerald-donald-interview/.

Sandoval, Chela. *Methodology of the Oppressed*. Minneapolis: University of Minnesota Press, 2000.

Santana, Dora Silva. "Transitionings and Returnings: Experiments with the Poetics of Transatlantic Water." *TSQ: Transgender Studies Quarterly* 4, no. 2 (May 2017): 181–190.

Scannell, R. Joshua. "Broken Windows, Broken Code." *Real Life*. August 29, 2016. http://reallifemag.com/broken-windows-broken-code/.

Scannell, R. Joshua. "What Can an Algorithm Do?" *DIS Magazine*, 2016. http://dismagazine.com/discussion/72975/josh-scannell-what-can-an-algorithm-do/.

Schlack, Sami. *Bodyminds Reimagined: (Dis)ability, Race, and Gender in Black Women's Speculative Fiction*. Durham, NC: Duke University, 2018.

Schneider, Susan, and Max Velmans. "Introduction." In *The Blackwell Companion to Consciousness*, edited by Max Velmans and Susan Schneider, 1–7. Oxford: Blackwell, 2007.

Scott, David. "The Re-enchantment of Humanism: An Interview with Sylvia Wynter." *Small Axe* 8 (September 2000): 119–207.

Silvera, Makeda. *Silenced: Talks with Working Class West Indian Women about Their Lives and Struggles as Domestic Workers in Canada*. Toronto: Sister Vision Press, 1989.

Simone, AbdouMaliq. *Improvised Lives*. Cambridge: Polity, 2019.

Simone, Nina. "Four Women." On *Wild Is the Wind*. Polygram, 1996, CD.

Simone, Nina. "I Got Life." On *Nuff Said*. RCA Studios, 1968, CD.

Sinnreich, Aram. *Mashed Up: Music, Technology, and the Rise of Configurable Culture*. Amherst: University of Massachusetts Press, 2010.

Smith, Malinda. "Gender, Whiteness, and the 'Other Others' in the Academy." In *States of Race: Critical Race Feminism for the 21st Century*, edited by Sherene Razack and Sunera Thobani, 37–58. Toronto: Between the Lines Press, 2010.

Smith, Neil. "There's No Such Thing as a Natural Disaster." Understanding Katrina: Perspectives from the Social Sciences. June 11, 2006. https://items.ssrc.org/understanding-katrina/theres-no-such-thing-as-a-natural-disaster/.

Smith, Neil, and Cindi Katz. "Grounding Metaphor: Towards a Spatialized Politics." In *Place and the Politics of Identity*, edited by Michael Keith and Steve Pile, 67–83. New York: Routledge, 1993.

Smyth, Joshua. "How to Calculate Dead Weight." *Sciencing*, accessed March 25, 2018. https://sciencing.com/calculate-dead-weight-7289046.html.

Spillers, Hortense. "Mama's Baby, Papa's Maybe: An American Grammar Book." In *Black, White, and in Color: Essays on American Literature and Culture*, 203. Chicago: University of Chicago Press, 2003.

Spillers, Hortense. "Mama's Baby, Papa's Maybe: An American Grammar Book." *Diacritics* 17, no. 2 (Summer 1987): 64–81.

Stallings, LaMonda. *Funk the Erotic: Transaesthetics and Black Sexual Cultures*. Urbana: University of Illinois Press, 2015.

Subramaniam, Banu. "Moored Metamorphoses: A Retrospective Essay on Feminist Science Studies." *Signs: Journal of Women in Culture and Society* 34, no. 4 (2009): 951–980.

Tasker, Yvone. *Fifty Contemporary Filmmakers*. London: Routledge, 2002.

Taylor, Christopher. "Plantation Neoliberalism." *New Inquiry*, July 8, 2014. https://thenewinquiry.com/plantation-neoliberalism/.

Thomas, Greg, and Sylvia Wynter. "Yours in the Intellectual Struggle." In *The Caribbean Woman Writer as Scholar*, edited by Keshia N. Abraham, 31–70. Coconut Creek, FL: Caribbean Studies Press, 2009.

Titchkosky, Tanya. "Life with Dead Metaphors: Impairment Rhetoric in Social Justice Praxis." *Journal of Literary and Cultural Disability Studies* 9, no. 1 (2015): 1–18.

Tom Magic Feet. "James Stinson 1969–2002—An Appreciation." *Spannered*, accessed October 7, 2013. http://www.spannered.org/music/774.

Traweek, Sharon. *Beamtimes and Lifetimes: The World of High Energy Physicists*. Cambridge, MA: Harvard University Press, 1992.

TV on the Radio. *Dear Science*. Interscope, 2008, CD.

Unknown Writer. *Liner Notes from Drexciya*. The Quest. Submerge, 1997, CD.

Vergès, François. "Creole Skin, Black Mask: Fanon and Disavowal." *Critical Inquiry* 23, no. 3 (Spring 1997): 578–595.

Walker, Alice. "Looking for Zora." In *In Search of Our Mothers' Gardens: Womanist Prose*, 93–116. New York: Harcourt and Brace, 1983.

Walker, Barrington. *Race on Trial: Black Defendants in Ontario's Criminal Courts*. Toronto: University of Toronto Press, 2010.

Wallace, David Foster. *Infinite Jest: A Novel*. Boston: Little, Brown, 1996.

Walvin, James. *The Zong: A Massacre, the Law, and the End of Slavery*. New Haven, CT: Yale University Press, 2011.

Weheliye, Alexander G. *Habeas Viscus: Racializing Assemblages, Biopolitics, and Black Feminist Theories of the Human*. Durham, NC: Duke University Press, 2014.

Weheliye, Alexander G. *Phonographies: Grooves in Sonic Afro-Modernity*. Durham, NC: Duke University Press, 2005.

Wells-Barnett, Ida B., and Jacqueline Jones Royster. *Southern Horrors and Other Writings: The Anti-Lynching Campaign of Ida B. Wells*. Boston: Bedford/St. Martins, Macmillan Learning, 1996.

West, Kanye. "Hey Mama." On *Late Registration*. Def Jam, 2005, CD.

Wilder, Craig Steven. *Ebony and Ivy: Race, Slavery, and the Troubled History of America's Universities*. New York: Bloomsbury, 2013.

Williams, Justin A. "Theoretical Approaches to Quotation in Hip-Hop Recordings." *Contemporary Music Review* 33, no. 2 (2014): 188–209.

Womack, Ytasha L. *Afrofuturism: The World of Black Sci-Fi and Fantasy Culture*. Chicago: Chicago Review Press, 2013.

Wonder, Stevie. "Sir Duke." On *Songs in the Key of Life*. Detroit: Tamla, 1976, CD.

Woods, Clyde. *Development Arrested: The Blues and Plantation Power in the Mississippi Delta*. London: Verso, 1998.

Wright, Richard. *Native Son*. New York: Signet, 1940.

Wynter, Sylvia. "1492: A New World View." In *Race, Discourse, and the Origin of the Americas: A New World View*, edited by Rex Nettleford and Vera Lawrence Hyatt, 5–57. Washington, DC: Smithsonian Institution Press, 1995.

Wynter, Sylvia. "Africa, the West and the Analogy of Culture: The Cinematic Text after Man." In *Symbolic Narratives/African Cinema: Audiences, Theory and the Moving Image*, edited by June Givanni, 25–76. London: British Film Institute, 2000.

Wynter, Sylvia. "Beyond Miranda's Meanings: Un/Silencing the 'Demonic Ground' of Caliban's 'Woman.'" In *Out of the Kumbla: Caribbean Women and Literature*, edited by Carole Boyce Davies and Elaine Savory Fido, 355–372. Trenton, NJ: Africa World Press, 1990.

Wynter, Sylvia. "Beyond the Categories of the Master Conception: The Counterdoctrine of the Jamesian Poiesis." In *C. L. R. James's Caribbean*, edited by Paget Henry and Paul Buhle, 63–91. Durham, NC: Duke University Press, 1992.

Wynter, Sylvia. "Beyond the Word of Man: Glissant and the New Discourse of the Antilles." *World Literature Today* 63, no. 4 (1989): 637–647.

Wynter, Sylvia. *Black Metamorphosis: New Natives in a New World* (unpublished ms., nd.)

Wynter, Sylvia. "The Ceremony Must Be Found: After Humanism." *boundary 2* 12, no. 3 (1984): 19–70.

Wynter, Sylvia. "Ethno or Socio Poetics." *Alcheringa/Ethnopoetics* 2, no. 2 (1976): 78–94.

Wynter, Sylvia. "The Eye of the Other." In *Blacks in Hispanic Literature: Critical Essays*, edited by Miriam DeCosta, 8–19. New York: Kennikat, 1977.

Wynter, Sylvia. "Is Development a Purely Empirical Concept or Also Teleological? A Perspective from 'We' the Underdeveloped." In *Prospects for Recovery and Sustainable Development in Africa*, edited by Aguibou Y. Yansané, 299–316. Westport, CT: Greenwood, 1996.

Wynter, Sylvia. "Jonkonnu in Jamaica: Towards the Interpretation of Folk Dance as a Cultural Process." *Jamaica Journal* 12 (1970): 34–48.

Wynter, Sylvia. "Maskarade." In *West Indian Plays for Schools*, edited by Sylvia Wynter, Easton Lee, and Enid Chevannes, 26–55. Vol. 2. Kingston: Jamaica Publishing House, 1979.

Wynter, Sylvia. "New Seville and the Conversion Experience of Bartolomé De Las Casas: Part One." *Jamaica Journal* 17, no. 2 (May 1984): 25–32.

Wynter, Sylvia. "New Seville and the Conversion Experience of Bartolomé De Las Casas: Part Two." *Jamaica Journal* 17, no. 3 (October 1984): 46–55.

Wynter, Sylvia. "Novel and History, Plot and Plantation." *Savacou* 5 (1971): 95–102.

Wynter, Sylvia. "On Disenchanting Discourse: 'Minority' Literary Criticism and Beyond." In *The Nature and Context of Minority Discourse*, edited by Abdul R. JanMohamed and David Loyd, 432–469. New York: Oxford University Press, 1990.

Wynter, Sylvia. "One-Love Rhetoric or Reality?—Aspects of Afro-Jamaicanism." *Caribbean Studies* 12, no. 3 (October 1972): 90–97.

Wynter, Sylvia. "On How We Mistook the Map for the Territory, and Reimprisoned Ourselves in Our Unbearable Wrongness of Being, of Désêtr." In *Not Only the Master's Tools: African American Studies in Theory and Practice*, edited by Lewis R. Gordon and Jane Anna Gordon, 107–169. London: Paradigm, 2006.

Wynter, Sylvia. "The Pope Must Have Been Drunk, the King of Castile a Madman: Culture as Actuality, and the Caribbean Rethinking Modernity." In *The Reordering of Culture: Latin America, the Caribbean, and Canada in the Hood*, edited by Alvina Ruprecht and Cecilia Taiana, 17–42. Ottawa: Carleton University Press, 1995.

Wynter, Sylvia. "Rethinking, 'Aesthetics': Notes towards a Deciphering Practice." In *Ex-iles: Essays on Caribbean Cinema*, edited by Mbye Cham, 238–279. Trenton, NJ: Africa World Press, 1992.

Wynter, Sylvia. "Towards the Sociogenic Principle: Fanon, Identity, the Puzzle of Conscious Experience, and What It Is Like to Be 'Black.'" In *National Identities and Sociopolitical Changes in Latin America*, edited by Mercedes F. Durán-Cogan and Antonio Gómez-Moriana, 30–66. New York: Routledge, 2001.

Wynter, Sylvia. "Unsettling the Coloniality of Being/Power/Truth/Freedom: Towards the Human, after Man, Its Overrepresentation—An Argument." *CR: The New Centennial Review* 3, no. 3 (2003): 257–337.

Young, Kevin. *The Grey Album: On the Blackness of Blackness.* Minneapolis: Graywolf, 2012.

belonging: geographic, colonial, planto-graphic, 32–33, 131, 155, 159–60, 161–62, 170; unorthodox belonging and unbe-longing, 5, 140, 169, 170, 172, 175–76, 181–82

Biko, Steve, 66, 70n

biocentricity: algorithms derived from attitudes of, 103–4, 106, 107n, 109–14; as an impetus for colonial behaviors, 27, 38, 153, 154–57, 159–61, 174–76; the assumptions underlying, 2, 126, 130–32, 135; the autopoietic quality of, 2, 126, 128, 132–33, 136; as the basis for justifying racial violence, 127, 148, 154–57; as the basis for racial oppres-sion, 127, 164–65, 174–76; biocentrism versus, 126n; biological determinism as an animating tool of, 45, 58n, 126, 133–35; black cultural production that questions and challenges, 171–77, 165–67, 169–70; black degradation and death as fundamental to, 46, 138, 139, 141–42, 144, 149; capitalism as a com-plement to, 37, 159–60; the Color Line imposed through, 42n–43n; Darwin-ian selection and dysselection, 60, 113, 114, 115, 126, 156; enfleshment, 40, 42n, 45, 49; evolutionary dysselection as an assumption of, 42n–43n, 50, 111, 113, 114, 126–13, 156, 165; fictive truths ema-nating from, 37, 44, 59, 113–14, 132–33, 134, 156, 174; identity-disciplines in academia, 37, 39–41, 44, 45, 49; the institutionalization of racism through, 37, 126–27, 132–33, 139, 143; the linear perspective of, 137–38; the Malthusian narrative, 38, 126; mechanical infra-structures based on, 131; the need to dislodge, 2, 74, 125–29, 186–87; pat-terning and coding as tools of, 106; positivism as a complement to, 59, 127, 139; scientific racism as an animating tool of, 126, 130–31; social construc-tionist arguments, 45, 134, 135, 138, 149. *See also* positivism; racism

biological determinism: as a tool for animating biocentric beliefs, 45, 58n, 126, 133–35; classificatory thinking and, 38, 131, 136; the shortcomings of, 1, 45, 129–30, 136–37. *See also* scientific racism

black creatives: Abdullah Haqq, 53n; anonymity as a tool for, 52–53; black creative praxes, 51, 67, 149; black cre-ative texts, 6, 7n, 37, 49, 51; Drexciya, 52–57; Ellen Gallagher, 53n, 55n, 83; M. NourbeSe Philip, 19n–21n, 128–29, 145–49; the production of as radical redefinition, 152–53; the work of, 1, 2, 20n–21n, 42n, 50–52

black diaspora: alienated reality, 155, 158–59, 161–62; attempts to list, cata-log, or map the, 168, 179–81; the behav-iors of scattered peoples, 158, 166, 173, 175; black diaspora spaces, 172–74, 182, 183; cultural mapping of the, 179–82; Dionne Brand on the, 61; geographic concepts of diaspora, 171–72, 175–76, 180; the geopolitical activities pro-duced through the, 72, 159, 168, 170; ungeographic time and space, 159, 168, 182–85; VèVè Clark on diasporic lit-eracy, 6, 7, 12, 29, 30, 34, 61, 141

black humanity: actions and cultural practices that reaffirm, 157–63, 165–67, 169–70; assaults on, 7, 125–29, 143–45, 154–55, 159–60; the association with violence as a misconstruing of, 105, 157; believing in, 12, 33, 73n, 107, 170; bios-mythoi nature and being human, 2n, 59n, 65, 72, 133, 137–38, 154, 159; black agency and the liberation of, 68n, 127–28, 134, 141–42; black bodies, 49, 50, 129, 134; black bodies versus black people, 40n, 63, 127–28, 130–32, 138, 155–56; black livingness and, 2, 13, 24, 27, 33, 68n, 141–45, 173, 186–87; the black sense of place, 11, 34, 106–8, 117, 119, 121, 170, 182; the blindness of academia regarding indigenous and, 38–39, 157n; the case of Davonte Flennoy, 103–4, 111, 120; diaspora ge-ography, 170–62, 182; indigenization,

158, 160; invention, reinvention, and repurposing by, 153n, 158–63; the labor of Drexciya, 57; the links between black intellectual life and, 50–52, 57, 64, 186–87; livingness in *Zong!*, 147–48; the multiethnic African trace within, 20n, 158, 160, 167; music as a self-affirming tool of, 153, 164–66, 169–56; narrative as a navigational tool of, 13, 22, 26–27, 31–32; premature and preventable death by racial violence, 143–45; as the rebellious impulse against oppression, 157–58; situating brutal historic experiences, 61–64, 125–29, 140–41, 172–73; the unmeasurability of, 121; unorthodox belonging and unbelonging, 5, 140, 169, 170, 172, 181–82; violence as a misconstruing of, 105; youth, mentoring, and money, 103–5. *See also* livingness
black intellectual life: as a resistance to the dominant knowledge system, 37–38, 42–43, 48, 50–52, 68n; black women intellectuals, 6, 29–30, 37–38, 58n–59n, 61–62; cultural production, 169–70; the devaluing of by others, 19n–21n, 25n–26n; Du Bois, 36, 65n, 107n, 179; Fanon on black consciousness, 19n, 60; Fanon's sociogenic principle, 39, 58, 135–36; Gilmore on the geography of liberation, 8–9, 66, 68n, 114; Glissant on history, 183–84; Glissant on the "sciences," 184–85; the link of to corporeal and affective labor, 3, 50–51, 186; as living the world and seeking liberation, 50, 57, 61–64, 68n, 186–87; materiality, 11, 33; Morrison, 11n, 49, 152, 179; Philip's *Zong!*, 128–29, 145–49; rebellion as praxis, 160–63; the role of methodology in, 44–46; sharing, 5n, 6, 13, 15–16, 17, 25, 27–28; Wynter on alienated reality, 155, 158–59, 161–62; Wynter on human creativity as a response to oppression, 151–54; Wynter on the bios-mythoi nature of humanity, 59n, 137–38, 165n

black method, 5, 9, 41, 170
black science fiction, 1, 2n, 55, 59n, 116
black studies: as a tool for challenging racism, 2, 4, 18, 19, 26–28, 30, 33; diasporic literacy and, 29, 30; feeling versus measuring and describing, 3, 9, 10, 15, 30, 38, 74, 117, 128; the importance of the nonworld to, 32–34; the interdisciplinary nature of, 9, 10, 12, 15, 135; referencing in, 26–27; the revolutionary potential of, 2, 4–5, 9–12, 15–16, 26–28, 37, 50, 71
Brand, Dionne, 61–63

capitalism: colonial-imperial-capitalist logics, 37, 38, 43, 113, 159, 182; predatory or corporate, 22n, 108, 139, 139n; racial, 33, 37, 38, 40n, 109n, 113, 139
citation: as a tool for racial liberation, 19, 26–30, 33; as a tool of racial and gender subordination, 20, 26n, 33; Carmen Kynard on, 26–27; the example of researching Bigger Thomas, 30; and the exposure of racialized sourcing, 25n; the gendered, racialized nature of some practices, 20–21, 25n–26n; the importance of in black intellectual life, 18, 27–30; as learning, counsel, and sharing, 17, 19, 26–30; the legitimizing role of, 22–23; the of ideas in books, 15; Sara Ahmed on practices, 20, 21n, 22, 29
Clark, VèVè, 6, 29–30
colonialism: colonial and plantographic geographies, 33, 34, 154–55, 158, 171, 174; colonial logic and knowledge systems, 3, 10, 27, 32, 38, 63, 130–32; counter-narratives to, 50–52, 61, 64n, 67, 69–70, 72, 157–62; the disruptive impacts of, 159, 171, 172, 181; enfleshment as a product of, 40, 42n; geographic belonging, 32–33, 131, 155, 159–60, 161–62, 170; the influence of on academic discipline, 40, 44, 50; nations and territories, 171, 174; place-making, 169, 187; positivism as a complement to, 33, 38, 174. *See also* displacement

consciousness: anxiety and unconscious awareness, 23; black, 58, 60–63, 66, 68–70, 161, 183; black music and, 66–67, 70; creative labor and, 56–57; embedding antiblack feelings, 156–57; experience and, 66; Fanonian black, 58–60; knowing and feeling racism, 60; the Middle Passage as shared unconscious memory, 32–33; racism and collective social, 156–57, 161, 162; recognizing and distancing violence, 62, 125, 127–29; sound and music, 66–67, 69–70; and the trauma of diasporic experience, 171–74, 176; the unconsciousness self of Frantz Fanon, 19n; Wynter on the responses to oppression, 164–65

conversation. *See* sharing

dance: as cultural practice, freedom, and rebellion, 141, 153n, 157–58, 161, 162, 166; as method-making, 46, 63, 141, 153n, 157, 158, 161–62; as story, 7, 8, 162, 166

data: assumptions and data gathering, 103–5, 131–33, 134–35, 174; black life construed through, 4, 39, 44, 50, 132; Carole Cadwalladr on computer ecosystems, 108n–9n; data grabbing and data mining, 108n–9n; experiential knowledge presented as, 36; frameworks for presenting, 48–49; Hartman on the *Zong* massacre data, 214; the objectification of black people through, 25n, 48–49, 135; statistical collection, 108–9

dehumanization: black resistance to, 17, 27–28, 34, 153–54, 157, 173; practices of, 11, 22n, 34, 154–55, 174–75

demonic ground, 2, 11n, 23, 43, 59n, 117

description: biocentric-based, 39, 41–42, 44–45, 134, 137, 149; the divisive potential of, 39, 134, 137, 149; the failure of to question, 39, 49, 134, 137, 149–50; the inability of to define, 125, 128, 149, 184; the use of in the "social construction" of race, 45, 134, 135

diasporic literacy, 6, 7, 12, 30, 34, 61, 141

discipline: as a practice of care, rigor, and monumental effort, 35, 56–57, 73–74; the physiological and psychic labor of, 3, 15, 50

disobedience: creative texts that foster, 51–52, 148, 149–50; the importance of, 52, 67, 72, 150; the importance of to method-making, 35, 41, 44, 45; the Middle Passage as impetus toward, 32; refusing unfreedom, 34, 61–63, 72. *See also* method and methodology; questioning; rebellion

displacement, 109n, 158, 171–73, 175–77, 181–83. *See also* colonialism

dispossession: biocentrically induced accumulation through, 3, 27, 34, 69, 74, 109n, 152, 159–60; black loss through, 7, 60, 72, 159

Donald, Gerald, 52, 53n, 56

Drexciya: the cosmogony of, 53n, 54–56; reactions to the music of, 53n, 54–57; the use of anonymity as a tool by, 52–53; the use of sound by, 56–57; visual depictions of Drexciyans, 53n

ecocidal practices, 2, 74, 139, 186

erasure, 22, 25n, 168, 183, 184

Fanon, Frantz: Fanonian black consciousness, 60, 135; the footnotes of, 19n; Sylvia Wynter's research on the sociogenic principle of, 58–61

feminists and feminism: black feminists, 1, 2, 27, 29; feminist science and technology, 1, 2, 129–32; the idea of excluding white patriarchs by, 20–22; Sara Ahmed on feminist knowledge worlds, 20, 21n, 27; the shortcomings of, 22n

freedom. *See* liberation

Gallagher, Ellen, 53n, 55n, 83

geography: absolute but uneven spaces, 10–11, 33, 34, 155; black geographies,

11, 32; black placelessness created by the Middle Passage, 155, 171–72; the black sense of place, 106–8; colonial and positivist, 33, 34; colonial, planto-graphic, positivist belonging, 32–34, 131, 155, 159–60, 161–62, 170; "creoliza-tion," 171; the cultural mapping of diasporic peoples, 180–82; dead, de-humanized spaces, 11, 43n, 157n, 174n; "diaspora" as understood in classic ge-ography, 171–73, 175–77, 179–80; dias-pora theory, 177–78; "displacement," 171; filial geographies, 32; geographic terms and politics, 10; Gilmore on the of liberation, 8–9, 66, 68n, 114; Glis-sant's racial of the Middle Passage, 32, 34; "glossary of terms," 171–77; home-land, 171, 172–74, 182; "hot spots," "hot lists," and "risky people," 103–4, 108, 112–15; human, 168–69, 174, 177–80, 181–82; interhuman geographies, 108; mapping, 168, 174, 176, 179, 180–81; migration, 171, 173, 176, 177; nation, 38, 63, 170, 171–72, 174–76, 177; the nonworld, 32–34; the produced by computer systems, 108n–9n; the pro-filing of places,104, 107–8; reference materials, 164–65; as story, 8, 13, 179; territory, 32, 110, 171, 174, 175, 179, 182, 185; ungeographic time and space, 159, 168, 182–85; white settlement as an establishment of place, 155, 174–74. *See also* space

Gilmore, Ruth Wilson, 8, 66, 114

Gilroy, Paul, 27n, 39n–40n, 54n, 109n, 118n, 140–41

Glissant, Édouard, 28n, 31–32, 34, 45, 66, 107, 169, 183–85

Hamadeh, Rana, 19n–21n

Haqq, Abdullah, 53n

history: the biocentric approach to, 38, 111; the brutal elements of black, 61–62; Glissant on "tormented chro-nology," 183–85; the multiple histories contained in *Zong!*, 147–48; personal

memory as, 14; the questioning of the 1960s, 37, 44; treatments of the *Zong* massacre, 140–45; Wynter's approach to the history of blackness, 43–44

humanity: the behaviors of scattered peoples, 158, 166, 173, 175; the bios-mythoi nature of, 59n, 137–38, 165n; as collective in deadweight measure, 142; diasporas, 172–76, 177; enflesh-ment, gender, and racial codes, 40n; geographic concepts of diaspora, 171–72; human geography, 168–69, 174, 177–80, 181–82; misreadings of Wynter's concept of "human," 42–43; new ways of being human, 24

ideas: collated names as substitutes for, 25; context, recontextualizing, and revisiting, 14, 141–28, 146–34; effec-tuating, 15, 18, 186–73; the importance of disliked authors and books in formulating, 14; intellectual inquiry as conversation about, 33, 71–74; method-making, 47–48; referencing and the formulation of, 16, 17, 19, 22, 26, 33–34; the sharing of relationally, 6, 17, 34, 44, 46, 50

identity-disciplines, 37, 40–41, 45

indigenous humanity. *See* black humanity

interdisciplinarity: as a tool for challeng-ing racism, 2, 4, 13, 53n, 117, 120, 121; black method, 5, 9, 41, 44, 57, 119, 170; the generative nature of, 2, 6, 7n, 8–9, 45, 48n, 51; the interplay between nar-rative and material worlds, 9–11; the of *Zong!*, 146–47

Iton, Richard, 58, 64n–65n, 67

knowing: Fanonian consciousness and racism, 60, 126n, 135n, 156n; forgetting and, 15, 20n, 22, 104, 120, 173; the how, where, who, and what underlying one's, 14, 23, 107, 120; the importance of unknowing to, 16–17, 34, 45, 72, 184;

knowing (*continued*)

  loops as mechanisms for coming to know, 14–15, 145–48; method-making, 41–48, 51, 57, 119; the physiological and intellectual efforts to achieve, 14–15, 113–14, 163; the role of worrying, 125; the white supremacist mode of, 155–57, 159–60

knowledge: the biocentric system of, 2, 43, 125–27, 131, 134, 174–75; black embodied, 3, 113–14; creativity as a means of breaching inequitable systems of, 153, 186–87; curiosity and wonder, 2–9, 44, 46, 48, 54, 150, 173; the disconnective influence of academic disciplines on, 35, 36; fictive truth, 37, 44, 59, 113–12, 132–33, 134, 156; geographic, 164–66; knowledge systems that reveal black life, 3, 27, 33, 106; the need to overturn false, racialized, 125–29, 139; positivist, 7, 33, 38, 57, 59, 174; the production and management of, 5, 17n, 146; racist, colonialist knowledge systems, 27, 32–33, 37, 130, 140, 141, 149, 163; radical theory-making versus existing systems of, 23–25, 73, 125–26; the role of materiality, 11–12, 20n, 33, 159–60; self-referential systems of, 42–43; situated, 25, 106, 130; subjectivity and, 17n, 149, 174; Sylvia Wynter on the dominant system of, 41–44; the system produced in *Zong!*, 146–48; theory as fictive, 7–8; tracking the accumulation of through loops, 14–15

labor: affective, 3, 51, 71–72, 74, 107n; creative, 5, 13, 20n–21n, 56–57, 65–67; the disappearance of after issuance, 15; the music of Drexciya, 56–57; the of aesthetically critiquing unfreedom, 61–62, 67–68; the physiological and psychic effort within, 3–4, 15, 50; the required for the praxis of liberation, 60–61, 67–70, 113–14; scholarly, intellectual, and neurological, 5, 19, 50,

71–72, 186; the underlying black intellectual life, 3, 50

learning: childhood referencing, 17n–18n; citations as, 26; learning outcomes, 36n; unknowing as a means of, 16, 146; *Zong!* as a capturing and unlearning of events, 146

liberation: as a site of possibility, 71–74; black bodies versus black people, 113–14; the black sense of place as a path toward, 11, 34, 106–8, 117, 119, 121, 182; black studies and the struggle for, 30–31, 33, 125–26; black through subversion, 8, 27, 160–67; diaspora geography and, 172–72, 175–76, 182; the dynamic nature of, 13, 66–67, 68n, 129, 141–42; liberatory thought and practices, 5, 7, 28, 31, 37, 50, 135; the physiological work underlying black, 3, 9, 15n, 50–51, 63, 72; the practice of, 3, 59–61, 69, 70n, 71, 149–50; the quality of as being here as well as there, 71–72, 128–29, 139, 172–73; questioning and rebelling, 49, 125–29, 153–54, 157–63; the role of sharing, 18, 25–29, 50; seeking and fashioning, 3, 6, 12, 23, 42–44, 47–48, 57

lists and cataloguing: academic reading, 25n–26n, 35n, 36; cataloguing, 168, 174, 179–80, 184–85; Glissant's repoliticizing of, 184–85; "hot spots," "hot lists," and "risky people," 103–4, 108, 112–15; subject, 164n, 179; that erase and objectify, 180, 184, 185

livingness: black as nonuniform and noncalculable for biocentrics, 103–4, 114, 117, 112, 145; black diasporic, 141, 145, 147, 165, 182; conversation and shared knowledge, 29, 33, 44, 50; the Drexciya approach to black, 57; the mnemonic function of story for black, 3, 6–7, 13, 73, 147–48, 186–87. *See also* black humanity; stories

loops: diachronic in Philip's *Zong!*, 145–32, 147, 148; the logic of racism, 131–35; as mechanisms for coming to know, 14–15, 139

A Map to the Door of No Return, 61–63, 176
memory: the biased nature of, 15, 175–77; the dynamic nature of, 6–7, 14, 56–57, 106, 148, 172–73, 179, 184
metaphor, 8–12
method and methodology: as an act of reworking, 73, 106–7, 169–70, 184; the approach of to categories and to knowledge, 35, 38, 44–45; curiosity and questioning as essential to, 41–44; interdisciplinary, 4–10, 44, 48n, 119; method-making, 41–48, 51, 57, 119; methodology as an act of disobedience and rebellion, 35, 41, 44; the music of Drexciya as, 57; the purpose and function of, 44–48. *See also* disobedience; rebellion
Middle Passage: the as a rupturing of identity and place, 32, 72, 154–55, 159, 172, 182–83; the as a source of later black rebellion, 153, 157, 144n, 160, 182, 183; the influence of the on the cosmogony of Drexciya, 53n, 55–56; the killing of slaves during the as commonplace, 55, 62, 105, 140–42, 153. *See also* plantation
modernity: as an outgrowth of slavery and capitalism, 139, 139n, 143, 174–75; consumerism and ownership as laudable, 155, 160, 168, 179; positivism as a complement to, 140–41, 144n; scientific expressions of, 58n, 136, 139, 140, 142; the slave ship as a technology of, 140; the tensions of with race, gender, and blackness, 14, 48, 58, 68n, 116, 171–72, 174–76, 177
music: as a way of being and living black, 65–67, 161–64; black as a response to racist oppression, 151, 153–54, 160–63; black as challenge and critique, 50–51, 64, 66–67, 166; black musical inventions and aesthetics, 151, 153, 163–64, 166, 169; Clyde Woods on black, 64–67; consciousness and, 66–67; Drexciya, 52–57; grooving to black, 154, 164, 165–67; listening, 56, 57, 69, 151, 153n, 154, 157–58, 161, 163–64; literature

concerning black, 151; in method-making, 46, 50–51, 65, 70, 154, 161–63; the neurological, affective power of, 50–51, 63, 165–66; reference and referencing in, 16n; remixes and mash-ups, 169–70; Richard Iton on love songs, 64n–65n; songs, 51–52, 64–65, 67–70, 169–70; "The Kick Drum is the Fault," 108–10; waveforms, 56, 66, 69, 151–54, 164, 166–67; Wynter's observations in *Black Metamorphosis*, 153–54, 161–63, 166–67. *See also* sound

narrative: as a tool for challenging racism, 4, 146–48; Barbara Christian on the use of for theorizing, 7n; biocentric, 148–49; counterhegemonic, 26–27, 113–18; counter-narratives, 51, 146–48, 175; Darwinism as fictive, 126; devices, 8, 9–10; the dynamic connection of to biology, 9; grooving to black, 15, 169; as impartial treatise, 7–8; interdisciplinarity and, 4–6; the interplay of with the material world, 10–11; Kevin Young on the twisting of, 8; the Malthusian, 38, 126; manifestations of the black, 7; science as, 59n, 129–33; the textual of books, bibliographies, and footnotes, 31; the use of in *Zong!*, 20n, 146–48. *See also* stories
nonworld, 32–34
normalization: the of racial violence, 118, 121, 144, 172, 174–76; the of racist, biocentric thinking, 21, 43, 106, 113, 133, 154–57, 161, 165; the *Zong* massacre as systemically typical and tolerable, 142–45

objectification: black rebellion against, 154–62, 173, 175; the case of the *Zong* massacre, 140–45; data and classification as tools of, 105, 107–8, 113–24, 135, 174, 180; the of black humanity in scholarship, 25n, 26n, 33, 41, 44–49, 129, 149–50, 184; the of black humanity through racism, 68, 131, 143, 159, 162, 174

oppression: as an underpinning of racist thinking and behaviors, 4, 113,
155–57, 171–72, 174–76; black music as
resistance to, 64–67, 153–55, 160–63;
rejecting unfreedom, 50, 61, 62, 121,
113, 147–48, 144n; resisting the dehumanizing effects of, 27–28, 157–63; the
work of identity-disciplines in undoing, 40

Philip, M. NourbeSe, 19n–21n, 23, 128–29,
145–48, 181; *Zong!* by, 19n–21n, 145–47
plantation: the as an inception point of
black rebellion, 153, 157n, 144–49, 182,
183, 186–87; the as a tool for creating
the black nonperson, 153, 154–57, 159;
oppression and violence made mundane through the, 62, 105, 106, 154–56;
the slave as a unit of labor on the,
154–55, 156, 159, 162; tours, 62. *See also*
Middle Passage
plantocratic thinking: accumulation and
dispossession, 3, 34, 72, 74, 109n, 152;
black objectification as a requirement
of, 41, 44–45, 154, 160; inequality and
racism, 64, 109–10, 114, 156, 156–58,
144, 162, 174–75; plantocratic logics, 3,
27, 63, 67, 152–53, 144n; the rebellion
against, 69–70, 106–7, 159–60, 162, 163,
165, 167
poetry: the extended poetry cycle of
Zong!, 146–48; as method-making,
63, 148
positivism: categorization, 38, 174; colonialism and, 33, 174–76; fictive truth,
37, 44, 59, 113–14, 132–33, 134, 156;
positivist geographies, 33, 174, 176, 165,
181–82; racism and, 113, 139, 165. *See
also* biocentricity; racism
possibility: the affective and physiological powers of, 71–73; black liberation
as, 71–74, 139, 145–46, 162; nonworlds,
unknowing and, 16–17, 32–34

questioning: the dynamic potential
of, 1, 4, 14, 29, 49, 53–54, 181–82; the

importance of vigilant, 45, 72, 106,
129; method and methodology as,
44–45, 105–6, 127–29, 161–62; the of
the global world system, 37, 41, 44, 72,
74; the potential of diachronic loops,
145–46, 147, 148; questions answered
by descriptions, 5, 46, 49; questions
with knowable answers, 23, 63; recon-
figuring as a tool of, 169–70, 183; Wynter's of who and what we are, 42n–43n,
44, 59–60, 137–38. *See also* disobedience; rebellion

race: enfleshment, 40, 42n, 45, 49,
106n; genetic variability, 43n, 110–11,
132; knowledge systems shaped by,
37, 126–27, 130–31; Paul Gilroy on,
39n–40n; racial taxonomies, 33, 131
racism: as a cause of displacement,
171–72, 173–74, 176; accumulation by
dispossession, 3, 34, 60, 69, 72, 109n;
apartheid, 28, 62, 130; the assignment
of less-than-human status to others,
37, 151–52, 154–55, 157; black unfreedom as a requirement of white freedom, 155–56, 160, 165; the conflating of
flesh with identity, 39, 40n; displacement as a product of, 144, 171, 172,
163, 181–82, 183; documentation as a
framework for, 105, 109–11; embedding
antiblack instincts, 155–57; erasure,
22, 25n, 159, 172–73, 175, 183–84; the
fostering effect of on black rebellion,
157–58, 164, 186–87; genocide, 2, 74,
139, 159–60, 172–73, 175; identity markers and racial differentiations, 38–39;
knowing and feeling, 60; observing
and critiquing without revering or describing, 46, 50–51, 62, 71, 106–7, 125;
practices, 22n, 62, 174–76, 181n; the
self-replicating influence of, 37, 48–49,
132–34, 136–37; white supremacist
logics, 27, 105–6, 113, 127–28, 132, 152,
154–55, 157. *See also* biocentricity; positivism; scientific racism
reading: Gilmore on cross-material, 8–9;

linking the metaphoric with the material, 9–10; materials and authors that one dislikes, 14, 34; reading across to counter scholarly objectification, 129, 139, 150; unknowing and, 16–17, 34

rebellion: against objectification, 44–45, 154–62; as a method of liberation, 49, 186–87; black music as, 161–67; the fostering of through black creative texts and praxes, 51–52, 144, 161; indigenization, 144, 160; invention, reinvention, and, 153n, 157–63; method and methodology as acts of, 35, 41, 44–48; the Middle Passage and plantation as points of inception for, 153, 157–58; the need for against objectification, 44–45; the subversive aspects of black, 8, 27, 160–67. See also disobedience; method and methodology; questioning

referencing: in black musics, 16n; in childhood development, 17n–18n; citing and, 17, 19, 25n, 26n; the formulation of ideas through, 16, 17, 19, 22, 26, 33–34; the function of in navigating the world, 18n, 19, 26; of place, 16n; as sharing knowledge, 17, 26–27, 31–34

relationality: aesthetic, 6–7, 125–29, 165–66, 169; as a path toward liberation, 39, 45, 51–52, 120–27, 129, 144n; the between black worldviews and biocentric knowledge, 152, 157–63, 164–65, 186–87; the black sense of place and, 106–7; invention and reinvention, 153n, 165, 169, 186; the of the brain-narrative-bios-mythois, 59n, 137–38; uncomfortable relationalities, 107, 159, 165. See also sharing

research: the recontextualizing power of, 14, 17, 40, 119–20; the shared, collaborative nature of, 15–16, 19, 31

scientific racism: as a tool for animating biocentric beliefs, 126–27, 130–35; the self-replicating quality of, 1, 3. See also biological determinism; racism

sharing: as a basis for promoting social change, 16, 18, 25, 27–29, 46–47, 66, 70; believing and, 12, 33, 72n; the citation as a tool for, 25–30; collective identities, 172–74, 176, 181; coming to know through, 14–15; conversation, 16–17, 19n, 28, 29, 71–73; delusions of separation that prevent, 28n; diasporic literacy and, 6, 29–30; friendship, 73, 186; inclusion and exclusion as wrongheaded, 30; music, 50–57, 67, 164–67; the nonworld as a referential knowledge system for, 32–34; the of stories, 6–7, 16, 73; reaffirmative communal behaviors, 153n, 157, 144, 161, 163; relationality, 6, 17, 50–52, 129. See also relationality

slavery: black oppression and, 139, 142–44; the contribution of to modernity, 139, 148; the defining influence of plantation, 152–56; the denial of black personhood through, 151–52, 153, 154, 155–56; mapping of the slave trade, 180–81; racist violence and, 146, 172, 175–76; the remaining infrastructures of, 62; Richard Iton on the legacies of coloniality and, 64; the slave as a unit of labor, 154–55, 156, 159, 162; transatlantic, 62, 64n, 148, 152, 159, 172, 174, 163, 181; the treatment of in Zong!, 146, 148

sound: being black as, 65, 69, 169–70; listening, 6, 8, 51, 54, 69, 164; the nonwordness of, 14, 154; Richard Iton on love songs, 64n; soundscapes, 64, 65; and story, 8, 63; the use of by Drexciya, 56–57; waveforms, 56, 66, 69, 151–54, 164, 166–67. See also music

space: black diaspora spaces, 168, 182, 183; the dead, dehumanized of "Otherness," 11, 43n, 157n, 174n; the for black method-making, 41, 52, 61, 63–64; Glissant on, 34; jurisdiction and regulation of, 174, 165–66; mapping and claiming, 169, 180; and the production of knowledge, 165–66; psychological, 10, 69–70, 165; territory, 32, 110, 171, 174, 175, 165, 182, 185. See also geography

Stinson, James, 52, 54n, 56

stories: black livingness and, 6–7, 12–13, 73n; devices that shape, 9–10; human beings as physiological-story-makers, 3n, 9; Kevin Young on the power of to resist racism, 8; as mnemonic devices, 3, 6–8, 13, 29, 73, 147–48, 186–87; the questioning, challenging power of, 3, 4–5, 8, 15–16, 71–72, 121, 169–70; the sharing of, 5n, 6–7, 16, 18–19, 29, 63, 71–74, 162–63; the ties between narrative and extraliterary sites in, 9–10; as tools for explaining and exploring the world, 4, 128–29. *See also* livingness; narrative

storytelling: the absence from biocentricity of the human capacity for, 2n, 126; the dynamism of biology with narrative in, 9, 17n, 59n; institutional, 33, 41; modes of, 7n, 8; the power of counterhegemonic narratives, 26–27, 73, 125–29; theory as, 7

struggle: the achievement of black liberation through, 30, 72–74, 140–41; black studies as a tool for, 28, 30, 37; the by blacks and indigenous peoples worldwide, 38, 175–76; diasporic literacy as a tool for, 6, 29–30, 34, 61; metaphors that map sites of, 9–12; the role of sharing in the black, 7, 25, 27; Wynter's emphasis on the importance of questioning, 41–44

territory. *See* space

theory: as a form of storytelling, 7–8, 73; radical theory-making, 23–25; spatial concepts, 10

unfreedom. *See* oppression

violence: the against black bodies, 72, 106, 127, 156, 181n; as a tool for embedding antiblack instincts, 156–57; as a tool for establishing nonbeings, 153, 155, 160; black creativity as a response to, 164–65; black humanity misread through, 105, 112, 118; the case of Davonte Flennoy, 103–4, 111, 120; the false beliefs underlying racial, 105, 127; genocide, 2, 74, 139, 159–60, 172–73, 175; the production of space through, 108, 109n, 175–76; psychological, 22n, 62, 164; racial that shapes memory, history, and behavior, 11, 12, 19, 28, 30, 152, 155–57; recognizing and distancing, 62, 125, 138, 139; the treatment of racist in *Zong!*, 146, 148; *Zong* massacre (1781), 19n, 139–45

visual arts: "Black Children" (plate), 95; "Black Ecologies. Coral Cities. Catch a Wave" (plate), 83; "Charmine's Wire" (plate), 87; ideas depicted through images, 14; "No Place, Unknown, Undetermined" (plate), 75; "Notes" (plate), 79; orbital photographs, 61, 62; painting, 8, 52, 140; photography, 8, 13, 70; "Polycarbonate, Aluminum (Gold), and Lacquer" (plate), 91; sculpture, 8, 52; "Telephone Listing" (plate), 99; "The Slave Ship" (1840) by J. M. W. Turner, 140

Woods, Clyde, 64–67

world: black challenges to the unkind, 4–5, 7, 23, 25, 27–30; black worlds and ways of being, 7, 17, 61, 68n, 72, 74; the depiction of the as unalterable, 2, 133, 174–75; the humanizing work of black artworlds, 2, 67, 149, 152, 164; the materiality of the analytical, 11, 12; the nonworld, 32–34; referencing as a means of navigating the, 17n–18n

Wynter, Sylvia: on the bios-mythoi nature of humanity, 59n, 137–38, 165n; *Black Metamorphosis*, 153–67; on blackness and black studies, 2, 36–38; on black rebellion as praxis, 160–61; the concept of alienated reality, 155, 144–45, 161–62; the concept of indigenization, 144, 160; the concern of with who and what we are, 42n–43n; on creative production as radical re-wording, 152–53; the "demonic model" of, 1–2, 23–25, 43, 59n, 117; the emphasis of on questioning the existing knowledge system, 37, 41–44, 136–37; on human storytelling, 9; the inter-disciplinarity of Wynter's intellectual approach, 2, 137–38; misreadings of her concept of "human," 42–43; on radical theory-making, 23–24; the rejection of the self-referential system by, 43, 136–37; research by on Fanon's sociogenic principle, 58–61; the species-ecological perspective of, 42, 136–37; on the widespread influence of scientific thinking, 136; the work of on neurobiology, 58–59n

Zong!: the creative labor underlying, 19n–21n, 136, 139, 145–47; the dia-chronic loops present in, 145–46, 147, 148; livingness in, 128–129 147–48

Zong massacre: the as historically pres-ent, 139; the commodification of black human beings as cargo, 140–41; the documentation of in the case of Gregson v. Gilbert (1783), 19n–20n; the explanation given for the killings, 140–41; the focus on numbers rather than on people in some accounts, 140, 142–43; NourbeSe Philip's com-memoration of in Zong!, 19n–21n, 139; Rana Hamadeh's commemoration of, 19n–21n; the violence as systemically typical and tolerable, 142–45; Walvin's history of the massacre, 140–43